THE GREAT BRITISH
BAKE OFF

THE GREAT BRITISH
BAKE OFF

How To Bake

THE PERFECT VICTORIA SPONGE
AND OTHER BAKING SECRETS

RECIPES BY
LINDA COLLISTER
FOREWORD AND PRACTICAL TIPS BY
MARY BERRY &
PAUL HOLLYWOOD

BBC
BOOKS

This book is published to accompany the television series entitled *The Great British Bake Off*, first broadcast on BBC TWO in 2011.

Executive Producer: Anna Beattie
Series Editor: Melissa Brown
Series Director: Andy Devonshire
Senior Producer: Jane Treasure
Producers: Claire Emerson, Emma Phillips
Unit manager: Caron Miles
Head of Production: Letty Kavanagh
BBC Commissioning Executive: Emma Willis

20 19 18 17 16 15 14

Published in 2011 by BBC Books, an imprint of Ebury Publishing.
A Random House Group Company

The Random House Group Limited Reg. No. 954009
Addresses for companies within the Random House Group can be found at www.randomhouse.co.uk
A CIP catalogue record for this book is available from the British Library.

ISBN 978 1 849 90268 7

The Random House Group Limited supports The Forest Stewardship Council (FSC®), the leading international forest certification organisation. Our books carrying the FSC label are printed on FSC® certified paper. FSC is the only forest certification scheme endorsed by the leading environmental organisations, including Greenpeace. Our paper procurement policy can be found at www.randomhouse.co.uk/environment

Commissioning editor: Muna Reyal
Project editor: Laura Higginson
Copy-editor: Norma MacMillan
Designer: Two Associates
Photographer: Cristian Barnett
Food Stylists: Katie Giovanni, Katy Greenwood, Lizzie Harris, Faenia Moore and Joy Skipper
Props Stylist: Cynthia Inions
Production: David Brimble

Colour origination by XY Digital Ltd
Printed and bound in Germany by Firmengruppe APPL, aprinta druck, Wemding

To buy books by your favourite authors and register for offers, visit www.randomhouse.co.uk

CONTENTS

Foreword by Mary Berry and Paul Hollywood   6
Introduction   8

Cakes   12
How to make the perfect Victoria Sandwich   16
Technical Challenge: Mary's Coffee and Walnut Battenburg   20

Biscuits and Teatime Treats   56
Technical Challenge: Mary's Brandy Snaps   60
How to make the perfect Almond Tuiles   64

Bread   100
How to make the perfect White Loaf   104
Technical Challenge: Paul's Focaccia   118

Pies and Savoury Pastry   142
How to make the perfect Shortcrust Pie   146
Technical Challenge: Paul's Pork Pie with Quails' Eggs   156

Tarts and Sweet Pastry   176
Technical Challenge: Mary's Tarte au Citron   180

Patisserie   206
How to make perfect Puff Pastry   210
Technical Challenge: Paul's Iced Fingers   240

Puddings and Desserts   246
How to make perfect Meringues   250
Technical Challenge: Mary's Chocolate Roulade   264

Celebration Cakes   282
How to make a Large Iced Fruit Cake   286

Conversion charts and cook's notes   316
Index   317

Mary's Foreword

This year's *The Great British Bake Off* was really special – we really got it down to a tee this series. Having twelve bakers this time, instead of ten, made for an even more exciting competition and as almost all the contestants had watched last year and knew what the series was about, the standard was noticeably higher.

We were on the look out for an all-round baker – someone who could handle every challenge thrown at them, someone who represented the very best home baker. All the contestants showed great promise in the early stages and we also decided to raise the stakes by providing them with three different challenges each week.

First they had to create a 'signature bake', a recipe they were proud of or a family favourite. It needed to be individual and creative as much as it had to be delicious and technically perfect. We told the bakers what the theme would be 1 week before filming so they could practise it before the bake-off.

Next, they had to rise to a 'technical challenge' from Paul and me – the recipes for all our technical challenges are featured throughout this book. The bakers didn't know what they were going to be baking until the day, when they received a basic recipe that included ingredients, quantities and a scant method – no technical advice, they had to work out the details themselves. No two bakes turned out the same.

The final challenge was the 'showstopper' and as the name implies, the bakers had to really impress us with a wow-factor bake. They were given the type of bake and how many to make, but it was up to them to add flavours. Our challenges were designed to demand a number of skills all at once. The bakers had 1 week to practise their showstopper bake, but this didn't mean everything went smoothly on the filming day. We had a few disasters!

Unfortunately, accidents did happen but Paul and I tried to be fair – there was a finished cake that slipped on to the floor. We didn't mark it down as we'd seen it completed and it was rescued so we were able to taste it. However, if a mixture curdled or pastry was burned then we weren't quite so forgiving!

The bakers were under a lot of pressure, but I think you can see how well we got along on set. The bakers really bonded, developing into a team, helping each other through each challenge and we were all genuinely sad when someone had to leave. I think that camaraderie is what makes *The Great British Bake Off* so unusual and charming to watch.

It's always a joy to work with Paul, who is a firm but fair judge and Mel and Sue always keep everything light and enjoyable, cheering and comforting the bakers and, of course, tasting the bakes – especially Sue! And with all the best bakers' recipes in this book, you can recreate the flavours of *The Great British Bake Off* at home, indulge with Mel and Sue, and see if you agree with the judges' comments!

Mary Berry

Paul's Foreword

The second series of *The Great British Bake Off* was fantastic to work on. This year we tested the bakers like never before, we pushed their technical ability to the limit to see who really had the know-how and the skills to win.

When Mary and I devised the recipes for the technical challenges it was important that we chose recipes that stretched the bakers and challenged their prowess in the kitchen. It's all good and well producing a Victoria Sandwich every week for the family, but when you're confronted with Pork Pies filled with quail's eggs and a time limit in which to make them, well this would scare anyone – especially working with a hot water crust pastry for the first time.

The first hurdle to jump, in my opinion, is equipment. Ovens can be notoriously unbalanced, so it is a good tip to buy a probe to check whether your oven is actually achieving the correct oven temperature. A good set of knives, baking trays and tins are also essential. There are so many pieces of kit you can buy now when baking, it's up to you to pick the ones you like but be consistent. It's very important when making sponges, for instance, following a recipe that calls for a 23cm tin, not to use a 26cm tin. The larger tin will not produce the desired results.

For me, modern baking needs digital scales. They are a must in the baking industry but will also become a strong ally when baking at home.

If you weigh up your ingredients correctly then you are 50 per cent on your way to baking something that looks and tastes great!

My technical challenges this year are Focaccia, Iced Fingers and Pork Pies and each recipe has its own issues. My Focaccia recipe has 400ml of liquid to 500g of flour, so you can imagine the look on all the bakers' faces. This recipe calls for a very different approach when mixing the dough and the introduction of the water is critical. The Iced Fingers created several problems because an enriched dough can be slow when proving (the use of warm milk helps). These went down a storm on set and were greatly appreciated by the crew. The Pork Pies were a very different type of challenge and called for a quail's egg to be placed in the centre of each pie – trickier than you might think!

In this series, there are two programmes in which Mary and myself get to show you how all the technical challenges should have been done. This was great fun for both of us and gave us the chance to show you, first hand, all the pitfalls you may encounter when baking the recipes.

Happy baking to all of you and enjoy the series.

Paul Hollywood

Introduction

Are you wondering how to perfect your Victoria Sandwich or create the lightest, flakiest puff pastry? With this book, *The Great British Bake Off* is here to help.

We've chosen recipes from the everyday to the celebratory, from the traditional to the avant-garde, from the simplest to the most sophisticated. Some are particularly great bakes to get children involved, while others require a little more time or skill, or look plain fabulous. To help you choose the right bake for every occasion, we've flagged up recipes that are 'good for kids' or 'great for celebrations'.

But this book is not just a collection of delectable recipes. It's also a helpful guide that covers the essentials of baking – the techniques, terms and ingredients – to help your baking taste, look and smell better than ever; to make your Victoria Sandwich worthy of Queen Victoria in all her majesty.

Mary Berry and Paul Hollywood's technical challenges, as faced by the bakers, are included in this book, together with step-by-step photography to ensure success at home. There are also step-by-step classic recipes, '**how to makes**', to help you master baking skills as well as the most successful recipes from the bakers, the '**best of the bake-off**'.

Chapter One is devoted to cakes. It shows you how to make a perfect creamed sponge – incorporating air into the ingredients by creaming and beating is central to its success. Master the perfect Victoria Sandwich and, once you're happy with the results, you'll have the confidence to try other cakes that build on these techniques and skills.

Whisked sponges, even lighter than creamed sponges, are made by whisking air into the eggs with the sugar and then folding in the other ingredients. There is a Lemon Cream Roll and Blood Orange Sponge recipe – both flourless – that use this method. This chapter also offers plenty of straightforward recipes, such as Quick and Simple Fruit Loaf and an Apricot Marzipan Loaf, which are good for beginner bakers, as well as a plethora of imaginative cupcake recipes from the bakers. At the other end of the scale are more time-consuming recipes for decorated sponges, including **Mary's Coffee and Walnut Battenburg (see page 21)**.

In **Chapter Two, Mary makes Brandy Snaps (see page 60)**: crisp, neatly rolled and glistening conker-brown. Almond Tuiles are similarly thin, crisp and shaped, although

made from a very different meringue-based mixture. Shortbread, a true test of a baker's skills, is here in several guises, including Two-chocolate Zebras (a striped dark and white chocolate version).

Many other classic biscuits are made by the same method of creaming butter with sugar (then working in an egg and other ingredients), but the one technique can lead to a wide range of results, such as Oat and Raisin, Chocolate Chunk, Walnut Crumbles and prettily decorated Iced Lemon Biscuits. Baking in quantity, without much fuss or expense, is the realm of traybakes and here you'll find Banana and Almond Slice and Sticky Maple-Apple Traybake. Glossy, jewel-like Florentines, finished with dark chocolate, chocolate-dipped Coconut Macaroons and the bakers' impressive macaroon displays add a touch of glamour to the tea table.

To make good bread you need another set of skills and **Chapter Three** is where you'll find everything you need to know. The simple White Loaf takes you through the basics step by step: mixing, kneading, rising and shaping the dough, and baking to get a good crust. Breadmaking isn't tricky and the ingredients are cheap, but it does demand patience. In this chapter the recipes range from a loaf made overnight the slow, old-fashioned way to a simple child-friendly recipe for Monkey Bread.

Paul's Focaccia (see page 119), is an Italian bread flavoured with olive oil, which is made from an unusual wet dough. A supreme test of a bread-baker's skill is the cake-like Rum Baba with its very fine and delicate crumb, and it's a thrill to eat the results. Once your hands are floury, once you know how good it feels to work the dough, once you've shared the results, you'll never stop making your own.

Chapter Four highlights the enduring British love for savoury pies, which combine excellent pastry with a flavour-packed filling. Shortcrust pastry provides the casing for countless pies and tarts, so this chapter begins with the technique for making perfect shortcrust and then showcases a classic double-crust beef pie.

Paul's Pork Pies are a traditional favourite (see page 157): crisp hot-water crust pastry cases filled with a well-seasoned pork mix concealing a tiny quail's egg. Rough puff pastry with its crisp, flaky layers, works well for robust farmhouse-style pies. It's quicker and easier to make than puff pastry, but still has all the buttery, rich taste; try it with a filling of pork, cider and apples. Ready-made filo is ideal for quickly assembled pastries like Mushroom and Gorgonzola Twists and the hearty Three Cheese and Spinach Pie.

Tarts and sweet pastry recipes fill **Chapter Five**: here you'll find beautifully presented recipes from the series including **Mary's Tarte au Citron (see page 181)**. Mary shares her method for making sweet rich shortcrust pastry in a food-processor. A processor is also used to make a pistachio-flavoured shortcrust for a glamorous but surprisingly easy Strawberry and Pistachio Tart.

By contrast, there are no shortcuts when making puff pastry, which is used for a luxurious version of baked apples made by wrapping strips of puff pastry around filled apples. The simplest tart of all has a base of biscuit crumbs and a darkly rich chocolate topping: it's Mud Pie not elegant, just irresistible!

Patisserie is as much art as craft, and learning the skills needed takes time. **Chapter Six** gives you a taste of what is involved. 'Laminated' pastries dominate here, by which I mean croissants and danish pastries, and the chapter opens with a step-by-step recipe for making puff pastry – the base for these breakfast favourites.

Puff is used for all kinds of pastries, including Millefeuilles filled with cream and raspberries. **Paul's Iced Fingers (see page 240)**, filled with jam and cream, are a classic British pastry shop treat, while choux pastry profiteroles and éclairs are here too, as well as a stunning Croquembouche from the programme.

Chapter Seven offers a selection of puddings and desserts to please everyone. Making the perfect meringue is a test for any baker, so we show you how to achieve success, every step of the way. Meringue forms the basis for a classic Pavlova and a Hot Lemon Curd Soufflé, both included here.

Mary's Chocolate Roulade (see page 265) is a dessert that's very hard to beat. And no apologies for the number of chocolate desserts, from the Queen of Sheba, a dense dark chocolate and almond cake that lives up to its grand name, to more homely Chocolate Fudge Hot-Pot Pudding and Chocolate Bread and Butter Pudding. There are cheesecakes too and a meringue-topped Lemon Ice Cream Meringue Pie,for when you want an impressive home-made treat without much effort.

Chapter Eight is all about celebrations, when the holidays and milestones of our lives are marked with a special meal, and a gorgeous cake or dessert to share as the centrepiece of the party table. The step-by-step recipe here shows you how to make, ice and decorate a large fruit cake that's perfect for a wedding or anniversary, as well as Christmas.

And if you want something a bit different there's a chocolate cake, covered in a fluffy marshmallow frosting, that can be scaled up and assembled in three tiers; there is also the best of the contestant recipes for a glorious tiered cake and cup cakes that can be iced and finished as elaborately as you wish, for any occasion. Smaller family celebrations such as Christmas demand traditional treats and so there's a classic Yule Log, a fruity Christmas Pudding and a chocolate-filled puff pastry Twelfth Night Cake for January 6th.

Baking is a science, but please don't be put off by this. As *The Great British Bake Off* shows, it is also really good fun. If you're a baking beginner or have been defeated by a bake in the past, remember the following three points.

Accuracy is essential because baking is largely chemistry, and chemistry demands precision. The wrong ingredients, or the wrong amounts, will lead to the wrong results. Some recipes will only work well if the ingredients are chilled, some only if they are at room temperature, or warm. The temperature of the oven is important, as is the timing: a casserole won't suffer from 5 minutes more or less in the oven but a batch of biscuits will.

Attention to detail is the difference between a decent baker and a great one. Getting seasonings, flavourings and colourings just right; taking care over pastry seams so they don't come apart in the oven; spreading the icing evenly – taking such pains pays off.

You need to trust your senses, maybe even more than your recipe. They will tell you when something is ready to come out of the oven – it will smell right or look nicely browned or feel crisp, or taste tender. Recipes can only be guides to cooking times.

One extra quality makes the big difference: you need to love what you're doing. It's the love you add that makes baking so creative, so satisfying and such fun. Once you've mastered the basic techniques you can enjoy adapting recipes, adding your own favourite ingredients, developing your own tricks and tips, and making your own masterpieces.

Happy baking!
Linda Collister

GOLDEN APRICOT AND MARZIPAN LOAF CAKE

BUTTERCREAM LEMON CURD

LEMON CREAM CAKE

SPECKLED MOCHA CAKE FRUIT LOAF

CAKES

CUPCAKES

COFFEE AND WALNUT BATTENBURG CAKE

VICTORIA SANDWICH

FARMHOUSE FRUIT CAKE

LEMON POPPYSEED MADEIRA CAKE

Home-made Cake = Treat

If you've never baked a cake from scratch before this is the place to start. Even experienced bakers may find some new ideas to try out. In this chapter there are cakes for any time of day – to go with a cup of tea or coffee, to fit into a lunchbox or to be dressed up for dessert. From super simple to super rich, they all taste splendid.

There are four main ways to make a cake: by whisking eggs with sugar, as when making a swiss roll or roulade; by creaming butter with sugar and beating in eggs, as when making a Victoria Sandwich; by melting butter and then stirring in the other ingredients, as when making a gingerbread or quick loaf cake; or by rubbing butter into flour and then mixing in the remaining ingredients, as when making something fairly robust like a fruit cake.

For cakes made by the whisking or creaming methods, there are few ingredients but they need plenty of beating (an electric mixer really helps), followed by the gentle folding-in of other ingredients such as flour. The classic Victoria Sandwich (see page 16) is a good challenge for creaming and beating skills. Success will be immediately obvious when you take the sponge out of the oven: if it has risen beautifully and has a light and tender but moist texture with an evenly coloured exterior you've passed the test.

The melting and rubbing-in methods produce cakes with a very different texture and appearance – the crumb is coarser and moister than that of whisked or creamed cakes, and the top may have a peak or be cracked. Cakes made by the melting or rubbing-in methods are much quicker but use more ingredients to add interesting textures and flavours.

Once you've mastered the basic techniques – and it only takes a few goes – you can start to mix and match with fillings and toppings, flavourings and finishes. If your attempt doesn't work out quite right first time, make a note to help you with your next cake. Mary's technical challenge for *The Great British Bake Off* contestants to make a Battenburg Cake (see page 21) involves not just baking two excellent sponges using the all-in-one creaming method, but the chequerboard assembly too. The finished cake must look as wonderful as it tastes.

Before you start, read through the recipe and get out all the equipment you'll need. Measure the tins to make sure they are the right size, then prepare them as instructed. The easiest way to grease tins is to brush them with melted butter. Paper linings – or non-stick baking paper – help stop cakes with delicate edges from sticking, so they will be easy to turn out as well as preventing overcooked or scorched crusts on cakes with longer cooking times. Non-stick tins, particularly springclip ones, are very useful as they make unmoulding so easy.

Always preheat the oven. Putting a cake mixture into a too-cool oven can melt the ingredients into a heavy mass, while a too-hot oven will give the cake a crisp brown crust and liquid centre. If you're baking more than one cake at a time, if possible, arrange them in the oven so one is not directly beneath the other and be ready to rotate them two-thirds through the cooking time, once they have started to colour. Accurate temperature is essential; for equipment lovers, you can purchase an oven thermometer to ensure the temperature is spot on.

Prepare all the ingredients listed so you have everything ready to use. Having butter and eggs at room temperature is essential for successful creaming and whisking – air is the free ingredient, and getting it, and trapping it in your cake batter is vital. Taking butter and eggs (and sometimes soured cream or buttermilk) out of the fridge an hour or so beforehand is best, but there are a couple of tricks that will help in an emergency. For hard, cold butter, cut it into even dice and microwave (on low) for 10 seconds only – you don't want the butter to become oily – then leave to stand for 10 minutes. For cold eggs, warm them, in their shells in a bowl of hand-hot water for 5 minutes (no hotter or they start to cook). Sift flour and any other dry ingredients – this not only removes lumps but adds air to the mix. Toast nuts and leave to cool – adding warm nuts to a cake mixture will melt the fat, losing all the air you've carefully beaten in.

When creaming and whisking, take your time and scrape down the bowl regularly so all the mixture is evenly beaten. Don't worry if the mixture starts to curdle when the eggs go in or if something doesn't go quite right. Your finished cake might look a bit different but it will still taste good.

Use a timer for baking but use your senses as well. Ovens do vary, so check for 'doneness' by sight (is the colour right? has the cake shrunk from the sides of the tin?) and touch (does it spring back when pressed?), as well as by the ultimate test with a skewer or cocktail stick: if it comes out clean when you stick it into the centre of the cake then you know your cake is ready.

Once out of the oven, some cakes should be left to firm up a little before turning out, while others are best quickly unmoulded – a round-bladed knife run around the inside of the tin aids easy removal. Cool on a wire rack so air can circulate on all sides. Many cakes are better made a day or so before cutting – this allows the flavours to develop and the crumb to firm up. Chocolate cakes, fruit cakes and gingerbread or spice cakes will be all the better for wrapping and keeping at least overnight.

If you've never made a cake before, start with the Quick and Simple Fruit Loaf (see page 29), which demonstrates basic skills you can build on. This cake tastes as good as it looks.

HOW TO MAKE THE PERFECT
VICTORIA SANDWICH

Our traditional afternoon tea cake, named after Queen Victoria, remains a classic. The sponge is made by the 'creaming' method – butter is creamed or beaten with the sugar, after which the eggs are gradually beaten in and finally the flour is carefully folded into the mixture. Good beating is the key to a good sponge.

Makes 1 large cake

For the sponge
225g unsalted butter, softened
225g caster sugar
4 large free-range eggs, at room temperature
½ teaspoon vanilla extract
225g self-raising flour, sifted
1 tablespoon milk, at room temperature

For the filling
6 rounded tablespoons good raspberry jam

To finish
caster or icing sugar

2 x 20.5cm sandwich tins, greased and the base lined with baking paper

✳ For a creamed sponge, the butter should be soft, rather than cold and hard, or warm and oily, so take it out of the fridge an hour or so in advance.

✳ The best sugar to use for a sponge is caster. Granulated sugar is too coarse and results in a crust speckled with tiny particles after baking. Muscovado sugars are too strong in flavour and colour, and their moist texture would makes the crumb of the cake a bit sticky.

✳ Make sure the eggs are at room temperature (see page 15). If they are too cold it will be harder for air to be whisked in, which makes it more likely that the mixture might curdle or separate, giving a heavy sponge.

✳ Self-raising flour is used because the chemical raising agents added to it give the sponge its lift and light texture. As an alternative you could use 225g plain flour plus 4 teaspoons baking powder. Bread flour is too strong for sponges – it has too much gluten, which will give a tough result.

✳ To avoid the wire cooling rack from marking the sponges, invert them, one at a time, onto a board covered with a sheet of baking paper, then remove the tin and lining paper. Set the upturned rack on the underside of the sponge, turn over together and remove the paper and board.

Mary's tip
If time is short, I soften the butter by cutting it into cubes, putting the cubes into a bowl of lukewarm tap water (approximately 28°C), then leaving the cubes for 10 minutes or until a cube can be easily squeezed.

1 Preheat the oven to 180°C/350°F/gas 4. Put the soft butter into a mixing bowl and beat with a wooden spoon or electric mixer for a minute until very smooth and creamy.

2 Gradually beat in the sugar, then keep on beating for 3 to 4 minutes or until the mixture turns almost white and becomes very fluffy in texture; scrape down the bowl from time to time. Break the eggs into a small bowl, add the vanilla and beat lightly with a fork just to break them up. Slowly add to the creamed mixture, a tablespoonful at a time, giving the mixture a good beating after each addition and frequently scraping down the bowl. This will take about 5 minutes. If the mixture looks as if it is about to curdle, add a tablespoon of the sifted flour and then continue adding the last portions of egg.

3 Sift the flour again, this time onto the mixture, and add the milk. Gently but thoroughly fold the flour into the egg mixture using a large metal spoon. Do this as lightly as possible so you don't knock out any of the air you have beaten in.

4 Stop folding when there are no streaks of flour visible in the mixture. Check that there isn't a clump of flour at the very bottom.

5 Spoon the mixture into the 2 tins so they are equally filled – you can do this by eye or by weighing the tins as you fill them.

6 Spread the mixture evenly in the tins, right to the edges.

7 Bake for 20 to 25 minutes or until a good golden brown and the sponges are springy when gently pressed with your fingertip. They should almost double in size during baking.

8 Remove the tins from the oven and leave for a minute – the sponges will contract slightly. Run a round-bladed knife around the inside of each tin to loosen the sponge, then turn out onto a wire rack and leave to cool.

9 Set one sponge upside down on a serving platter and spread over the jam. Gently set the other sponge, golden crust up, on top. Dust with sugar. Store in an airtight container and eat within 5 days. (See page 13 for the finished cake.)

TECHNICAL CHALLENGE
MARY'S COFFEE AND WALNUT BATTENBURG

The original pink and white Battenburg cake was made to honour the marriage of Queen Victoria's granddaughter to Prince Louis of Battenberg in 1884. This cake is a delightful change, but still in keeping with tradition.

Makes 1 small to medium cake

100g unsalted butter, softened
100g caster sugar
2 large free-range eggs, at room
temperature
100g self-raising flour
½ teaspoon baking powder
50g ground almonds
few drops of vanilla extract
3 teaspoons milk
1½ teaspoons coffee granules
25g walnuts, chopped

For the coffee butter icing
100g icing sugar
40g unsalted butter, softened
½ teaspoon coffee granules
1½ teaspoons milk

To finish
225g white marzipan
icing sugar, for dusting
about 5 small walnut pieces

1 x 20cm square, shallow cake
tin, greased; non-stick
baking paper

✳ The mixture for traditional sponge cakes, such as that for the Victoria Sandwich on page 16, are beaten thoroughly to incorporate air. Sponges made by the all-in-one method, as here, use self-raising flour plus extra baking powder to make up for the lack of beating and help the mixture to rise.

✳ To help you roll out the marzipan to the correct size to wrap the assembled cake, cut 2 pieces of string – one that is the length of the assembled cake and one that will wrap all the way around it. Use these as measuring guides.

✳ Brush off any crumbs from the marzipan and worktop before wrapping the cake, to be sure that the outside of the cake will have a smooth, neat finish.

Mary's tip
A brilliant new product now available is parchment-lined foil. Being stiffer than standard non-stick baking paper (also called baking parchment) the foiled paper stands up firmly and keeps its shape, which will make lining the Battenburg tin a lot easier.

1 Preheat the oven to 160°C/325°F/gas 3. Cut out a rectangle of baking paper that is 20cm wide and 28cm long. Fold the paper in half widthways. Open out the paper and push up the centre fold to make a 4cm pleat. Line the base of the tin with the paper, making any adjustments to ensure the pleat runs down the centre of the tin.

2 Put the soft butter, sugar, eggs, flour, baking powder and ground almonds into a large mixing bowl and beat with a wooden spoon for 2 to 3 minutes or until smooth, slightly lighter in colour and glossy looking.

3 Spoon slightly more than half the mixture into a separate bowl and add the vanilla and 1½ teaspoons of the milk. Mix well, then set aside. Stir the coffee with the remaining milk until it has dissolved (no need to heat the milk), then add this to the first bowl of mixture together with the chopped walnuts. Spoon the vanilla mixture into one half of the tin and the coffee-walnut mixture into the other half.

4 Level the surface of each half with a knife. Be sure that the pleated paper divider is still straight and in the middle. Bake for 35 to 40 minutes or until the 2 sponges are well risen and springy to the touch and have shrunk slightly from the sides of the tin. Take out of the oven and cool in the tin for a few minutes, then run a round-bladed knife around the inside of the tin to loosen the sponges and turn them out onto a wire rack. Peel off the lining paper and leave the sponges to cool completely.

5 Trim the crisp edges off the cooled sponges using a serrated knife, then cut each lengthways into 2 equal strips. To make the butter icing, sift the icing sugar into a medium bowl. Add the butter. Stir the coffee and milk together until the coffee has dissolved, then pour into the bowl. Beat everything together with a wooden spoon until soft and smooth.

6 Lay a vanilla sponge strip and a coffee-walnut strip side by side and use a little of the butter icing to stick them together. Spread a bit more icing on the top. Stick the remaining 2 strips together with icing. Lay these on top of the icing on the other 2 strips, placing them so they will create a chequerboard effect on the ends. Spread a bit more icing over the top of the assembled chequerboard.

7 Roll out the marzipan on a worktop to make an oblong that is the length of the cake and sufficiently wide to wrap around it (use the pieces of string as your measuring guide). Lay the iced side of the cake on the marzipan oblong, positioning it so when you lift up one long side of the marzipan it perfectly covers one side of the cake (this way the join will be neatly in the corner). Reserve a teaspoonful of the icing and spread the rest over the remaining 3 sides of the cake (not the ends).

8 Roll the cake over in the marzipan, pressing to cover it neatly. Brush the corner join lightly with water and press it to seal. (Try to avoid touching the marzipan with wet fingers as they will mark it.) Turn the cake over so the join is underneath. Trim a slim slice from each end of the cake to neaten and show off the chequerboard effect. Smooth the marzipan over with your hands so their warmth will give it a smooth finish.

9 While the marzipan is still soft, crimp the edges by pinching the marzipan between your thumb and first finger at a slight angle and at regular intervals. Score the top of the cake with long diagonal lines using a sharp knife. Sift over some icing sugar to lightly dust the top, then lay the walnut pieces down the centre, securing with the reserved butter icing.

BEST OF THE BAKE-OFF
Cherry Bakewell Cup Cakes

Makes 12

For the cup cakes
150g unsalted butter, very soft
150g caster sugar
100g self-raising flour
3 large eggs, at room temperature, beaten
½ teaspoon baking powder
60g ground almonds
1 tablespoon milk, at room temperature
4 tablespoons raspberry jam

For the icing
250g icing sugar
about 3 tablespoons strained fresh lemon juice
12 glacé cherries (non-dyed), rinsed and dried

1 x 12-hole muffin tray, lined with paper muffin or cup-cake cases

Preheat the oven to 190°C/375°F/gas 5. Beat the butter with an electric mixer until creamy. Add all the other ingredients for the cup cakes, except the jam, and beat until light and creamy.

Spoon the mixture into the cup-cake cases, dividing it evenly. Level the mixture in each case using your fingertip. Bake for 15 to 20 minutes or until golden brown and firm to the touch, and a skewer inserted into the centre of a cup cake comes out clean. Remove each cup cake from the tray and place on a wire rack. Leave to cool completely.

To make the icing, sift the icing sugar into a mixing bowl and work in enough of the strained lemon juice to make a thick, but spoonable and runny icing. Set aside.

Using an apple corer, remove the centre from each cup cake, cutting only two-thirds of the way down. Stir the jam with a teaspoon until it is a little runny, then carefully spoon into the holes in the cup cakes until the jam just reaches the top (don't over-fill).

Beat the icing using a teaspoon, then spoon it over the top of each cup cake to flood the surface until the icing reaches the sides of the paper case. Take care that the jam doesn't become mixed into the icing. Add a cherry to the middle immediately and leave to set.

Mary's tip
When using glacé cherries, make sure they are washed and dried really well, otherwise the syrup they are kept in will leak into your icing, if being used to decorate the cake, or cause the cherries to sink to the bottom of the sponge cake during baking.

BEST OF THE BAKE-OFF
Chocolate and Orange Cup Cakes

Makes 12

50g dark chocolate
  (70% cocoa solids),
  broken up
120g plain flour
1 teaspoon baking power
140g caster sugar
40g unsalted butter,
  softened and diced
1 large egg, at room
  temperature
120ml full-fat milk, at
  room temperature
1 unwaxed orange
3 tablespoons granulated
  sugar
orange chocolate
  shavings, to decorate

For the buttercream
4 tablespoons full-fat
  milk
50g white chocolate
125g unsalted butter,
  softened
500g icing sugar, sifted

1 x 12-hole muffin tray,
  lined with paper muffin
  or cup-cake cases; a
  piping bag fitted with
  a star tube

Preheat the oven to 180°C/350°F/gas 4. Melt the chocolate in a heatproof bowl set over a pan of steaming hot but not boiling water (don't let the base of the bowl touch the water). Remove the bowl from the pan, stir the chocolate until smooth and leave to cool.

Put the flour, baking powder and caster sugar in a food-processor and pulse to mix. Add the butter and process until the mixture has a sandy texture. Mix the egg into the milk, then slowly add to the processor through the feed tube, while the machine is running. Scrape down the sides. Add the melted chocolate to the bowl and run the machine until thoroughly combined. Divide the mixture among the cup-cake cases. Bake for 15 to 20 minutes or until just firm to the touch.

Meanwhile, pare a long strip of peel from the orange and reserve for the buttercream. Cut the orange in half and squeeze out the juice. Mix the granulated sugar into the juice.

Pierce the hot cup cakes in several places with a skewer or cocktail stick. Spoon over the orange syrup. Leave to soak in for 5 minutes, then lift the cup cakes from the tray and cool on a wire rack.

Heat the milk in a small pan or the microwave. Add the strip of orange peel to the hot milk and leave to infuse until cold; discard the peel. Melt the chocolate as above and cool.

Using an electric mixer, beat the butter until creamy. Gradually beat in the icing sugar and the cooled milk using low speed. Finally, beat in the cooled melted chocolate.

Pipe the buttercream onto the cup cakes. Add chocolate shavings to decorate.

Quick and Simple Fruit Loaf  EASY FOR KIDS

This is possibly the easiest cake you'll ever make – all you have to do is melt the butter and mix together all the ingredients. Made with a bag of luxury dried fruit mixture, the loaf cake will look very pretty.

Makes 1 large loaf cake

175g unsalted butter
150g caster sugar
400g plain flour
good pinch of salt
4 teaspoons baking
    powder
300g luxury dried fruit
    mix
125ml full-fat or
    semi-skimmed milk, at
    room temperature
2 large free-range eggs,
    at room temperature

1 x 900g loaf tin, about
    26 x 12.5 x 7.5cm,
    greased and lined with
    a strip of greaseproof
    paper

Preheat the oven to 180°C/350°F/gas 4. Put the butter and sugar into a medium-sized pan and heat gently, stirring occasionally, until the butter has melted.

Sift the flour, salt and baking powder into a mixing bowl and stir in the dried fruit. Beat together the milk and eggs until thoroughly combined, then pour into the flour mixture. Add the melted butter and mix well with a wooden spoon.

Transfer the mixture to the prepared tin and spread evenly. Bake for about 1 hour or until the top is a good golden brown and a skewer inserted into the centre comes out clean. Remove the tin from the oven and set on a wire rack. Leave to cool for 20 minutes, then gently turn out the loaf onto the rack and leave to cool completely.

Wrap in foil or greaseproof paper and keep for 24 hours before cutting. Store in an airtight container and eat within 5 days.

Tip: If you want to add a topping, brush the cooled cake with the apricot jam glaze mixture on page 36, or spoon over a runny glacé icing (see page 223).

Gorgeous Lemon Cream Cake GOOD FOR *Celebrations*

This cake has the 'wow' factor, which makes it ideal for a summery birthday cake. The soft, light sponge layers, made from a whisked egg mixture, are rather like a swiss roll. Set aside plenty of time to make this because there are several stages, and the cake is at its best when it has had time to stand.

Makes 1 large cake

For the sponge
6 large free-range eggs, at room temperature
175g caster sugar, plus extra for sprinkling
175g plain flour

For the lemon syrup
100g caster sugar
2 large unwaxed lemons

For the filling
250ml double cream, well chilled
2 tablespoons caster sugar
500g Lemon Curd (see page 32)
400g ricotta

To finish
50g flaked almonds, toasted
2 tablespoons Lemon Curd (see page 32)

2 x 20.5cm sandwich tins, greased and the base lined with baking paper

Preheat the oven to 180°C/350°F/gas 4. Break the eggs into a large mixing bowl. Whisk using an electric mixer until frothy, then whisk in the sugar. Continue whisking on high speed for about 5 minutes or until very thick and pale in colour and the whisk leaves a ribbon-like trail. The mixture will massively increase in volume.

Sift one-third of the flour onto the mixture and carefully fold in with a large metal spoon. Repeat to add the remaining flour in 2 batches, folding until there are no visible streaks of flour. Divide the mixture between the tins and spread evenly. Bake for about 20 minutes or until well risen to the top of the tins, a good golden brown and firm to the touch.

Remove from the oven. Run a round-bladed knife around the inside of the tins to loosen the sponges. Cover a wire rack with a sheet of baking paper and sprinkle with a little caster sugar. Carefully turn out the sponges onto the paper and leave to cool completely.

Meanwhile, make the lemon syrup. Put the sugar and 100ml water into a small pan. Grate the zest from 1 lemon and add. Carefully peel the zest from the second lemon and cut into fine shreds; cover and set aside for the decoration. Halve both lemons and squeeze the juice. Add 3 tablespoons of juice to the pan. Heat gently, stirring frequently, until the sugar has dissolved, then bring to the boil and simmer for 2 minutes to make a light syrup. Leave to cool.

To make the lemon cream filling, whip the cream until thick. Add the sugar and whip until soft peaks form. Stir the lemon curd gently, then mix one-third of it with the ricotta. When thoroughly combined, fold this into the whipped cream to make a very smooth, thick mixture. Cover and chill for at least 30 minutes but no more than an hour.

When ready to assemble the cake, slice each sponge in half horizontally to make 4 thin layers. If necessary trim the sponges to neaten. Set one layer, cut surface up, on a serving plate. Brush or spoon one-quarter of the lemon syrup over the sponge and leave to soak in for a couple of minutes.

Recipe continues on page 32

Transfer just under half the lemon cream filling mixture to another bowl (this will be used to cover the cake); cover and chill. Using a palette knife, spread one-third of the remaining lemon cream over the soaked sponge. Carefully spread one-third of the remaining lemon curd on top of this. Set a second layer of sponge on top, again cut side up. Repeat with the lemon syrup, lemon cream and lemon curd. Add the third sponge layer with filling as before, then top with the final layer of sponge, this time cut side down. Brush the top of the cake with the last of the lemon syrup. Cover and chill the cake for 30 minutes.

Cover the top and sides of the cake with the reserved lemon cream. Press flaked almonds around the sides. Decorate the top with dashes of lemon curd and the reserved lemon shreds; or fill a small piping bag with the lemon curd and pipe swirls or a lattice or 'Happy Birthday'. Chill overnight in an airtight container. Remove from the fridge 30 minutes before serving. Store in the fridge and eat within 3 days.

Lemon Curd

Not just for spreading on bread, lemon curd makes a great filling for cakes and swiss rolls and for a quickly assembled hot soufflé (see page 272).

Makes about 560g

125g unsalted butter, softened
225g caster sugar
finely grated zest and juice of 3 medium unwaxed lemons
3 large free-range eggs, at room temperature, beaten

Put the butter, sugar, and lemon zest and juice into a heatproof bowl. Set over a pan of simmering water (the base of the bowl should not touch the hot water) and stir gently with a wooden spoon until the mixture is smooth and melted, and you can no longer see or feel any grains of sugar.

Remove the bowl from the pan. Strain the eggs into the mixture (straining removes any membranes or pieces of shell) and stir well. Replace the bowl over the simmering water and stir until the mixture becomes very thick and opaque. Take your time and don't turn up the heat, because if the mixture comes close to boiling the eggs will scramble. The lemon curd is ready when you can draw a finger through the mixture on the wooden spoon and see a clear path.

Immediately remove the bowl from the heat and transfer the lemon curd to a clean bowl or screw-topped jar. Leave to cool, then cover and chill. The lemon curd can be stored in the fridge for up to 2 weeks.

Flourless Lemon and Cream Roll

This moist whisked sponge is made with ground almonds instead of flour. It is filled with lemon curd and whipped cream, and will taste like a rich lemon mousse if left to stand for a couple of hours before cutting.

Makes 1 medium cake

For the sponge
4 large free-range eggs, at room temperature
125g caster sugar, plus extra for sprinkling
finely grated zest and juice of 2 medium unwaxed lemons
100g ground almonds

For the filling
6 tablespoons Lemon Curd (see opposite)
200ml double or whipping cream, well chilled

1 swiss roll tin, about 20.5 x 31cm, greased and the base lined with baking paper

Preheat the oven to 180°C/350°F/gas 4. Separate the eggs, putting the yolks into one mixing bowl and the whites into another. Add the sugar and lemon zest to the yolks and whisk with an electric mixer for about 3 minutes or until paler in colour and very thick and mousse-like in texture. Carefully fold in the ground almonds and lemon juice using a large metal spoon.

Whisk the egg whites until they stand in stiff peaks, then gently but thoroughly fold into the yolk mixture in 3 batches.

Transfer the mixture to the prepared tin and spread evenly. Bake for about 20 minutes or until the top is golden brown and the sponge feels just firm but springy. Set the sponge, in its tin, on a wire rack. Cover with a sheet of greaseproof paper and then a damp tea towel – this helps prevent the roll from cracking when you roll it up. Leave to cool completely.

Turn out the sponge onto a sheet of greaseproof paper sprinkled with caster sugar. Trim off the crusty edges with a sharp knife, then make a shallow cut across the sponge about 2cm from one short end (this will help form a tighter and neater spiral). Spread the lemon curd over the sponge, just to the edges. Whip the cream until firm, then spread it over the lemon curd to within 3cm of the edges.

Gently roll up the sponge from the end with the cut, using the greaseproof paper to help you. The sponge may crack a little. Carefully transfer the roll to a serving plate and sprinkle with more caster sugar. Cover and chill for about 2 hours or until ready to serve. This is best eaten with 24 hours.

Speckled Mocha Cake GOOD FOR *Celebrations*

A gorgeous, richly flavoured creamed-sponge cake, this is flecked with dark chocolate and filled with a mocha butter icing. It will become more moist and richer in taste as it matures, so for the best results make it a day in advance of cutting.

Makes 1 medium cake

For the sponge
175g unsalted butter, softened
175g caster sugar
3 large free-range eggs, at room temperature
175g self-raising flour
¼ teaspoon baking powder
1½ tablespoons instant coffee, dissolved in 2 tablespoons water
50g dark chocolate (70% cocoa solids)

For the filling
50g dark chocolate (70% cocoa solids)
1 tablespoon instant coffee, dissolved in 1 tablespoon water
50g unsalted butter, softened
100g icing sugar, sifted

To finish
icing sugar, for dusting
chocolate coffee beans, to decorate (optional)

2 x 20.5cm sandwich tins, greased and the base lined with baking paper

Preheat the oven to 180°C/350°F/gas 4. Put the butter into a mixing bowl and beat with a wooden spoon or electric mixer for about 1 minute or until really creamy. Gradually beat in the sugar. Continue beating until the mixture becomes very pale and fluffy in texture.

Beat the eggs with a fork just to mix, then gradually add to the butter mixture, beating well after each addition. Sift the flour and baking powder into the bowl and gently fold into the mixture with a large metal spoon, followed by the coffee. Grate the chocolate and mix in gently.

When thoroughly combined, divide the mixture between the 2 tins and spread evenly. Bake for 20 to 25 minutes or until the sponges spring back when gently pressed. Run a round-bladed knife around the inside of the tins to loosen the sponges, then turn out onto a wire rack and leave to cool completely.

To make the filling, roughly chop the chocolate and put into a heatproof bowl with the coffee. Set over a pan of steaming hot but not boiling water (don't let the base of the bowl touch the hot water) and leave to melt. Remove the bowl from the pan and stir the chocolate gently, then add the butter and icing sugar. Beat well until smooth. Leave the filling mixture until it is firm enough to spread.

Sandwich the 2 sponges together with the filling. Set the cake on a serving plate and dust with sifted icing sugar. If you like, decorate with a few chocolate coffee beans in the centre. Store in an airtight container and eat within 5 days.

Lemon Poppyseed Madeira Cake

A fine Madeira cake should have a moist, close texture and taste of good butter. The mixture needs plenty of beating to incorporate as much air as possible and to avoid a solid, dense crumb.

Makes 1 medium cake

250g plain flour
1 teaspoon baking
    powder
good pinch of salt
2 teaspoons poppyseeds
225g unsalted butter,
    softened
200g caster sugar
finely grated zest of
    1 large unwaxed lemon
3 large free-range eggs,
    at room temperature,
    beaten
2 tablespoons fresh
    lemon juice

1 x 20cm round, deep
    cake tin or springclip
    tin, greased and lined
    with baking paper

Preheat the oven to 170°C/325°F/gas 3. Sift the flour, baking powder and salt into a bowl. Stir in the poppyseeds and set aside until needed.

Put the soft butter into a mixing bowl and beat well for 1 minute using a wooden spoon or an electric mixer. Gradually beat in the sugar and then the lemon zest. Continue beating for about 5 minutes or until the mixture is very pale and fluffy.

Gradually beat in the eggs, adding just a tablespoonful at a time and beating well after each addition. To prevent the mixture from curdling, add a tablespoonful of the sifted flour mixture with the last portion of egg. Beat in the lemon juice, then carefully fold in the remaining flour mixture with a large metal spoon until thoroughly combined.

Transfer the mixture to the prepared tin and spread evenly. Gently bang the tin on the worktop to remove any pockets of air. Using the back of the metal spoon, make a slight hollow in the centre so the cake will rise evenly.

Bake for 1 to 1¼ hours or until firm to the touch and golden brown; a skewer inserted into the centre of the cake should come out clean. Set the tin on a wire rack and leave to cool completely, then remove the cake from the tin and peel off the lining paper. If not eating immediately, wrap in fresh paper and store in an airtight container for up to 4 days.

Paul's tip
When making sponges ensure that all the ingredients are the same temperature, as this will give you a better rise.

Golden Apricot and Marzipan Loaf Cake

 EASY FOR KIDS GOOD FOR *Celebrations*

The combination of soft-dried apricots and chunks of marzipan produces a richly flavoured, moist loaf cake. It's easily made by rubbing butter into flour and then stirring together with the rest of the ingredients, adding the diced marzipan to the mixture in the tin. The cake is pretty and special enough to bake in a round tin for a Golden Wedding celebration.

Makes 1 large loaf cake

For the cake mixture
300g self-raising flour
good pinch of salt
150g unsalted butter,
    cool and firm, but not
    rock-hard
100g golden caster sugar
100g soft-dried apricots
150g sultanas
2 large free-range eggs
½ teaspoon vanilla
    extract
150ml full-fat or
    semi-skimmed milk
150g marzipan

To finish
2 tablespoons apricot
    jam
1 tablespoon boiling
    water
2 tablespoons flaked
    almonds

1 x 900g loaf tin, about
    26 x 12.5 x 7.5cm (or
    a 20cm round, deep
    cake tin), greased and
    the base lined with
    baking paper

Preheat the oven to 180°C/350°F/gas 4. Sift the flour and salt into a mixing bowl. Cut the butter into small pieces; add to the bowl and toss in the flour. Rub the pieces of butter into the flour between the tips of your fingers until the mixture looks like fine crumbs. (You can also do this stage in a food-processor.)

Stir in the sugar. Roughly chop the apricots or cut into small chunks with kitchen scissors. Add to the bowl with the sultanas and mix well. Beat the eggs with the vanilla and milk until thoroughly combined. Add to the bowl and mix with a wooden spoon to make a stiff cake mixture that should just drop off the spoon with a shake of the wrist.

Spoon one-third of the mixture into the prepared tin and spread evenly. Cut the marzipan into 1.5cm cubes and arrange half on top of the cake mixture. Cover with half of the remaining mixture, spreading it evenly. Arrange the rest of the marzipan cubes on this layer. Spread the rest of the cake mixture on top to evenly fill the tin.

Gently bang the tin on the worktop to get rid of any pockets of air. Bake for 1 to 1¼ hours or until a skewer inserted into the centre comes out clean (it's best to test in several different places, because it's hard to avoid the marzipan). Transfer the tin to a wire rack. Run a round-bladed knife around the inside of the tin to loosen the cake, then leave to cool for 15 minutes before carefully turning out and cooling completely on the wire rack.

To finish, gently warm the apricot jam with the water, stirring to make a sticky glaze. Brush this over the top of the cake. Scatter the flaked almonds over the cake. Leave to set. Store in an airtight container and eat within 5 days.

Hazelnut and Chocolate Cake GOOD FOR *Celebrations*

Chocolate cakes made with nuts often taste more of chocolate than anything else; however, here the flavour of the roasted hazelnuts really comes through. The cake is moist but not dense and not too sweet – it would also be good for dessert, served with crème fraîche or vanilla ice cream.

Makes 1 medium cake

150g blanched hazelnuts
(hazelnuts with their
skins removed)
175g dark chocolate
(70% cocoa solids),
roughly chopped
200g caster sugar
2 tablespoons plain flour
100g unsalted butter,
softened
5 large free-range eggs,
at room temperature,
separated
good pinch of salt

For the topping
50g blanched hazelnuts
25g dark chocolate
(70% cocoa solids)

1 x 22cm springclip tin,
greased and the base
lined with baking paper

Preheat the oven to 180°C/350°F/gas 4. Spread out the hazelnuts in an ovenproof dish or small tin and toast in the oven for 10 minutes or until light golden brown. Leave to cool completely.

Put the chocolate into a heatproof bowl and set over a pan of steaming hot but not boiling water (don't let the base of the bowl touch the hot water). Melt gently, stirring occasionally. Remove the bowl from the pan and leave to cool.

Tip the cooled hazelnuts into the bowl of a food-processor with 50g of the sugar and the flour. 'Pulse' until the mixture looks like a fairly fine powder – stop the machine before it forms a paste.

Put the butter into a large mixing bowl and beat with a wooden spoon or an electric mixer until creamy. Gradually beat in all but 2 tablespoons of the remaining sugar. Continue beating until the mixture becomes paler and light in texture. Add the egg yolks one at a time, beating well after each addition. Using a large metal spoon fold in the cooled melted chocolate followed by the nut mixture.

Put the egg whites into a large bowl with the pinch of salt and whisk until they stand in stiff peaks. Whisk in the reserved 2 tablespoons of sugar, then fold into the chocolate-nut mixture in 3 batches.

Spoon the cake mixture into the prepared tin and spread evenly. Scatter the whole blanched hazelnuts over the top. Bake for about 45 minutes or until a skewer inserted into the cake, halfway between the side of the tin and the centre, comes out clean (the centre of the cake should still be soft and moist).

Transfer the tin to a wire rack. Run a round-bladed knife around the inside of the tin, then carefully unclip the tin side – the cake will be fragile. Leave to cool completely. The cake will firm up as it cools.

Melt the chocolate for the topping as above. Spoon it into a small piping bag and make a zig-zag pattern over the top of the cake. Store in an airtight container and eat within 4 days.

BEST OF THE BAKE-OFF
Rhubarb and Custard Cup Cakes

Makes 12

80g unsalted butter,
   very soft
270g caster sugar
240g plain flour
1 tablespoon baking
   powder
¼ teaspoon salt
240ml full-fat milk
2 large eggs, at room
   temperature
½ teaspoon vanilla
   extract

For the filling
75ml whipping cream
75ml full-fat milk
½ vanilla pod, split open
1 large egg yolk
25g caster sugar
15g cornflour
3 tablespoons rhubarb
   compote

For the buttercream
90g caster sugar
2 large egg whites, at
   room temperature
250g unsalted butter,
   softened
1 teaspoon vanilla extract

1 x 12-hole muffin, lined
   with paper muffin or
   cup-cake cases; piping
   bag and star tube; a
   sugar thermometer

Preheat the oven to 200°C/400°F/gas 6. Using an electric mixer, beat together the butter, sugar, flour, baking powder and salt until the mixture has a sandy consistency. In a bowl or jug combine the milk, eggs and vanilla. Gradually add three-quarters of this to the butter mixture, beating constantly, and beat until smooth. Scrape down the sides of the bowl, then add the remaining milk mixture and beat until smooth again.

Divide the mixture among the paper cases, filling them about two-thirds full. Bake for 18 to 20 minutes or until firm and golden brown. Remove from the oven and allow to cool for 1 to 2 minutes in the tray, then transfer to a wire rack and leave to cool completely.

Meanwhile, make the filling. Put the cream and milk in a pan. Scrape the seeds from the vanilla pod into the pan; add the pod too. Heat gently until hot but not boiling. In a bowl, beat the egg yolk with the sugar until very pale and fluffy. Add the cornflour and mix in. Remove the vanilla pod from the hot cream mixture, then pour it into the egg mixture, whisking constantly. Pour back into the pan and cook, stirring, over low heat for 1 to 2 minutes or until the custard thickens. Pour into a large bowl and leave to cool.

For the buttercream, put all but 1 tablespoon of the sugar in a small heavy pan with 4 teaspoons water and dissolve the sugar over low heat. Raise the heat to medium and boil the sugar syrup undisturbed until a sugar thermometer registers 115°C/240°F.

While the syrup is boiling, whisk the egg whites in a large, free-standing electric mixer until they hold soft peaks. Beat in the reserved tablespoon of sugar. Beating on medium speed, gradually add the hot syrup in a slow steady stream, then continue beating for 8 to 10 minutes or until the meringue is stiff and smooth and completely cold.

With the mixer still on medium speed, beat in the butter a 1cm lump at a time until thick and smooth. (The mixture may curdle but will become smooth again as you beat in more butter.) Finally, add the vanilla extract and beat until combined.

Cut a small hollow in the top of each cup cake and put in a little rhubarb compote. Pipe the custard over the compote, then pipe the buttercream over the top. Decorate with rhubarb and custard sweets. You could use whipped cream instead of the buttercream for a less sugary version.

Quick Chocolate Fudge Cake  EASY FOR KIDS

All the chopping and mixing here is done quickly and effortlessly in a food-processor. You just need to have everything weighed and ready before you start – the tin prepared, flour sifted, coffee made (in a cafetière or using instant coffee) and eggs beaten. During baking the mixture turns into a very moist, brownie-like sponge that is not too sweet. The topping is simple too – just melt and mix.

Makes 1 large cake

For the sponge
100g pecan halves
100g plain flour
1 teaspoon baking powder
½ teaspoon bicarbonate of
   soda
75g dark chocolate (70%
   cocoa solids), broken up
2 tablespoons cocoa
   powder
200g light brown
   muscovado sugar
100ml hot black coffee
2 large free-range eggs,
   at room temperature,
   beaten
175g unsalted butter,
   softened and cut into
   pieces
125ml soured cream

For the icing
75g dark chocolate (70%
   cocoa solids), broken up
25g unsalted butter
3 tablespoons icing sugar
2 tablespoons black coffee

1 traybake tin or cake tin,
   25.5 x 20.5 x 5cm,
   greased and the base
   lined with greased paper

Preheat the oven to 160°C/325°F/gas 3. Arrange the pecans in the base of the prepared tin, pressing them onto the greased paper.

Sift the flour with the baking powder and bicarbonate of soda; set aside. Put the chocolate into the bowl of a food-processor with the cocoa and 100g of the sugar. Process until the mixture looks sandy-textured. With the machine running pour in the hot coffee through the feed tube and process until the chocolate has melted. Stop the machine and scrape down the sides of the bowl.

Add the eggs and the rest of the sugar, and process for 30 seconds. Scrape down the bowl again, then add the butter and run the machine for a minute. Scrape down the bowl once more. Add the soured cream and the flour mixture, and process just until the mixture becomes a smooth, streak-free batter.

Spoon the mixture into the tin on top of the nuts. Bake for about 45 minutes or until the sponge has started to shrink away from the sides of the tin, and a skewer inserted into the centre comes out clean. The top will have a crust but will be only just firm.

Remove from the oven. Run a round-bladed knife around the inside of the tin to loosen the sponge, then leave to cool completely in the tin. When cold, set a board on top of the tin and invert. Lift off the tin and the lining paper – the nutty base of the cake is now the top.

To make the icing put the chocolate into a small, heavy-based pan with the butter, icing sugar and coffee. Set on the lowest possible heat and stir gently until melted and smooth. Remove from the heat and leave until thick enough to spread. Cover the top of the cake with the icing and leave to set before cutting. Store in an airtight container and eat within 4 days.

Banana Fudge Layer Cake GOOD FOR *Celebrations*

Here, a creamed vanilla sponge mixture is baked in three layers, then sandwiched with a thick, creamy fudge and sliced bananas – definitely a cake for those with a sweet tooth! If you enjoy the taste of salted caramels, add ¼ teaspoon sea salt flakes to the fudge mixture.

Makes 1 large cake

For the sponge
175g unsalted butter, softened
150g caster sugar
25g light brown muscovado sugar
3 large free-range eggs, at room temperature, beaten
175g self-raising flour
½ teaspoon vanilla extract
1 tablespoon milk, at room temperature

For the filling and topping
175g light brown muscovado sugar
150g unsalted butter
75g double cream
2 ripe medium bananas

3 x 20.5cm sandwich tins, greased and the base lined with baking paper

Preheat the oven to 180°C/350°F/gas 4. Put the soft butter into a mixing bowl and beat with a wooden spoon or an electric mixer until creamy. Gradually beat in the 2 sugars and beat well until the mixture turns paler in colour and becomes light and fluffy in texture.

Gradually add the eggs, beating well after each addition; add a tablespoon of the flour with the last portion of egg to prevent the mixture from curdling. Sift the remaining flour into the bowl and fold into the mixture with a large metal spoon. Combine the vanilla extract with the milk and fold in.

Divide the mixture equally among the 3 prepared tins and spread evenly. Bake for 18 to 20 minutes or until light golden brown and just firm to the touch; if necessary, rotate the tins after 15 minutes in the oven so the cakes cook evenly. Run a round-bladed knife around the inside of each tin, then turn out the sponges onto a wire rack. Leave to cool completely.

Meanwhile, make the fudge mixture. Put the sugar, butter and cream into a medium pan and set over low heat. Stir frequently until the butter has melted. Turn up the heat slightly and simmer for 3 minutes, stirring frequently to prevent the mixture from catching on the base of the pan.

Remove from the heat and stir vigorously for 30 seconds. (Add the sea salt flakes, if using.) Leave to cool, occasionally giving the mixture a gentle stir. It is ready to use once it has become spreadable – in warm weather you may need to put it in the fridge for just a few minutes to firm up.

Spread one-third of the fudge mixture on top of each cake; select one to be the top layer and swirl the fudge decoratively with a round-bladed knife. Slice the bananas very thinly and arrange on top of the fudge on the 2 other layers. Sandwich the layers together with the swirled fudge layer on the top. Store in an airtight container and eat within 4 days.

Devil's Food Cake

The flavour of this dark chocolate sponge cake develops and improves as it matures, so make it a day or so before serving. You could also use a white American-style marshmallow frosting to ice this cake (see page 310).

Makes 1 large cake

For the sponge
4 tablespoons cocoa powder
175ml boiling water
1 teaspoon bicarbonate of soda
100g dark chocolate (70% cocoa solids)
125g unsalted butter, softened
350g caster sugar
2 large free-range eggs, at room temperature
1 teaspoon vanilla extract
300g plain flour, sifted
125ml soured cream, at room temperature

For the filling and topping
300g dark chocolate (70% cocoa solids), broken up
300ml soured cream, at room temperature
100g good-quality white chocolate, broken up

2 x 20.5cm sandwich tins, greased and the base lined with baking paper; non-stick baking paper or a re-usable silicone sheet

Preheat the oven to 180°C/350°F/gas 4. Put the cocoa into a heatproof bowl and mix to a smooth liquid with the boiling water. Stir in the bicarbonate of soda and leave to cool.

Break up the chocolate into another heatproof bowl and set over a pan of steaming hot but not boiling water (don't let the base of the bowl touch the hot water). Leave to melt gently. Remove the bowl from the pan. Stir the chocolate until smooth, then leave to cool.

Put the soft butter into a large mixing bowl and beat for a minute with a wooden spoon or an electric mixer until creamy. Gradually beat in the sugar, then beat thoroughly for 4 to 5 minutes or until very light. Beat the eggs and vanilla with a fork until broken up, then add to the butter mixture a tablespoon at a time, beating well after each addition.

Fold in the flour in 3 batches, alternately with the soured cream. Mix the cocoa liquid into the melted chocolate, then fold into the cake mixture. When thoroughly combined – no streaks visible – divide the mixture between the 2 tins and spread evenly.

Bake for about 30 minutes or until risen and just firm, and a skewer inserted into the cakes comes out clean. Run a round-bladed knife around the inside of the tins to loosen the sponges, then turn out onto a wire rack and cool. When cold, slice each one horizontally in half, to make 4 layers.

To make the filling and topping, melt the chocolate as before. Remove the bowl from the pan and stir in the soured cream. Reserve half of the chocolate cream for covering the cake. Set one sponge layer, cut side up, on a serving platter. Spread with one-third of the remaining chocolate cream. Layer up the rest of the sponges in the same way, ending with a sponge layer, crust side up. Spread the reserved chocolate cream over the top and sides of the cake. (If the chocolate cream starts to stiffen before you have finished covering the cake, set the bowl over a pan of steaming hot water for a few seconds and stir gently until softened.)

Melt the white chocolate, then spread, fairly thinly, onto a sheet of baking paper and leave to set. Break into long, thin shards and scatter over the cake. Store the cake in an airtight container in a cool spot (not the fridge).

Chocolate Chilli Cake

A plain and fairly simple chocolate loaf cake, unadorned and yet that little bit different: the 'secret' ingredient is hot chilli sauce. Add a few drops to make it interesting or ¼ teaspoon if you enjoy a warm spicy 'kick'. The texture is soft, light and moist – it's good eaten warm with custard and makes a good cake for a picnic.

Makes 1 large loaf cake

250ml semi-skimmed or full-fat milk
100g dark chocolate (70% cocoa solids), broken up
¼ teaspoon ground ginger
¼ teaspoon Tabasco sauce (or to taste)
250g plain flour
1 tablespoon cocoa powder
2 teaspoons baking powder
½ teaspoon bicarbonate of soda
150g unsalted butter, softened
300g light brown muscovado sugar
1 tablespoon black treacle
3 large free-range eggs, at room temperature
cocoa powder or icing sugar, for dusting

1 x 900g loaf tin, about 26 x 12.5 x 7.5cm, greased and the base lined with baking paper

Preheat the oven to 180°C/350°F/gas 4. Heat the milk in a small pan until scalding hot but not boiling. Remove from the heat and add the chocolate, ginger and Tabasco. Stir or whisk gently until melted and smooth. Leave to cool. Meanwhile, sift the flour, cocoa powder, baking powder and bicarbonate of soda into a bowl. Set aside until needed.

Put the soft butter into a mixing bowl and beat with a wooden spoon or an electric mixer until creamy. Make sure the sugar is free of lumps, then gradually beat it into the butter, followed by the treacle. Beat thoroughly for 4 to 5 minutes or until the mixture looks much paler and fluffier in texture.

Beat the eggs with a fork just to mix, then gradually add to the mixture, beating well after each addition. Using a large metal spoon, stir in the flour mixture in 3 batches, alternately with the cold chocolate milk. When thoroughly combined pour into the prepared tin and spread evenly.

Bake for 55 to 60 minutes or until firm and a skewer inserted into the centre comes out clean. Leave to cool in the tin for 5 minutes – the cake will shrink slightly – then turn out onto a wire rack and cool completely. For the best flavour, wrap the cake in foil and keep for a day before cutting. Dust with cocoa powder or icing sugar before serving.

Tip: Make sure the chocolate milk is cold before mixing it into the creamed mixture or it will melt the butter.

BEST OF THE BAKE-OFF
Earl Grey Cup Cakes

Makes 12

For the cup cakes
200ml semi-skimmed
    milk
2 Earl Grey tea bags
115g unsalted butter,
    softened
225g caster sugar
2 large eggs, at room
    temperature
250g plain flour mixed
    with 1 teaspoon
    baking powder

For the icing
75g unsalted butter,
    softened
grated zest and juice of 2
    large unwaxed lemons
375g icing sugar, sifted

1 x 12-hole muffin, lined
    with paper muffin
    or cup-cake cases; a
    piping bag fitted with a
    star tube (optional)

Preheat the oven to 180°C/350°F/gas 4. Heat the milk in a pan until it is steaming hot. Remove from the heat, add the tea bags and leave to infuse for 2 minutes. Squeeze the bags gently, then remove them. Measure 150ml milk and leave to cool to room temperature (if the milk is warm it will melt the butter in the cake mixture).

In a large mixing bowl, beat the butter with the sugar until creamy. Add the eggs, one at a time, beating in well. Add one-third of the flour to the creamed mixture and beat well. Pour in one-third of the measured tea-infused milk and beat again. Repeat until all the flour and milk have been added.

Carefully spoon the mixture into the cup-cake cases, dividing evenly so they are all about two-thirds full. Bake for about 20 minutes or until a skewer inserted into the centre of a cup cake comes out clean. Remove from the oven and leave the cakes in the tray for about 10 minutes, then transfer to a wire rack to cool.

To make the icing, beat the butter with 5 tablespoons of the lemon juice and half the icing sugar until smooth. Gradually add the remainder of the icing sugar, beating well until smooth and creamy. Taste and add a little more juice if needed. Pipe or spread swirls of icing onto the cupcakes and decorate with the lemon zest.

Blood Orange Sponge Cake

When blood oranges appear in the shops, you know spring is around the corner. They are usually medium-sized, with a tough skin, vivid scarlet flesh and juice that tastes slightly tarter than you might expect. Their season is quite short, so make the most of them. This very light whisked sponge is made without flour or butter – the rich flavour and moist texture come from the almonds and the orange soaking syrup.

Makes 1 medium cake

For the sponge
6 large free-range eggs,
  at room temperature
175g caster sugar
finely grated zest of
  2 blood oranges
100g ground almonds
75g flaked almonds

For the syrup
100g caster sugar
juice of 4 blood oranges

To finish
1 blood orange, peeled
  and thinly sliced
25g flaked almonds

1 x 22cm springclip tin,
  greased and the base
  lined with baking paper

Preheat the oven to 180°C/350°F/gas 4. Separate the eggs, putting the yolks into one large mixing bowl and the whites into another. Add the sugar and grated orange zest to the egg yolks and beat with an electric mixer until very thick and mousse-like – this will take about 3 minutes. Using a large metal spoon, stir in the ground almonds.

Whisk the egg whites until they stand in stiff peaks. With a large metal spoon fold them into the yolk mixture in 3 batches, adding the flaked almonds with the last batch of whites.

Spoon the mixture into the prepared tin and spread evenly. Bake for 45 minutes or until the sponge is golden brown and springy when lightly pressed; during baking the mixture will puff up like a soufflé and then gradually sink.

While the sponge is baking, make the soaking syrup. Put the sugar and orange juice into a medium pan. Heat gently, stirring frequently until the sugar has dissolved, then bring to the boil. Simmer for 2 to 3 minutes to make a light syrup.

As soon as the sponge is cooked, remove it from the oven and set it, still in the tin, on a large plate. Run a round-bladed knife around the inside of the tin to loosen the sponge. Prick the sponge all over with a skewer, then spoon the hot syrup over the cake, reserving 2 tablespoons. As the sponge cools it will absorb all the syrup.

When ready to serve, remove the cake from the tin and decorate the top with the orange slices. Spoon the reserved syrup over the orange slices, then scatter the flaked almonds over them. The cake can be kept, well covered, in a cool place (not the fridge) for 24 hours. Serve at room temperature.

Strawberry and White Chocolate Cream Cake

GOOD FOR
Celebrations

A summertime celebration deserves a special cake for dessert. The sponge for this gorgeous cake is made with melted white chocolate, which adds deep flavour but not heaviness. It is filled with whipped cream and ripe strawberries soaked in an orange syrup, then finished off with more cream, berries and white chocolate.

Makes 1 large cake

For the sponge
150g good-quality white chocolate, broken up
200g unsalted butter, diced and softened
3 large free-range eggs, at room temperature
150g caster sugar
finely grated zest of ½ unwaxed orange
200g self-raising flour

For the filling and topping
400g ripe strawberries
finely grated zest and juice of ½ unwaxed orange
1 tablespoon caster sugar (or to taste)
200ml double or whipping cream, well chilled
50g good-quality white chocolate, to decorate

2 x 20.5cm sandwich tins, greased and the base lined with baking paper

Preheat the oven to 180°C/350°F/gas 4. Put the chocolate into a heatproof bowl. Set over a pan of steaming hot but not boiling water (don't let the base of the bowl touch the hot water) and melt very gently, stirring frequently. Remove the bowl from the heat and stir until smooth. Add the butter and stir until it has melted.

Put the eggs into a mixing bowl and whisk with an electric mixer until frothy. Add the sugar and orange zest and whisk on high speed until the mixture is very thick and mousse-like, and the whisk leaves a ribbon-like trail when lifted from the bowl. This takes about 4 minutes.

Give the chocolate and butter mixture a stir, then add to the egg mixture and stir briefly – it should be just combined. Sift the flour into the bowl and gently fold in using a large metal spoon.

Divide the mixture between the prepared tins and spread evenly. Bake for 20 to 25 minutes or until the sponges are light golden brown and springy to the touch. Run a round-bladed knife around the inside of the tins to loosen the sponges, then turn out onto a wire rack and leave to cool.

When ready to assemble the cake, wipe the strawberries with kitchen paper and hull. Save one-third (the good-looking ones) for decoration; thinly slice the rest into a bowl. Add the orange zest and juice and the sugar and mix gently. Leave for 10 to 30 minutes to allow the flavours to develop. Meanwhile, whip the cream until thick.

Set one sponge, browned top down, on a serving plate. Spoon the sliced strawberries and juice onto the sponge to cover evenly. Spread half the whipped cream on top. Set the second sponge, browned top up, on the cream. Carefully spread the rest of the cream over the top, then decorate with the reserved strawberries, cut into halves.

Keep the cake chilled, in an airtight container, until ready to serve (up to 12 hours). Remove from the fridge 30 minutes before serving and decorate the top with curls or gratings of white chocolate.

Sticky Orange Marmalade Cake

A really good Seville orange marmalade – home-made or a top brand – with an intense bittersweet flavour plus decent chunks of peel, transforms a simple creamed sponge mixture into an old-fashioned treat.

Makes 1 medium cake

For the sponge
175g unsalted butter, softened
175g caster sugar
3 large free-range eggs, at room temperature, beaten
175g self-raising flour
pinch of salt
½ teaspoon baking powder
3 tablespoons chunky Seville orange marmalade
2 tablespoons full-fat or semi-skimmed milk

To finish
3 tablespoons chunky Seville orange marmalade
100g icing sugar
2 tablespoons warm water

1 x 20cm round, deep cake tin or springclip tin, greased and the base lined with baking paper

Preheat the oven to 180°C/350°F/gas 4. Put the soft butter into a mixing bowl and beat with a wooden spoon or electric mixer for 1 minute or until creamy. Gradually beat in the sugar, then continue beating until the mixture becomes paler and fluffy.

Gradually add the eggs, beating well after each addition; add a tablespoon of the flour with the last portion of egg. Sift the remaining flour, the salt and baking powder into the bowl and gently fold into the mixture with a large metal spoon. When thoroughly combined add the marmalade and milk and stir in.

Spoon the mixture into the prepared tin and spread evenly. Bake for 50 to 55 minutes or until a good golden brown and firm to the touch. Run a round-bladed knife around the inside of the tin to loosen the cake, then carefully turn out onto a wire rack. Gently warm the second portion of marmalade and brush over the top of the warm cake. Leave to cool completely.

Sift the icing sugar into a bowl, add the warm water and mix to a smooth, runny icing using a wooden spoon. Spoon the icing over the cake and let it run down the sides – the chunks of marmalade will stick up through the icing. Leave until set before cutting. Store in an airtight container and eat within 5 days.

BEN

Double-Chocolate Marbled Loaf Cake

Adding melted dark and white chocolate turns a Madeira-style creamed cake mixture into a wonderful loaf that looks as good as it tastes. Once the chocolate is added to the sponge mixture it will start to firm up, so you will need to work fairly quickly.

Makes 1 large loaf cake

For the sponge
250g unsalted butter, softened
250g caster sugar
4 large free-range eggs, at room temperature
1 teaspoon vanilla extract
250g self-raising flour
good pinch of salt
75g dark chocolate (70% cocoa solids), roughly chopped
75g good-quality white chocolate, roughly chopped
1 tablespoon cocoa powder

To finish
25g dark chocolate (70% cocoa solids), roughly chopped
25g good-quality white chocolate, roughly chopped
30g unsalted butter, diced

1 x 900g loaf tin, about 26 x 12.5 x 7.5cm, greased and lined with a strip of greaseproof paper

Preheat the oven to 170°C/325°F/gas 3. Put the soft butter into a bowl and beat with a wooden spoon or electric mixer for 1 minute or until creamy. Gradually beat in the sugar and beat thoroughly until the mixture turns pale and fluffy.

Beat the eggs with the vanilla just until combined, then gradually add to the creamed mixture, beating well after each addition; add 1 tablespoon of the flour with each of the last 2 portions of egg to prevent the mixture from curdling. Sift the rest of the flour with the salt into the bowl and gently fold in with a large metal spoon. Transfer half the mixture to another bowl.

Put the dark chocolate into a heatproof bowl and set over a pan of steaming hot but not boiling water (don't let the base of the bowl touch the hot water). Melt gently, stirring frequently. Remove the bowl from the pan and leave to cool while you melt the white chocolate in the same way.

Sift the cocoa powder into one bowl of cake mixture. Add the cooled melted dark chocolate and mix gently until thoroughly combined. Carefully stir the cooled melted white chocolate into the other bowl of cake mixture. Spoon both mixtures into the prepared loaf tin, adding tablespoonfuls of each mixture alternately. Gently bang the tin on the worktop to eliminate any pockets of air, and carefully smooth the surface. Draw a chopstick or table knife through the two mixtures, swirling, to marble them.

Bake for about 1¼ hours or until a skewer inserted into the centre of the cake comes out clean. Set the tin on a wire rack and leave to cool for 20 minutes, then carefully turn out the cake onto the rack and leave to cool.

To finish, put the dark chocolate into one heatproof bowl and the white chocolate into another. Add half of the butter to each bowl, then melt gently as above. Using a teaspoon (or a small piping bag), drizzle the 2 chocolate mixtures over the top of the cooled cake. Leave to set, then wrap the cake in greaseproof paper or foil and leave for a day before slicing. Store in an airtight container and eat within 5 days.

Butter Icing

This is a simple but useful icing for filling and topping small cakes and sponges. It can be spread on top of the cakes or spooned into a piping bag fitted with a star tube and piped in swirls or rosettes. You can colour the icing by adding edible food colouring a couple of drops at a time. For a coffee icing, replace the milk with cold, very strong black coffee.

Makes enough to decorate 24 fairy cakes or 12 larger cup cakes, or to fill and top a 20cm sponge cake

125g unsalted butter, softened
400g icing sugar
3–4 tablespoons milk

To flavour
1 teaspoon vanilla extract
  OR 3 tablespoons
  cocoa powder

Put the soft butter into a mixing bowl and beat with a wooden spoon or an electric mixer until paler in colour and very creamy. Sift the icing sugar into the bowl. Add the milk and the vanilla or cocoa, depending on whether you want a vanilla or chocolate icing. Beat (on low speed if using an electric mixer) until very smooth and thick.

Use the icing immediately, or cover and chill. (If the icing is too firm after chilling, leave it to soften at room temperature until it is easy to spread or pipe.)

Buttercream

This icing is considerably richer, lighter and creamier than simple Butter Icing (see opposite page), but slightly trickier to make. For the best results, you need to use a sugar thermometer.

Makes enough to decorate 24 fairy cakes or 12 larger cup cakes, or to fill and top a 20cm sponge cake

85g caster sugar
2 large free-range egg yolks
150g unsalted butter, very soft but not runny

To flavour
1 teaspoon vanilla extract OR 75g dark chocolate (70% cocoa solids), melted and cooled, OR 1–2 tablespoons cold, very strong black coffee; a sugar thermometer

Put the sugar and 4 tablespoons water into a small heavy-based pan and heat gently, without boiling, until the sugar dissolves. Bring to the boil and boil until the temperature reaches 110°C/225°F on a sugar/cooking thermometer (often called the fine thread stage). This will take about 5 minutes. Don't let the syrup start to caramelize.

Meanwhile, put the egg yolks into a heatproof bowl and mix briefly. Stand the bowl on a damp cloth to keep it from slipping. Pour the hot sugar syrup into the bowl in a thin, steady stream, whisking constantly with an electric mixer. Keep whisking until the mixture becomes very thick and mousse-like, pale in colour and completely cold.

Gradually whisk in the soft butter followed by the vanilla, chocolate or coffee (to taste). Spoon or pipe the buttercream onto the cakes. In warm weather, chill the decorated cakes just until the icing is firm.

CHOCOLATE CRACKLES

COCONUT MACAROONS

STICKY MAPLE APPLE TRAYBAKE

WALNUT CRUMBLES DROP SCONES

BISCUITS

AND TEATIME TREATS

FLORENTINES ALMOND TUILES

STEM GINGER SHORTBREAD

BANANA AND ALMOND SLICE

Simple Pleasures

There's something comforting about making biscuits. The ingredients and equipment are basic and inexpensive, and if you can stand a bit of a mess there's not much that can go wrong. The simplest of recipes are often the best-loved. But you do need to take a bit of care to ensure consistency, to make a batch of biscuits similar in shape, size, colour and thickness. And of course sometimes what appear to be simple biscuits need some skill – for example, making Tuiles (see page 64), which sound easy, is a real challenge. The batter has to be just the right consistency and the baking time spot on, so the biscuits are even in colour and can be moulded into curved shapes.

Biscuits are as much about texture as taste – they can be crisp and brittle, chewy and moist, crumbly and short, sticky and soft. The differences in method and ingredients change the final outcome. The three main methods for biscuit-making are rubbing butter into flour, as if making a very rich shortcrust pastry, for a robust dough that's easy to roll and cut into shapes; creaming butter with sugar just enough to give a short, crumbly texture (rather than beating in a lot of air as for a sponge), to make shortbread; and melting butter, often with sugar and syrups, before working in flour and other ingredients. The latter method is the one used to make Brandy Snaps (see page 60), Mary's technical challenge for the *Great British Bake Off* contestants. Mary picked this recipe to test the bakers' consistency and accuracy – every brandy snap must look similar in size, colour and thickness, even though they are baked in small batches.

Biscuit mixtures and doughs can be dropped by the spoonful onto a baking sheet, thinly spread into neat circles, or rolled out and cut into shapes with special biscuit cutters. Traybakes, which may be quickly stirred-together mixtures, often using oil rather than butter for speed, or made using standard cake methods, are poured or pressed into a tin and cut into bars or wedges after baking. It is easy with both biscuits and traybakes to make a large quantity in very little time.

A really good baking sheet is an essential piece of equipment. If you choose one that's heavy duty and good quality – make sure it is the right size for your oven – it should give you a lifetime of baking. Very cheap 'bargain' buys will turn out to be a disappointment as they usually buckle in the oven, resulting in misshapen, scorched biscuits. An accurate kitchen timer is also vital – a minute more or less with a large fruit cake is not that crucial, but with a biscuit it can alter the result. Wire cooling racks are useful, though in an emergency the grill-pan rack comes in handy. If you plan to make scores of biscuits and cookies then a tiered or stacked rack will save space.

Before you start preheat the oven, making sure that the temperature is accurate, and arrange the shelves according to your oven guide. When it comes to preparing the baking sheets, some recipes call for them to be lined with non-stick baking paper, though you can also use the newer re-usable silicone sheets (the thinner type designed for biscuits and pastry). For other recipes the sheets are lightly brushed with soft or melted butter or left ungreased.

Measure the ingredients accurately, because if you vary them the recipe will change too. More often than not, it's butter that provides the main flavour – shortbread relies on it – and a spread will not work in the same way. If you change the sugar the recipe will change in taste, texture and appearance; for example, muscovado sugar will give a more chewy result than caster sugar. Wholemeal flour will give a drier, more dense biscuit than white flour, and chocolate with a low percentage of cocoa solids, or 'chocolate' cake covering, will not behave and taste the same as dark chocolate with 70 per cent cocoa solids.

Many biscuit doughs need to be well chilled before baking to make sure that the biscuits keep their shape and the butter doesn't melt and ooze out before the starch and protein in the flour have time to do their work. It's important to leave enough space between the biscuits on the baking sheet to allow for spreading in the oven or the biscuits may merge. For the best results bake one sheet at a time, and be ready to rotate the sheet so the biscuits colour evenly. Baking time depends on size, so make sure the biscuits on each sheet are all a similar size and thickness. It's a good idea to bake a trial biscuit or two first to check on the oven temperature, the baking time and the baking sheet preparation. Leave the sheet to cool completely before adding the next batch of raw dough so it doesn't start to melt.

How biscuits are cooled after baking varies from recipe to recipe. Brandy snaps and tuiles are made in small batches because they need to be lifted off the baking sheet fairly swiftly as it comes out of the oven and shaped while still warm. Other biscuits need time to firm up before they are lifted off the sheet and onto a wire rack or they will crumble. Some biscuits will instantly become crisp, while others will turn crisp as they cool, and some are designed to have softer, chewier centres.

Homely or elegant, it's up to you.

THE GREAT BRITISH
BAKE OFF

TECHNICAL CHALLENGE
MARY'S BRANDY SNAPS

Made from store-cupboard ingredients, these crisp, golden, lacy biscuits always look impressive. For a special dessert, dress them up by dipping the ends in melted chocolate and filling with whipped cream.

Makes 14–15

50g butter
50g demerara sugar
50g golden syrup
50g plain flour
½ teaspoon ground
 ginger
½ teaspoon lemon juice

To finish
dark or milk chocolate,
 melted
finely chopped nuts,
 such as pistachios, or
 toasted flaked almonds
whipped cream

2 baking sheets, lined
 with baking paper

* Brandy snaps are shaped by rolling them gently around the handle of a wooden spoon (a thickish handle works well). Oil the handle, to make it easy to slide the shaped biscuits off, then lay it on a wire rack, ready to use.

* Only use non-stick baking paper to line the baking sheets. The brandy snaps will stick if greaseproof paper is used.

* Bake one sheet of biscuits at a time: once they are baked, you will need to work fast to shape them, so wait until the first batch comes out of the oven before putting the next one in.

* If while you are rolling the brandy snaps, the other biscuits on the baking sheet have firmed too much to shape, put them back in the oven for a few seconds to soften again.

Mary's tip
One piece of equipment that is critical to good baking is a well-made set of scales. For me, digital scales are exceedingly reliable and accurate and take up very little space. It means that small quantities, such as the ingredients for Brandy Snaps, can be precisely measured.

1 Preheat the oven to 180°C/350°F/ gas 4. Put the butter, sugar and syrup into a small, heavy-based pan. Heat gently until the butter has melted and the sugar has dissolved, stirring occasionally – this will take about 15 minutes over low heat. Don't let the mixture boil or it might crystallize. To check if the sugar has dissolved completely, pull the spoon across the bottom of the pan: you shouldn't hear any gritty granules being scraped along.

2 Remove from the heat and leave the mixture to cool for 2 to 3 minutes. Sift the flour and ginger into the pan, add the lemon juice and stir well to mix thoroughly.

3 Make 4 biscuits at a time on each baking sheet. For each biscuit, drop a rounded teaspoonful of the mixture onto the sheet to make a neat round, using a second spoon to help. Space the biscuits about 10cm apart.

4 If the mixture in the pan becomes too firm to spoon out neatly, you can roll it into small, smooth balls in your hands, set them on the baking sheets and flatten slightly with your fingertips.

5 Bake for 10 to 15 minutes or until the mixture has spread out to make a thin biscuit that looks lacy and is a dark golden colour. Remove from the oven and leave for a minute or so to firm up slightly.

6 The biscuits need to be just firm enough to remove from the baking sheet, but still pliable enough to shape. To check, release a biscuit from the baking paper around the edges using a small palette knife. If ready, lift off the biscuit using a fish slice.

7 Quickly roll the warm biscuit, lacy side out, around the handle of the oiled wooden spoon and press the join lightly to seal. Slide the brandy snap off the spoon onto the wire rack, join down, and leave it to cool and firm up. Repeat until all the mixture has been used up. When cold, store the brandy snaps in an airtight tin or container (they will keep for at least a week).

8 To make chocolate-dipped brandy snaps, melt the chocolate in a heatproof bowl over a pan of steaming hot but not boiling water. Lay a piece of non-stick baking paper on a wire rack or tray. Dip about half of each brandy snap in melted chocolate (or coat by spooning on the chocolate).

9 Dip the chocolate-coated end into the nuts or sprinkle them over the chocolate. Set the brandy snaps on the baking paper and allow the chocolate to set. Both plain and chocolate-dipped brandy snaps can be filled with whipped cream; do this just before serving. Use a piping bag fitted with a large star nozzle to pipe the cream neatly into each brandy snap. (See page 57 for the finished bake.)

THE GREAT BRITISH
BAKE OFF

HOW TO MAKE PERFECT
ALMOND TUILES

Ideal with a delicate sorbet or ice cream, these crisp, wafer-fine biscuits are named after the curved roof tiles found on old houses. Although they don't take long to make they do need a bit of concentration and it's always best to bake a trial biscuit first so you can adjust the mixture and timing if necessary.

Makes about 28

2 large free-range
   egg whites, at room
   temperature
125g caster sugar
75g unsalted butter,
   melted and cooled
½ teaspoon vanilla
   extract
75g plain flour, sifted
75g flaked almonds

2 baking sheets, greased

＊ Because flour varies in dryness from brand to brand and egg whites vary in size you may need to adjust quantities in the batter. If it is thick and hard to spread, and the outside of the biscuit is coloured before the centre is cooked, you need to add a little more lightly beaten egg white. If the mixture spreads all over the baking sheet in the oven and burns, it is too thin and you need to work in a little more flour.

＊ The baking time is crucial because the biscuits have to be baked to just the right point – if they are overcooked they will be hard to shape. If necessary, rotate the sheets in the oven halfway through the cooking time so the biscuits bake evenly.

Mary's tip
The cooked tuiles will need to be stored in an airtight container lined with kitchen paper. Layer kitchen paper between the biscuits too – this will prevent them from becoming soft.

1 Preheat the oven to 180°C/350°F/gas 4. Put the egg whites into a large mixing bowl. Whisk with a hand whisk or electric mixer until they form stiff peaks. Whisk in the sugar a tablespoon at a time. Scrape down the sides of the bowl, then whisk in the cooled butter and vanilla. Sift the flour again, this time into the bowl, and fold in with a large metal spoon. Add the almonds and fold in.

2 Drop a rounded teaspoonful of the mixture onto a prepared baking sheet and spread into a thin disc about 10cm across using the back of the spoon. Add 2 or 3 more discs of batter to the baking sheet, spacing them well apart. Bake for 5 to 6 minutes or until a very pale gold and just brown around the edges.

3 Remove from the oven. Using a palette knife, immediately loosen each wafer-thin biscuit from the sheet and drape it over a rolling pin. It will rapidly firm up into a curved shape. Remove and set aside. If the biscuits firm too much while they wait to be removed from the sheet, return to the oven for a minute to soften.

4 Continue baking batches of biscuits, letting the baking sheets cool and then lightly greasing them each time.

5 To make basket shapes, which are perfect for filling with ice cream, sorbet or fresh berries, gently mould the warm biscuits over an orange rather than the rolling pin. Remove as soon as set and hard.

Paul's tip
Melt white chocolate and brush the insides of the tuiles, then leave to cool and fill with cream rippled with raspberries.

Walnut Crumbles

Crisp and buttery, these biscuits are studded with plenty of nuts. For a change, you could replace the walnuts with macadamias or lightly toasted hazelnuts or pecans.

Makes 24

100g unsalted butter, softened
100g caster sugar
40g demerara sugar
1 large free-range egg, at room temperature
½ teaspoon vanilla extract
250g self-raising flour
85g walnut pieces, chopped smaller

To finish
15g walnut pieces

1–2 baking sheets, lightly greased

Preheat the oven to 180°C/350°F/gas 4. Put the soft butter into a mixing bowl with both sugars and beat well with a wooden spoon or an electric mixer. Lightly beat the egg with the vanilla, then beat into the butter mixture. Sift the flour into the bowl and work in with a wooden spoon or your hands. Add the chopped walnuts and work in.

Using floured hands, divide the mixture into 24 even-sized pieces and shape each into a ball. Set the balls well apart on the prepared baking sheets and flatten with a fork. Scatter the walnut pieces over the biscuits and gently press in. Bake for about 10 minutes or until golden with light brown edges.

Remove from the oven and leave the biscuits on the baking sheets for a couple of minutes to firm up, then transfer to a wire rack and leave to cool completely. Store in an airtight container and eat within 5 days.

Royal Icing for Piping

Using royal icing for piping will give your biscuits a brilliant white – and more professional – finish than a simple glacé icing. You could use royal icing instead of glacé icing for the Iced Lemon Biscuits opposite.

1 large free-range egg white, at room temperature
drop of lemon juice
about 275g icing sugar, sifted

Using a wooden spoon, beat the egg white with the lemon juice until well mixed, then gradually beat in enough icing sugar to make a smooth, stiff icing that can be piped. Press a piece of clingfilm onto the surface of the icing to keep it moist until ready to use.

Iced Lemon Biscuits

GOOD FOR
Celebrations

These pretty biscuits can be made into any shape you like, then iced simply or elaborately, with a lemon glacé icing or royal icing (see opposite page).

Makes about 24 x 8cm daisy shapes

For the dough
150g unsalted butter, softened
100g caster sugar
finely grated zest and juice of 1 large unwaxed lemon
75g full-fat cream cheese
300g plain flour
good pinch of salt
good pinch of baking powder

For the glacé icing
100g icing sugar
lemon juice (see recipe)

shaped biscuit cutters; 1–2 baking sheets, greased

Put the soft butter into a mixing bowl and beat with a wooden spoon or electric mixer until creamy. Add the sugar and lemon zest and beat thoroughly until light and fluffy. Beat in 2 teaspoons of the lemon juice followed by the cream cheese. Save the rest of the lemon juice for the icing.

Sift the flour, salt and baking powder into the bowl and work in with a wooden spoon or your hands to make a firm dough. Shape into a thick disc, wrap in clingfilm and chill for 30 minutes.

Preheat the oven to 180°C/350°F/gas 4. Unwrap the dough and roll out on a lightly floured worktop until slightly thicker than a pound coin. Dip the biscuit cutter in flour, then cut out shapes.

Gather up the trimmings, re-roll and cut out more shapes, flouring the cutter as needed. Arrange slightly apart on the prepared baking sheets (bake in batches if necessary).

Bake for 12 to 15 minutes or until just turning golden brown around the edges; rotate the sheets halfway through the baking time so the biscuits cook evenly. Remove from the oven and leave the biscuits on the baking sheets to cool and firm up for 3 minutes, then transfer to a wire rack and leave to cool completely.

To make the glacé icing, sift the icing sugar into a mixing bowl. Using a wooden spoon stir in 2½ teaspoons of the saved lemon juice to make a thick, smooth icing that can be piped. If you want to make a runnier icing for spreading, or to fill in the space between piped lines, work in a little more lemon juice until the icing will run slowly off the back of the wooden spoon when it is held up above the bowl.

Spoon the icing into a small piping bag and use to decorate the biscuits. Leave until firm. Store in an airtight container and eat within 5 days.

BEST OF THE BAKE-OFF
Melting Moments

Makes 16 pairs

250g unsalted butter,
 softened
60g icing sugar, sifted
½ teaspoon vanilla
 extract
250g plain flour
60g cornflour
red food colouring (the
 gel type works best)
icing sugar, for dusting

For the filling
125ml full-fat or semi-
 skimmed milk
2 tablespoons plain flour
125g caster sugar
125g unsalted butter,
 softened
½ teaspoon vanilla
 extract, or less to taste
about 2 tablespoons
 seedless raspberry jam

2 baking sheets, lined
 with baking paper; a
 piping bag fitted with
 a star tube

Using a wooden spoon or electric mixer, beat the butter with the icing sugar until pale and fluffy. Add the vanilla and beat for a few seconds. Sift the flour and cornflour together into the bowl and mix until smooth.

Paint a straight line of red food colouring on the inside of the piping bag, from the tube to the opening of the bag. Spoon the biscuit mixture into the piping bag.

Pipe into 32 swirls on the baking sheet. Each swirl should be about 5cm across and 2.5cm high. Chill in the fridge or freezer for 15 minutes to firm.

Meanwhile, preheat the oven to 180°C/350°F/gas 4. Bake the biscuits for about 12 minutes or until they are pale golden. Leave for a few minutes on the baking sheet to set slightly before transferring to a wire rack to cool.

To make the filling, heat the milk with the flour in a small pan, whisking constantly until the mixture boils and thickens. Whisk over very low heat for a minute to cook out the taste of the flour, then pour the mixture onto a plate. Cover closely with clingfilm to prevent a skin from forming and leave until completely cold.

Beat together the sugar and butter until very pale and fluffy – about 10 minutes by hand or 4 minutes with an electric mixer. Add the thickened milk mixture and beat until light, creamy and almost white. Add the vanilla. If the mixture is very soft, cover and chill until it is firm enough to pipe.

To assemble, spread a little jam on the bases of half the biscuits. Pipe small swirls of the filling onto the bases of the remaining biscuits and sandwich pairs together. Lightly dust with icing sugar.

HOLLY

IAN

Chocolate Chunk Cookies

The classic home-made chocolate chip cookie is short and buttery, with thin, crisp edges and a softer centre. And it should look irregular and hand-made. The all-important chocolate should be either dark, with 70 per cent cocoa solids, chopped into chunks, or top-quality dark chocolate chips.

Makes 24

125g unsalted butter, softened
50g caster sugar
50g light brown muscovado sugar
1 large free-range egg, at room temperature
½ teaspoon vanilla extract
150g plain flour
good pinch of salt
½ teaspoon baking powder
50g pecan or walnut pieces
100g chocolate pieces (see above)
icing sugar, for dusting

1–2 baking sheets, lightly greased

Preheat the oven to 190°C/375°F/gas 5. Put the soft butter into a mixing bowl and beat with a wooden spoon or an electric mixer until creamy. Add the sugars and beat well until the mixture looks fluffy. Lightly beat the egg with the vanilla, then gradually beat into the mixture.

Sift the flour, salt and baking powder into the bowl and mix in with a wooden spoon. When thoroughly combined work in the nuts and chocolate pieces.

Put heaped teaspoons of the dough onto the prepared baking sheets, spacing well apart to allow for spreading. (Bake the biscuits in batches, if necessary.) Bake for 8 to 10 minutes or until the biscuits are lightly golden with darker brown edges; rotate the sheets halfway through the baking time so the biscuits cook evenly.

Remove from the oven and leave the biscuits on the baking sheets to cool and firm up for a couple of minutes, then transfer to a wire rack and leave to cool completely. Dust with icing sugar. Store in an airtight container and eat within 4 days.

BEST OF THE BAKE-OFF
Christmas Shortbread and Marzipan Biscuits

Makes 25

300g plain flour
6 tablespoons rice flour
125g caster sugar
250g unsalted butter,
  chilled and diced
125g white marzipan
2 tablespoons icing
  sugar, sifted

1–2 baking sheets, lined
  with baking paper

Sift the plain flour and rice flour into a bowl. Add the caster sugar and stir to mix. Add the butter and rub into the dry ingredients to make a firm shortbread dough.

Divide the dough into 25 portions and roll each into a ball. Divide the marzipan into 25 pieces and roll each into a tiny ball. Press a ball of marzipan into each ball of dough and carefully seal the dough over the marzipan to enclose completely. Place on the prepared baking sheets and chill for 20 minutes.

Preheat the oven 170°C/325°F/gas 3. Bake the biscuits for about 25 minutes or until they are light golden around the edges. Remove from the oven and leave to firm up on the baking sheets for 5 minutes, then transfer to a wire rack to cool completely.

Dredge with icing sugar before serving.

Stem Ginger Shortbread

Shortbread is still a favourite and a test of a cook's skill. Good butter is the key to a wonderful taste, while a combination of plain flour and either rice flour, ground rice or cornflour gives the crisp but short (not tough) texture.

Makes 20

200g unsalted butter, softened
100g caster sugar, plus extra for sprinkling
260g plain flour
40g rice flour, ground rice or cornflour
½ teaspoon ground ginger
good pinch of salt
50g chopped glacé ginger

1–2 baking sheets, greased

Put the soft butter into a mixing bowl and beat with a wooden spoon or electric mixer until creamy. Gradually beat in the sugar and continue to beat thoroughly until the mixture looks lighter in colour and fluffy.

Sift the flour with the rice flour (or ground rice or cornflour), ground ginger and salt into the bowl. Add the chopped ginger and work all the ingredients together with your hands until thoroughly combined. Form the dough into a log shape about 20cm long and wrap in clingfilm. Chill for 20 to 30 minutes or until firm.

Preheat the oven to 170°C/325°F/gas 3. Unwrap the log and slice across into 20 rounds using a large sharp knife. Arrange slightly apart on the prepared baking sheets (bake in batches if necessary).

Bake for about 20 minutes or until firm but not coloured. Remove from the oven and sprinkle with caster sugar, then leave on the baking sheets to cool and firm up for a couple of minutes. Transfer to a wire rack and leave to cool completely. Store in an airtight container and eat within a week.

Speckled Chocolate Shortbread
Make up the dough as in the main recipe above, adding ½ teaspoon vanilla extract to the butter before beating in the sugar and omitting the ground ginger and the chopped glacé ginger.

After slicing the dough into rounds, set them slightly apart on baking sheets lined with non-stick baking paper. Grate 50g well-chilled dark chocolate (70 per cent cocoa solids) and carefully sprinkle over the tops of the shortbread rounds. Bake as in the main recipe, omitting the caster sugar sprinkling.

Pistachio Shortbread
Make up the dough as in the main recipe above, omitting the ground ginger and chopped glacé ginger. Roughly chop 50g shelled unsalted pistachios and work into the dough with the flour mixture. Shape and bake as in the main recipe.

Paul's tip
A great recipe for kids, use a variety of cutters to entertain them and try hearts for Valentine's Day!

Double Chocolate Buns

Not as sweet or as delicate as cupcakes, and richer than muffins, these old-fashioned buns don't need icing – there's plenty of chocolate in the mixture. For the best results use a really good white chocolate rather than chocolate chips.

Makes 12

250g plain flour
50g cocoa powder
1 teaspoon baking
    powder
1 teaspoon bicarbonate
    of soda
125g unsalted butter,
    softened
125g caster sugar
2 large free-range eggs,
    at room temperature
½ teaspoon vanilla
    extract
250ml soured cream, at
    room temperature
100g good-quality white
    chocolate, coarsely
    chopped
icing sugar, for dusting

1 x 12-hole muffin tray,
    lined with paper muffin
    cases

Preheat the oven to 200°C/400°F/gas 6. Sift the flour, cocoa powder, baking powder and bicarbonate of soda into a mixing bowl and set aside until needed.

Put the soft butter into another mixing bowl and beat with a wooden spoon or an electric mixer until creamy. Add the sugar and beat until the mixture turns paler and fluffy. Beat the eggs with the vanilla, then gradually add to the mixture a tablespoon at a time, beating well after each addition.

Using a large metal spoon, fold in the flour mixture in 3 batches alternately with the soured cream. When thoroughly combined, mix in the chopped chocolate – the mixture will be quite heavy but not stiff.

Spoon the mixture evenly into the paper cases. Bake for 20 to 25 minutes or until the buns are just firm to the touch. Turn out onto a wire rack and leave to cool. Dust with icing sugar before serving. These are best eaten the same day.

Drop Scones

These griddle scones, made from a rich, sweet pancake batter, are also called scotch pancakes. You don't need any special equipment – just a frying pan – and they take only a few minutes to whip up.

Makes about 16

110g plain flour
¾ teaspoon bicarbonate
  of soda
1½ teaspoons cream of
  tartar
good pinch of salt
1 tablespoon caster sugar
1 tablespoon golden
  syrup
1 large free-range egg,
  beaten
125ml full-fat or
  semi-skimmed milk
butter, for cooking

Sift the flour, bicarbonate of soda, cream of tartar, salt and sugar into a mixing bowl. Add the golden syrup, egg and milk and whisk briefly to make a thick, smooth batter. Avoid overwhisking the mixture or the scones will be tough.

Heat a large griddle (flat not ridged), or heavy cast-iron frying pan or non-stick frying pan, and add just enough butter to grease the pan. Add about 1½ tablespoons of batter to the pan to make a drop scone 7–8cm in diameter. Cook for 2 minutes or until the top has started to set and the underside is golden brown.

Turn the scone over and cook for another 2 minutes or until the other side is also golden. This is your test scone: the inside should be cooked but not dry so adjust the heat as needed; if the scone is a bit heavy or solid work a little more milk into the batter.

Cook the rest of the scones in batches of 3 or 4, keeping the cooked scones warm in a clean cloth. Eat warm as soon as possible, or next day lightly toasted, with butter and honey or jam.

Chocolate Crackles

These very dark and rich chocolate biscuits are rolled in icing sugar just before baking. As they cook the surface cracks to look like crazy paving. Chocolate with 70 per cent cocoa solids works best in this recipe – a much higher percentage will give a hard dry biscuit, a much lower one will make the biscuits too sweet.

Makes 30

100g dark chocolate
(70% cocoa solids),
roughly chopped
100g unsalted butter,
softened
150g light brown
muscovado sugar
1 large free-range egg, at
room temperature
½ teaspoon vanilla
extract
175g self-raising flour
½ teaspoon bicarbonate
of soda
2–3 tablespoons icing
sugar

1–2 baking sheets,
greased

Put the chopped chocolate into a large heatproof bowl and set over a pan of steaming hot but not boiling water (don't let the base of the bowl touch the hot water). Leave to melt gently. Remove the bowl from the pan and stir in the butter. When the mixture is completely smooth stir in the muscovado sugar. Leave to cool for 5 minutes.

Beat the egg with the vanilla just until combined, then add to the bowl. Sift the flour and bicarbonate of soda into the bowl and mix thoroughly with a wooden spoon. Cover the bowl with clingfilm and chill for about 1 hour or until firm.

Preheat the oven to 200°C/400°F/gas 6. Divide the chocolate dough into 30 even-sized pieces and roll into neat balls. Spoon the icing sugar into a shallow dish. Roll the balls, one at a time, in the sugar to coat thickly. Set the balls on the prepared baking sheets, spacing well apart to allow for spreading. (Bake the biscuits in batches, if necessary.)

Bake for 10 minutes for a softer biscuit, or 12 minutes for a crisp result. Remove from the oven and leave on the sheets for a minute, then transfer to a wire rack and leave to cool completely. The biscuits will continue to firm up as they cool. Store in an airtight container and eat within 5 days.

Two-chocolate Zebras

These incredibly rich, stripey shortbread biscuits are perfect with chocolate mousse (see page 270) or a cup of coffee. For the best flavour choose good-quality chocolates and take care when melting them.

Makes 40

45g dark chocolate
    (70% cocoa solids),
    roughly chopped
45g good-quality white
    chocolate, roughly
    chopped
125g unsalted butter,
    softened
100g caster sugar
1 large free-range egg,
    at room temperature
½ teaspoon vanilla
    extract
250g plain flour
½ teaspoon baking
    powder
good pinch of salt

1–2 baking sheets, lined
    with baking paper

Put the chopped dark chocolate into a small heatproof bowl and set over a pan of steaming hot but not boiling water (don't let the base of the bowl touch the hot water). Leave to melt gently. Remove the bowl from the heat and set aside to cool until needed. Melt the white chocolate in the same way, watching it carefully so it doesn't overheat.

Put the soft butter into a mixing bowl and beat with a wooden spoon or an electric mixer until creamy. Beat in the sugar and continue beating until the mixture is pale and fluffy. Beat the egg with the vanilla until just combined, then gradually beat into the butter mixture. Sift the flour, baking powder and salt into the bowl and work in with a wooden spoon until thoroughly combined into a dough.

Divide the dough in half and put one half into another bowl. Work the melted dark chocolate into one portion of dough, and the white chocolate into the other.

Form the white chocolate dough into a brick-like shape and set between 2 sheets of clingfilm. Roll out to a 20 x 15cm rectangle. Slide onto a tray and chill for 30 minutes. Repeat with the dark chocolate dough.

To assemble the biscuits set the white chocolate rectangle on the worktop or a cutting board. Peel off the top sheet of clingfilm. Peel off the top sheet of clingfilm from the dark chocolate rectangle and invert it on top of the white chocolate dough. Gently press the two doughs together. Peel off the uppermost sheet of clingfilm. Using a large sharp knife, neaten up the rectangle so it is exactly 20 x 15cm, then cut lengthways into 3 strips, each 20 x 5cm. Stack up the 3 strips to make a thin brick-like shape. Wrap and chill for 20 minutes.

Preheat the oven to 180°C/350°F/gas 4. Cut the dough brick across into 5mm slices and set these slightly apart on the prepared baking sheets (bake in batches if necessary). Bake for 8 to 10 minutes or until lightly golden around the edges. Remove from the oven and leave the biscuits to cool and firm up on the sheets for a couple of minutes, then transfer to a wire rack and leave to cool completely. Store in an airtight container and eat within 5 days.

BEST OF THE BAKE-OFF
Macaroon Mocktails

To serve these pretty macaroons, place two or three of each flavour into martini glasses, and fill a large glass pitcher with an assortment of flavours. If you don't want to make the pineapple filling for the Piña Colada macaroons, you can substitute 120g ready-made pineapple jam. Each macaroon recipe makes 20 pairs.

Piña Colada Macaroons

3 medium egg whites, at
   room temperature
225g icing sugar, sifted
55g ground almonds
45g desiccated coconut

For the pineapple filling
100g tinned pineapple
   (drained weight)
75g caster sugar
125ml double cream,
   whipped

2 or more baking sheets,
   lined with baking
   paper; a piping bag
   fitted with a 1cm plain
   tube

With an electric mixer, whisk the egg whites to soft peaks. Gradually whisk in half the sugar and continue whisking for about 2 minutes or until the mixture is very thick and glossy. In a small bowl, combine the remaining sugar with the almonds and coconut, then carefully fold into the egg whites using a large metal spoon.

Spoon the macaroon mixture into the piping bag and pipe in 4cm diameter circles on the baking sheets. Flatten any peaks with the tip of a knife, then leave to stand for 20 minutes to allow a skin to form on the surface of the macaroons.

Preheat the oven to 150°C/300F/gas 2. Bake the macaroons for 14 to 18 minutes or until they have risen and are firm to the touch. Transfer to a wire rack to cool completely.

For the pineapple filling, blitz the pineapple in a food-processor until coarsely chopped, then combine with the sugar in a small pan. Cook over medium heat, stirring constantly, until the sugar has dissolved and the mixture thickens to a jam-like consistency. Remove from the heat and allow to cool.

Gently fold 4 tablespoons of the cooled jam into the whipped cream and use to generously sandwich pairs of macaroons together. Once assembled, eat the same day.

For recipes for Mojito and Cranberry Cooler flavoured macaroons, turn to page 86

Mojito Macaroons

3 medium egg whites, at
    room temperature
225g icing sugar, sifted
green gel food colouring
105g ground almonds

For the lime sauce
2 teaspoons cornflour
60g caster sugar
juice of 2 limes

For the mint cream
1 teaspoon finely
    chopped mint leaves,
    or to taste
125ml double cream,
    whipped
1–2 tablespoons icing
    sugar, sifted

Make the macaroon mixture as for the Piña Colada Macaroons, folding
in a little food colouring to tint it a pale green colour before mixing in the
ground almonds (omit the desiccated coconut). Bake as above.

To make the lime sauce, combine the cornflour with the sugar in a
small pan and mix in the lime juice and 2 tablespoons water. Cook over
medium heat, stirring constantly, until the sugar has dissolved and the
sauce thickens. Remove from the heat and allow to cool, then chill.

Gently fold the chopped mint into the whipped cream, then fold in the
lime sauce and sweeten with icing sugar to taste. Use to sandwich pairs of
macaroons together.

Cranberry Cooler Macaroons

3 medium egg whites, at
    room temperature
225g icing sugar, sifted
orange gel food
    colouring
105g ground almonds

For the filling
grated zest of ½ orange
150ml double cream,
    whipped
3–4 tablespoons
    cranberry sauce
1–2 tablespoons icing
    sugar, sifted (optional)

Make the macaroon mixture as for the Piña Colada Macaroons, folding
in a little food colouring to tint it a rose pink colour before mixing in the
ground almonds (omit the desiccated coconut). Bake as above.

For the filling, gently fold the orange zest into the whipped cream. Fold
in cranberry sauce to taste and sweeten with icing sugar, if necessary.
Use to sandwich pairs of macaroons together.

Banana and Almond Slice

Most banana cakes are made with walnuts or, sometimes, pecan nuts. Here, ground and flaked almonds combine with ripe bananas to make a rich and well-flavoured sponge that doesn't need to be topped with icing or spread with butter, and that will improve on keeping.

Cuts into 20 pieces

50g flaked almonds
175g unsalted butter, softened
250g caster sugar
½ teaspoon vanilla extract
3 large free-range eggs, at room temperature, beaten
50g ground almonds
225g self-raising flour
150ml soured cream
2 ripe medium bananas

1 traybake tin or cake tin, 25.5 x 20.5 x 5cm, greased and the base lined with greased baking paper

Preheat the oven to 180°C/350°F/gas 4. Scatter half the flaked almonds over the greased paper lining in the tin; save the rest for the topping.

Put the soft butter into a mixing bowl and beat until creamy with a wooden spoon or an electric mixer. Gradually beat in the sugar and continue beating thoroughly until paler in colour and fluffy in texture. Beat in the vanilla, then gradually add the eggs, beating well after each addition. Using a large metal spoon, fold in the ground almonds.

Sift about one-third of the flour into the bowl and fold in. Add about one-third of the soured cream and fold in. Repeat with half the remaining flour followed by half of the soured cream. Finally, mix in the last portion of flour and then the soured cream.

Using a fork, roughly mash the bananas so they still have a bit of texture. Stir into the cake mixture. Spoon the mixture into the tin and spread evenly. Scatter over the reserved flaked almonds. Bake for 50 to 60 minutes or until a good golden brown and a skewer inserted into the centre of the cake comes out clean.

Remove the tin from the oven and set it on a wire rack. Run a round-bladed knife around the inside of the tin to loosen the sponge, then leave to cool before turning out. Cut into pieces to serve. Store in an airtight container and eat within 4 days.

Little Stem Ginger Gingerbreads  EASY FOR KIDS

These dark and sticky individual gingerbreads, made with plenty of spices and chunks of glacé ginger and baked in paper muffin cases, are hard to resist. Although there are many ingredients, the recipe is a simple melt-and-mix one. If you like you can decorate the tops with the glacé icing on page 223.

Makes 12

175g plain flour
1 teaspoon bicarbonate
  of soda
1 teaspoon ground
  cinnamon
1 teaspoon ground mixed
  spice
1 tablespoon ground
  ginger
good pinch of salt
100g unsalted butter
2 tablespoons golden
  syrup
2 tablespoons black
  treacle
50g chopped glacé
  ginger
100ml full-fat or
  semi-skimmed milk
100g dark brown
  muscovado sugar
1 large free-range egg,
  at room temperature,
  beaten

1 x 12-hole muffin tray,
  lined with paper
  muffin cases

Preheat the oven to 180°C/350°F/gas 4. Sift the flour, bicarbonate of soda, cinnamon, mixed spice, ground ginger and salt into a mixing bowl.

Gently melt the butter with the syrup, treacle and glacé ginger in a small pan. Remove from the heat and leave to cool. In another pan warm the milk and sugar, stirring frequently until the sugar has dissolved.

Leave the milk and sugar to cool until lukewarm, then pour into the flour mixture, followed by the butter mixture and the beaten egg. Mix well with a wooden spoon to make a thick, sticky batter.

Spoon the mixture into the 12 muffin cases, filling them evenly; the mixture will rise considerably in the oven. Bake for 18 to 20 minutes or until firm to the touch.

Lift the gingerbreads out of the tray onto a wire rack and leave to cool completely. Store in an airtight container and eat within 4 days.

Carrot and Pistachio Traybake

Carrot cakes flavoured with plenty of spice and topped with a rich lemony cream are always popular, and easy to make. This recipe uses pistachios – their bright flavour and colour work well with the carrots – but you could use walnut pieces instead.

Cuts into 20 pieces

For the sponge
225g self-raising flour
1 teaspoon baking powder
1½ teaspoons ground
    cinnamon
¼ teaspoon freshly grated
    nutmeg
½ teaspoon each ground
    ginger and mixed spice
good pinch of salt
200g light brown
    muscovado sugar
finely grated zest of
    ½ unwaxed lemon
75g unsalted pistachios,
    roughly chopped
3 large free-range eggs
150ml sunflower oil
350g carrots, grated

For the topping
200g full-fat cream cheese
50g unsalted butter,
    softened
150g icing sugar, sifted
finely grated zest of
    ½ unwaxed lemon
juice of 1 lemon
25g unsalted pistachios

1 traybake tin or cake tin,
    25.5 x 20.5 x 5cm,
    greased and the base lined
    with baking paper

Preheat the oven to 180°C/350°F/gas 4. Sift the flour, baking powder, all the spices and the salt into a large mixing bowl. Mix in the sugar, lemon zest and chopped pistachios with a wooden spoon. Beat the eggs with the oil until well mixed, then add to the bowl together with the grated carrots and mix thoroughly.

Transfer the mixture to the prepared tin and spread evenly. Bake for about 45 minutes or until a skewer inserted into the centre of the cake comes out clean.

Set the tin on a wire rack and run a round-bladed knife around the inside of the tin to loosen the sponge. Leave it to firm up for about 5 minutes, then carefully turn out onto the wire rack and leave to cool completely.

Meanwhile, make the topping. Beat the cream cheese, butter, icing sugar, and lemon zest and juice together with a wooden spoon or electric mixer until very smooth and creamy. (In warm weather you may need to chill the topping mixture until it is firm enough to spread.)

Spread and swirl the mixture over the top of the sponge. Roughly chop the pistachios and scatter evenly over the topping. Cut into pieces for serving. Store in an airtight container in a cool spot and eat within 4 days.

Coffee and Walnut Traybake

There are plenty of nuts to balance the rich combination of strong coffee and good butter in both the sponge and topping here. The flavours develop and become rounder a day or so after baking so it's worth making this in advance.

Cuts into 20 pieces

For the sponge
125g unsalted butter, softened
125g caster sugar
2 large free-range eggs, at room temperature, beaten
150g self-raising flour
1 tablespoon instant coffee, dissolved in 1 tablespoon hot water
75g walnut pieces

For the topping
200g icing sugar
85g unsalted butter, melted
2 tablespoons instant coffee, dissolved in 2 tablespoons hot water
3 tablespoons whipping or single cream
25g walnut pieces

1 traybake tin or cake tin, 25.5 x 20.5 x 5cm, greased and the base lined with baking paper

Preheat the oven to 180°C/350°F/gas 4. Put the soft butter into a mixing bowl and beat with a wooden spoon or electric mixer until creamy. Add the sugar and beat well until the mixture turns paler in colour and light in texture.

Gradually add the eggs, beating well after each addition. Sift the flour into the bowl and add the coffee liquid. Carefully fold the ingredients together with a large metal spoon. When thoroughly combined, fold in the walnut pieces.

Transfer the mixture to the prepared tin and spread evenly. Bake for about 20 minutes or until the top is a good golden brown and springs back when lightly pressed.

Remove from the oven and run a round-bladed knife around the inside of the tin to loosen the sponge. Set the tin on a wire rack and leave the sponge to cool for 20 minutes before turning out onto the rack. Leave to cool completely.

To make the topping, sift the icing sugar into a mixing bowl. Add the warm melted butter, coffee liquid and cream and mix well with a wooden spoon to make a smooth icing. Leave until thick enough to spread (in warm weather chill the topping for a few minutes), then swirl over the top of the sponge.

Scatter over the walnut pieces. Leave until firm, then cut into pieces with a sharp knife. Store in an airtight container and eat within 4 days.

Sticky Maple-Apple Traybake

Tart-sweet Bramley apples are baked into a very light sponge that is bursting with flavour and finished with an easy-to-make creamy maple topping.

Cuts into 20 pieces

400g Bramley apples
¾ teaspoon ground
    cinnamon
2 teaspoons maple syrup
125ml sunflower oil
150g light brown
    muscovado sugar
½ teaspoon vanilla
    extract
grated zest of ½ lemon
2 large free-range eggs
50g walnut pieces
275g plain flour
½ teaspoon baking
    powder
1 teaspoon bicarbonate
    of soda
good pinch of salt
2 large free-range
    egg whites, at room
    temperature

For the topping
75g unsalted butter,
    softened
75g light brown
    muscovado sugar
3 tablespoons maple
    syrup
175g full-fat cream
    cheese

1 traybake tin or cake
    tin, 25.5 x 20.5 x 5cm,
    greased and the base
    lined with baking paper

Preheat the oven to 180°C/350°F/gas 4. Peel and core the apples, then cut into 1cm chunks. Put into a bowl, sprinkle with the cinnamon and toss until combined. Drizzle over the maple syrup and set aside.

Put the oil, sugar, vanilla and lemon zest into a mixing bowl and whisk thoroughly with a wire hand whisk or an electric mixer. Lightly beat the eggs with a fork to break them up, then add to the bowl and whisk for a couple of minutes until the mixture looks thick and slightly mousse-like.

Stir in the nuts and the apple mixture using a large metal spoon. Sift the flour, baking powder, bicarbonate of soda and salt into the bowl and fold in – the mixture will be quite stiff.

Put the egg whites into another bowl and whisk until stiff peaks form. Fold into the apple mixture in 3 batches. Transfer the mixture to the prepared tin and spread evenly.

Bake for 30 to 35 minutes or until a good golden brown and a skewer inserted into the centre of the cake comes out clean. Transfer the tin to a wire rack. Run a round-bladed knife around the inside of the tin to loosen the sponge, then leave to cool before turning out.

To make the topping, beat the butter with the sugar and maple syrup until smooth and creamy. Beat in the cream cheese.

Spread evenly over the top of the cooled sponge. Leave in a cool spot to firm up, then cut into pieces. Store in an airtight container, in a cool spot, and eat within 4 days.

Coconut Macaroons

These macaroons are moist and chewy and not too sweet, with a good chocolate base. They are easy to make – everything is simply mixed together – and the pyramids are fun to shape with your fingers. Sweetened shredded coconut, available in supermarkets alongside desiccated coconut, works best in this recipe.

Makes 14

200g sweetened
    shredded coconut
1 large egg white, at
    room temperature
¼ teaspoon vanilla
    extract
good pinch of salt
100ml coconut milk

To finish
100g dark chocolate
    (70% cocoa solids),
    roughly chopped

1 baking sheet, lined with
    baking paper

Put the coconut into a mixing bowl. In a smaller bowl lightly beat the egg white with the vanilla and salt until slightly frothy, then add to the coconut. Add the coconut milk and mix all the ingredients together with a wooden spoon until thoroughly combined. Cover the bowl and leave to stand at room temperature for 30 minutes.

Preheat the oven to 180°C/350°F/gas 4. Give the mixture a stir, then spoon a tablespoon onto the prepared baking sheet. Dip your fingers in cold water and shape the mixture into a pyramid. (Coconut milk varies in consistency from brand to brand so if the mixture seems very damp and falls apart, return it to the bowl and work in more sweetened coconut a tablespoon at a time; if the mixture seems very dry and won't stick together add more coconut milk.) Continue shaping the coconut pyramids, spacing them slightly apart on the sheet to allow for spreading.

Bake for 25 to 30 minutes or until the peaks of the pyramids are golden brown and firm. Remove from the oven and leave the macaroons to cool on the baking sheet.

Meanwhile, put the chopped chocolate into a small heatproof bowl and melt gently over a pan of steaming hot but not boiling water (don't let the base of the bowl touch the hot water). Remove the bowl from the pan.

Carefully peel the macaroons off the lining paper and dip the bases in the melted chocolate – the least messy way to do this is by balancing each macaroon on 2 forks. Leave to set on a clean sheet of non-stick baking paper. Store in an airtight container and eat within 4 days.

Tip: Mix the contents of the tin of coconut milk well before measuring, because the creamy and watery parts separate on standing.

Oat and Raisin Biscuits  EASY FOR KIDS

These simple biscuits are always popular. For the best results use regular porridge oats rather than instant oats or porridge mix. Jumbo oats will give the biscuits a slightly chewy texture and lacy appearance. For a change, you could replace the vanilla with several gratings of nutmeg.

Makes 30

125g unsalted butter,
   softened
150g light brown
   muscovado sugar
1 large free-range egg,
   at room temperature
1 tablespoon full-fat or
   semi-skimmed milk
½ teaspoon vanilla
   extract
100g self-raising flour
75g raisins
150g porridge oats

1–2 baking sheets,
   greased

Preheat the oven to 180°C/350°F/gas 4. Put the butter and sugar into a mixing bowl and beat with a wooden spoon or electric mixer until pale and fluffy in texture. In another bowl beat the egg with the milk and vanilla until just combined, then beat into the butter mixture. Add the flour, raisins and oats to the bowl and mix thoroughly with a wooden spoon.

Put heaped teaspoonfuls of the mixture onto the prepared baking sheets, spacing well apart to allow for spreading. (Bake in batches if necessary.) Bake for 12 to 15 minutes or until the biscuits are lightly browned around the edges.

Remove from the oven and leave the biscuits to cool and firm up on the sheets for a couple of minutes, then transfer to a wire rack and leave to cool completely. Store the biscuits in an airtight container and eat within 5 days.

BEST OF THE BAKE-OFF
Mint Chocolate Macaroons

Makes 27 pairs

For the macaroon mixture
125g ground almonds
125g icing sugar
2 teaspoons cocoa powder
4 medium egg whites, at
   room temperature
125g caster sugar

For the centre filling
50ml double cream
75g good-quality milk
   chocolate, chopped

**For the mint-chocolate
   cream**
50ml double cream
100g good-quality white
   chocolate, chopped
dot of mint-green paste
   food colouring
few drops of peppermint
   flavouring

To finish
100g good-quality white
   chocolate
dot of mint-green paste
   food colouring

2 or more baking sheets,
   lined with baking paper;
   a piping bag with a 1cm
   plain tube and a 0.5cm
   plain tube; lolly sticks
   (optional)

Sift the ground almonds, icing sugar and cocoa into a mixing bowl, pressing any lumps through. Set aside.

With an electric mixer, whisk the egg whites in a large bowl until soft peaks form. Gradually whisk in the caster sugar and continue whisking for 2 minutes or until stiff and glossy. Using a large metal spoon, fold in the sifted ingredients in 3 batches.

Spoon the mixture into the piping bag fitted with the 1cm tube and pipe in 4cm discs on the prepared baking sheets; you should make 54 discs. Leave to stand for 20 minutes to allow a skin to start to form. Wash the piping bag and tube.

Meanwhile, preheat the oven to 150°C/300°F/gas 2. Bake the macaroons for 14 to 18 minutes or until firm to the touch and they will easily peel off the paper. Cool on the sheets for 10 minutes, then transfer to a wire rack. Leave until cold.

To make the centre filling, heat the cream until steaming hot, then pour over the chocolate in a heatproof bowl. Leave for 2 minutes, then stir until smooth and melted. Cool until firm enough to pipe. Spoon into the piping bag fitted with the 1cm tube. Pipe a 'button' (no larger than 2cm) of the mixture in the centre of the undersides of half the macaroons. Wash the piping bag again.

For the mint-chocolate cream, heat the cream and melt the chocolate as before. Add a few dots of paste food colouring to tint the mixture green and add peppermint flavouring to taste. Cool until firm enough to pipe. Spoon into the piping bag fitted with the 0.5cm tube and pipe a ring around each chocolate 'button'. Lightly press the macaroons, base to base, to the plain macaroons. Wash the piping bag and tube.

To finish, melt the remaining white chocolate in a bowl set over a pan over steaming hot but not boiling water. Tint it green with a dot of paste food colouring, then spoon into the piping bag fitted with the 0.5cm tube. Pipe a swirl onto each macaroon. Leave to set, then cover tightly and keep in a cool place. These are best eaten after 2 days.

Variation: For Chocolate Orange Macaroons, replace the green food colouring with orange, and the flavouring with orange.

Florentines

These pretty nut and chewy fruit biscuits are made in the same way as Brandy Snaps (see page 60) and are just as tricky. Once cold, the fragile biscuits are spread with a thick layer of chocolate – you can use dark or white, or some of each – which holds everything together. Despite their name, the recipe doesn't come from Florence, although candied fruit is much used there. Glacé ginger can replace the candied peel if you're fond of its warm spicy flavour.

Makes 12

50g blanched almonds
(almonds with their
skins removed)
50g glacé cherries
25g chopped mixed peel
50g large sultanas or
raisins, or crystallized
fruits
25g plain flour
75g unsalted butter
75g golden syrup
100g dark chocolate
(70% cocoa solids) or
good-quality white
chocolate, broken up

2 baking sheets, non-
stick, greased, or lined
with baking paper or a
re-usable silicone sheet

Preheat the oven to 180°C/350°F/gas 4. Prepare all the ingredients so they are ready to use: chop the almonds fairly finely; roughly chop the cherries, then combine with the peel and sultanas (if using crystallized fruits chop into pieces the same size as the cherries); sift the flour.

Put the butter and golden syrup into a medium pan and melt gently. Remove from the heat and stir in all the prepared ingredients (not the chocolate).

Put a tablespoonful of the mixture onto one of the prepared baking sheets and gently flatten it out to a round about 7cm in diameter. Repeat with the rest of the mixture to make 12 biscuits, spacing well apart to allow for spreading.

Bake for about 8 minutes or until a good golden brown. Remove from the oven and leave to cool on the baking sheets for 5 minutes or until firm, then carefully transfer to a wire rack and leave to cool completely (the biscuits are very fragile so handle with care).

To finish, put the chocolate into a heatproof bowl and set over a pan of steaming hot but not boiling water (don't let the base of the bowl touch the water). Leave to melt gently. Remove the bowl from the pan.

Spread a thick layer of melted chocolate over the flat underside of each Florentine. If you like, use a serrated icing spatula or a fork to make a wavy pattern in the chocolate. Leave to set, chocolate side up, on a sheet of non-stick baking paper. Store in an airtight container.

RUSTIC LOAF WHITE FOCACCIA

HAZELNUT APRICOT AND LOAF RUM BABA
HONEY WHOLEMEAL LOAF

BREAD

BLACK OLIVE AND THYME BREAD BREAD

MONKEY BREAD

PICNIC LOAF STICKY BUNS

PIZZA DOUGH

LONDON LOAF SODA BREAD

Hands On

Making bread is all about using your hands: to mix, knead and shape the dough and, finally, to test the baked loaf. Once you know how good it feels to handle a batch of dough and then watch as it is transformed into a crusty loaf that tastes as wonderful as it smells, you'll become hooked.

You don't need many ingredients to make a good loaf – just flour, yeast, salt and water – so it's fairly cheap and it's not particularly difficult. But you do need plenty of time – hours not minutes, although it's not all hands-on time. There are four main stages: mixing and kneading, rising, shaping and baking. The challenge is to make a fine loaf with a good, even shape and colour, the perfect crust and a good chewy crumb with plenty of flavour.

If you've never tried to make bread before, a good place to start is with a simple White Loaf (see page 105). It's made from just the four basic ingredients and doesn't need a tin. Once you've baked a loaf you're happy with and got to grips with the skills needed, you can move on to more adventurous recipes, such as Paul's technical challenge, a Focaccia (see page 119). The dough for this is different from a traditional bread dough – it's very lively and vigorous, enriched with olive oil.

Flour for breadmaking is usually ground from wheat, unless the label says otherwise. Those labelled as 'bread flour' or 'strong flour' are the ones to look for as they are milled from wheat with a higher proportion of protein to starch than the flour used for cakes and pastry. As flour is the main ingredient for bread it's worth choosing something good. A high-quality flour will give a superior result, but steer clear of 'bargain' or 'basic' flours, which can give a disappointing result and inferior flavour (see page 112 for more details about wholemeal flour). Use a flour that's appropriate for the recipe – for instance, it's unlikely you'll get a true baguette or ciabatta using a high-gluten Canadian flour (labelled 'extra strong' or 'very strong') instead of flour made from softer French or European wheat with a lower gluten content. And plain flour does not have enough gluten to make a loaf the size of one made from bread flour.

Yeast is what makes bread rise. It may not look like it, but yeast is a living organism, and given the chance – with some moisture, a little warmth and food (in the form of flour or sugar) – it will start to grow. As it grows it produces carbon dioxide, which expands and pushes up the dough.

There are two kinds of yeast for baking: dried and fresh (the standard substitution is 15g fresh yeast for 7g dried). Fine-powdered dried yeast, which is sold in 7g sachets – labelled as 'fast-action', 'easy-bake', easy-blend' or 'instant' – is mixed into the flour before the liquid is added. This kind of yeast can work with one rising instead of the usual two. Fresh yeast, which is available (cheaply) from large supermarkets with in-store bakeries, is mixed with the liquid and then added to the flour. Whether you use fresh or dried yeast, just remember that yeast can be killed if it gets too hot, so keep liquids at blood temperature or below.

Salt adds flavour, but also helps the gluten in the flour to form the structure of the dough. Add it judiciously – too much salt can make a loaf tough, while too little will yield a loaf that is a bit smaller and lacking flavour. Sea salt flakes give more flavour for their weight so you can use less. Before adding, crush to a coarse powder with your fingers to help the salt dissolve.

Water is most often used to bind the ingredients into a dough (filtered tap water works just fine). Some recipes also add milk, buttermilk or eggs to give a softer, richer crumb.

Thorough kneading is a major key to success for most loaves as the dough is worked so the gluten in the protein of the flour is developed and arranged into neat bundles of strands (rather than a messy ball), which become capable of stretching around the bubbles of carbon dioxide gas produced by the growing yeast. This is the scaffolding the dough relies upon for rising, and can't be skimped if you are after perfection – an under-kneaded dough can give a sad-looking, flat and dense loaf. If you are kneading the dough by hand, set the timer for 10 minutes and get to work. To test if it is thoroughly kneaded, take a small piece and stretch it between your fingers to make a thin, translucent sheet; if it won't stretch out or it tears easily, then knead a while longer.

The next stage is to leave the dough to rise. The temperature of the dough and the room determine the speed of the rise. The usual temperature is a warm 24–27°C (75–80°F), but the dough can be given a slower rise at a cooler temperature, which will result in a loaf with more flavour and a chewier texture. If there's too much warmth, the dough will rise too fast for any flavour to develop. In addition to the temperature, the dough needs to be kept humid, so cover the bowl or leave it in a steamy moist (but not hot) spot.

Once risen, the dough is punched down to break up large air bubbles that could wreck the structure of the dough, making it uneven or misshapen later on. And then the dough is shaped. A tin gives a neat appearance, while a free-form loaf baked on a hot baking sheet or baking stone will look more rustic. Before baking, the shaped dough is given a second rising so it just doubles in size – again, a warm but not hot spot and a little humidity are needed. The dough is usually lightly covered to prevent the top from drying out and forming a tough skin.

Now comes the final stage: baking your loaf. Many bakers like to create a burst of steam as the loaf goes into the oven (see page 105), to help keep the outside moist – initially to give the dough the chance to puff up and then to achieve a good crunchy crust (unless a softer crust is wanted, as for baps, challah and so on). Towards the end of the baking time rotate the loaf so it colours on all sides, and always test for 'doneness' – don't rely on the timer or the colour of the crust. To test most loaves, remove from the oven and turn out onto your hand (protected with a thick oven glove), then tap on the underside of the loaf with your knuckles. A hollow sound indicates that the loaf is cooked through, whereas a dull thud means it needs more time.

Once you've made a few loaves you can adapt a recipe, adding your own improvements. The recipes in this chapter are more guidelines than strict instructions – bread has a mind of its own. Think of breadmaking as one long learning experience. And a large reward from a mere bag of flour.

HOW TO MAKE A PERFECT
WHITE LOAF

A crusty loaf with a slightly chewy crumb and plenty of flavour isn't hard to make and you only need three ingredients – good bread flour, yeast and salt plus water. You'll make this loaf time and again.

Makes 2 medium loaves

700g strong white bread
    flour
2 teaspoons sea salt
    flakes, crushed
1 x 7g sachet fast-action
    dried yeast OR 15g
    fresh yeast
about 450ml lukewarm
    water

1 or 2 baking sheets;
    non-stick baking
    paper; a roasting tin

* You can use either dried or fresh yeast to make this loaf. Fresh yeast comes in the form of a greyish-brown, clay-like lump with a distinct aroma; it can be stored, tightly wrapped in a sealed plastic box in the fridge, for a good week. To use it, crumble into a small bowl and mix to a smooth liquid with about 7 tablespoons of the measured water (or other liquid specified), then add to the flour along with the remaining water.

* The temperature of the water is crucial to success – too hot and the yeast will be killed, too cold and its growth will be slowed right down. 'Lukewarm' means around blood temperature – 38°C/98.6°F: it should be comfortable to dip your little finger in. Because flours vary from miller to miller, it is impossible to give an exact quantity of water needed for any bread recipe – you have to use your own judgement as you are mixing the dough.

* Most bread doughs, including this one, can be mixed and kneaded by hand or using a large, free-standing electric mixer with the dough hook attachment. Kneading is hard work, and the mixer does come in handy: you can reduce the kneading time to 4 to 5 minutes, using the lowest possible speed. But be aware that over-kneading – impossible by hand, too easy by machine – can result in the dough collapsing in the oven or produce a holey loaf.

* Creating a burst of steam in the oven at the start of baking will help achieve a delicious crisp crust. When you turn the oven on, put an empty roasting tin in the bottom of the oven to heat up. Then when you put the loaf in to bake, pour cold water into the tin and quickly close the oven door.

1 Put the flour and salt into a large mixing bowl. Add the dried yeast. Mix well, then make a well in the centre.

2 Pour the lukewarm water into the well. (If using fresh yeast, mix it with the liquid – see page 105 – then add to the flour.)

3 Mix the flour into the water to make a soft but not sticky dough. If there are dry crumbs or the dough feels stiff and dry, work in a little more lukewarm water; if it feels sticky and starts to stick to your fingers, work in a little more flour.

4 Turn out the dough onto a lightly floured worktop and knead thoroughly for 10 minutes. To knead, first stretch the ball of dough away from you by holding one end down with your hand and using the other hand to pull and stretch out the dough as if it were an elastic band.

5 Then gather the dough together back into a ball. Give it a quarter turn and repeat the stretching and gathering-back movements. As the dough is kneaded it will gradually change its texture and appearance and will start to feel pliable yet firm and look smooth and silky.

6 Return the ball of dough to the bowl and cover with a snap-on lid, damp tea towel or clingfilm, or slip the bowl into a large plastic bag. Leave to rise until doubled in size – this will take about an hour in a warm kitchen, 2 hours at normal room temperature, 3 hours in a cool larder or overnight in the fridge.

7 Punch down the risen dough with your knuckles to deflate it. Turn it out onto a lightly floured worktop and knead gently for a minute so the gas bubbles are evenly distributed – this prevents holes in the baked loaf (some rustic loaves skip this step as the holes are a feature). Divide the dough into 2 equal portions and shape each into a ball.

8 Roll each ball around under your cupped hand until very smooth and neat, then set it on a sheet of non-stick baking paper. Dust with flour. Cover the loaves lightly with clingfilm or a damp tea towel and leave to rise until just doubled in size – about 1 hour at normal room temperature. Towards the end of the rising time preheat the oven to 230°C/450°F/gas 8. Put one or two baking sheets into the oven to heat up (you may be able to fit both loaves onto one large sheet, but bear in mind they will spread a bit) and put a roasting tin at the bottom of the oven.

9 Uncover the loaves and sprinkle with a little more flour, then slash the top of each with a sharp knife. Transfer them, on the paper, to the hot baking sheet(s) and put into the oven. Pour a cup of cold water into the hot roasting tin to produce a burst of steam and bake for 15 minutes. Rotate the sheets if needed so the loaves brown evenly, then reduce the oven temperature to 200°C/400°F/gas 6 and bake for a further 15 to 20 minutes or until a good golden brown and the loaves sound hollow when tapped underneath. Leave to cool on a wire rack.

JANET

BEST OF THE BAKE-OFF
Cheese and Onion Tear and Share Loaf

Makes 1 loaf

450g strong white bread
   flour
1½ teaspoons sea salt
   flakes, crushed
1 teaspoon caster sugar
1 x 7g sachet fast-action
   dried yeast
about 300ml lukewarm
   water
2 tablespoons vegetable
   or olive oil, plus extra
   for brushing
1 onion, halved and
   thinly sliced
120g mature Cheddar,
   grated

1 baking sheet, lined with
   baking paper

Sift the flour, salt and sugar into a large bowl and stir in the yeast. Make a well in the centre and pour in the water with 1 tablespoon of the oil. Mix the liquid into the dry ingredients to form a soft but not sticky dough, adding more water as needed. Cover with clingfilm and leave to rest for 10 minutes.

Turn out the dough onto a lightly floured worktop and knead for about 5 minutes or until smooth and elastic. Shape into a ball and place in an large oiled bowl. Cover with oiled clingfilm and leave to rise in a warm place for about 1 hour or until the dough has doubled in size.

Heat the remaining oil in a pan over medium-low heat and cook the onion gently for about 15 minutes or until soft but not coloured. Remove from the heat and leave to cool.

Punch down the dough and knead until smooth. Divide into 19 even pieces and shape each into a 7.5cm diameter disc. Divide the onion and 50g of the cheese among the discs. Wrap the dough around the cheese and onion filling to form balls, pinching the dough over the filling to seal completely.

Arrange the balls seam-side down on the prepared baking sheet in a honeycomb structure (3, 4, 5, 4, then 3 balls per row), leaving a 2cm gap between each ball. Cover with a large upturned roasting tin and leave to rise in a warm place for 30 to 40 minutes or until doubled in size.

Towards the end of the rising time, preheat the oven to 190°C/375°F/gas 5. Sprinkle with the remaining cheese and bake for 25 to 30 minutes or until risen and evenly golden brown; rotate the baking sheet after 15 minutes, if necessary, to ensure even browning. Brush with oil, then transfer to a wire rack and leave to cool completely.

A Good Rustic Loaf

There are lots of interesting combinations of flours and seeds or grains available these days, and it's fun to experiment with them. Loaves made with wholegrain or seeded flours have a moist, open texture and good crust. Some wholegrain flours contain very hard grains, such as wheat or spelt berries, which add good flavour and texture to a loaf, but can make it more difficult to eat. This can be fixed by giving the dough several risings, including one long overnight one. If you don't like seeded loaves, why not try using a stoneground spelt flour – it makes delicious bread.

Makes 2 medium loaves

To start the dough
250g strong wholegrain seeded bread flour or spelt bread flour
½ teaspoon fast-action dried yeast (from a 7g sachet) OR 5g fresh yeast

To finish
1 x 7g sachet fast-action dried yeast OR 15g fresh yeast
about 500g strong wholegrain seeded bread flour or spelt bread flour
300ml lukewarm water
2 teaspoons sea salt flakes, crushed
2 tablespoons olive oil

2 baking sheets; non-stick baking paper; a roasting tin

To start off the dough put the flour into a large mixing bowl or the bowl of a large, free-standing electric mixer. If using dried yeast, mix it into the flour, then make a well in the centre and pour in 200ml water (at room temperature). (If using fresh yeast see page 105.)

Work the flour and liquid together with your hands to make a very soft, sticky dough. Continue working the dough for 2 to 3 minutes or until it starts to become elastic and slightly firmer. Cover the bowl with a snap-on lid or clingfilm and leave at room temperature for 8 to 12 hours. The dough will rise up and then fall back.

The next day, if using dried yeast combine it with 250g of the flour. Add the lukewarm water to the dough in the bowl and work in by stirring and squeezing the dough through your fingers to make a very thick batter. Work in the yeast and flour mixture. If using fresh yeast, crumble it into the lukewarm water and mix well, then add to the dough in the bowl together with the 250g flour. Mix as above.

Continue working the dough well until it feels very elastic – about 5 minutes by hand or a couple of minutes using the dough hook attachment of the mixer on low speed. Cover the bowl as before and leave in a warm place for about 2 hours or until the dough has doubled in size.

Uncover the dough and add the salt and oil. Using your hand or the dough hook, gradually work in enough of the rest of the flour to make a soft but not sticky dough. The amount of flour needed will vary according to the type you use. Turn out the dough onto a floured worktop and knead thoroughly by hand for 5 minutes, or a couple of minutes using the dough hook on the lowest speed, until the dough feels firmer but is still very pliable. Return to the bowl if necessary, cover as before and leave to rise in a warm place for 1 hour.

Gently tip the dough onto a lightly floured worktop and divide in half. Flour your hands, then shape each piece into an oval about 25cm long and transfer to a sheet of non-stick baking paper. Cover lightly and leave to rise in a warm place for 30 minutes.

Towards the end of the rising time, preheat the oven to 230°C/450°F/ gas 8. Put the baking sheets and an empty roasting tin into the oven to heat up.

Uncover the loaves and lift them, on their paper, onto the heated baking sheets and then into the oven. Pour a cupful of cold water into the hot roasting tin to create a burst of steam (this helps achieve a crunchy crust), and quickly shut the oven door. Bake for 30 minutes or until the loaves are a good golden brown and sound hollow when tapped on the underside. Cool on a wire rack.

Tip: Adding a little 'aged' or 'saved' dough is a good trick for giving a depth of flavour to a simple mixture – not quite a sourdough but more interesting than a quickly made loaf. Keep back a portion of the mixed dough (before a loaf is shaped), wrap well and keep in the fridge for 3 to 4 days. When you come to make a fresh loaf, bring the saved dough to room temperature, then work it into the fresh batch of kneaded dough before the first rising.

Paul's tip

Add pumpkin, sunflower, sesame and poppy seeds to this great recipe. It will taste delicious – use 50g of each.

Glazes and Toppings

Add a touch of distinction to your loaf with a glaze or topping, which can be applied before or after baking and will change the appearance, taste and texture of the crust.

Glazes

* You will need a good non-moulting pastry brush (the new rubbery or silicone types are excellent and can be cleaned in the dishwasher).

* Two thin coats of glaze will give a better, more even result than one thick one.

* If you are brushing an uncooked loaf with glaze, make sure you do not 'glue' the dough to the rim of the tin or baking sheet – you will have problems turning out the cooked loaf, and it may prevent the loaf from expanding in the oven (the all-important 'oven-spring').

* The classic glaze for a golden shiny crust is egg. Beat an egg, at room temperature, with ¼ teaspoon salt then carefully brush over the dough just before baking. A richer brown glaze – for butter- and egg-rich doughs, such as challah and brioche – is made by using an egg yolk beaten with a large pinch of salt. This will give the crust a wonderfully rich taste too.

* Brushing the top of a dough with semi-skimmed or full-fat milk before baking will give a slightly shiny, golden sheen, which is useful if you want to sprinkle the loaf with seeds or sugar. Brushing with cream will give a softer, golden crust.

* Dusting an unglazed loaf with flour gives an attractive country feel to bread. Loaves made with stoneground flours and those with large flecks, look best of all.

* Bread can also be glazed after baking: for a soft top, brush lightly with melted butter as soon as the loaf or rolls come out of the oven. You can also use olive oil.

* For a sweet glaze – for tea breads and buns – carefully dissolve 3 tablespoons sugar in 4 tablespoons hot milk, without letting the mixture boil. Brush the hot glaze over the bread while it's still hot.

Toppings

* After the dough is shaped, and before its second rising, it can be rolled in seeds, nuts, cereals or grated cheese. Just before baking, try sprinkling a topping onto a glazed dough. Some toppings scorch easily so be ready to reduce the oven temperature, or loosely cover the top of the loaf with a sheet of greaseproof paper, if it is getting too brown.

* Lightly brush the top of the loaf or rolls with water, milk or egg glaze, then sprinkle with: **seeds** (linseeds, sesame, pumpkin or sunflower, poppy or nigella seeds); **cereals** (wheat, barley, rye or spelt flakes, cracked wheat, flaked oats or oatmeal, cornmeal); **chopped nuts** (walnuts, pecans, almonds, hazelnuts, which all taste and look good but scorch easily); **herbs** (rosemary and thyme work best); **sea salt flakes**; **sugar** (crystals or demerara sugar); **coarsely grated cheese**.

Old-fashioned London Loaf

This recipe for a good-looking white loaf was a great favourite with traditional London bakers, and was often called a slow-rise or 12-hour bread. It uses a tiny amount of yeast and is left to ferment overnight; the result is a well-flavoured loaf with a thin, crisp crust and firm, close crumb, which makes it easy to slice.

Makes 1 large loaf

500g strong white bread
flour
1½ teaspoons sea salt
flakes, crushed
10g unsalted butter, cut
into tiny pieces
½ teaspoon fast-action
dried yeast (from
a 7g sachet) OR
5g fresh yeast
300ml water, at room
temperature
1 tablespoon milk, for
brushing
2 teaspoons poppyseeds,
for sprinkling

1 x 900g loaf tin, about
26 x 12.5 x 7.5cm,
greased with butter;
a roasting tin

Combine the flour and salt in a large mixing bowl or the bowl of a large, free-standing electric mixer. Cut the butter into tiny pieces, add to the bowl and rub into the flour with the tips of your fingers until the butter disappears.

If using dried yeast: mix it into the flour. Make a well in the centre and pour in the water. If using fresh yeast: crumble it into the water and stir together; make a well in the centre of the flour and pour in the yeast liquid.

Using your hand or the dough hook attachment of the mixer, mix the flour into the liquid until the dough just comes together. If there are dry crumbs and the dough feels stiff and dry, work in a little more water; if it is very sticky and sticks to your fingers, add a little more flour.

Turn the dough out onto a lightly floured worktop and knead thoroughly for 10 minutes by hand, or for 4 minutes in the mixer using the dough hook on the lowest possible speed, to make a smooth, silky and firm yet pliable dough.

Return the dough to the bowl, if necessary, and cover tightly with a snap-on lid or clingfilm, or slip the bowl into a large plastic bag. Leave to rise very slowly in a cool room for no less than 8 hours and no more than 12 hours – overnight is ideal. The dough should have doubled in size.

Punch down the dough and turn out onto a lightly floured worktop. Knead the dough very gently for a minute, then cover with a sheet of clingfilm and leave to relax for 15 minutes.

Recipe continues on page 115

Press and flatten the dough with your knuckles to make a rectangle slightly longer and wider than your tin. Keeping one short side joined up, cut the rectangle down its length into 3 strips of equal width.

Plait the strips and press the ends together to join firmly. Lift the plaited dough into the buttered tin, tucking the ends under. Slip the tin into a large plastic bag and slightly inflate it so the plastic doesn't stick to the dough, or cover the tin lightly with a damp tea towel.

Leave to rise in a warm place until the dough reaches the top of the tin – 1½ to 3 hours depending on the initial temperature of the dough and of the room.

Towards the end of the rising time preheat the oven to 220°C/425°F/ gas 7. Put a roasting tin into the oven to heat up.

Uncover the risen loaf. Brush gently with milk and sprinkle with poppy seeds, then put into the oven. Pour a cup of cold water into the hot roasting tin to create a burst of steam (this helps to achieve a crunchy crust), then quickly shut the oven door.

Bake for 30 minutes. Remove the tin from the oven and, wearing oven gloves, turn out the loaf. Return the loaf to the oven, straight onto the shelf without the tin, and bake for a further 5 minutes. Carefully remove the loaf from the oven and tap the base to check that it is cooked. Leave to cool on a wire rack.

Tip: For a change, sprinkle the top of the glazed loaf with sesame seeds or porridge oats, even oatmeal.

THE GREAT BRITISH BAKE OFF

TECHNICAL CHALLENGE
PAUL'S FOCACCIA

A bread that tastes as good as it looks, this makes a fine accompaniment to antipasti and soups as well as for dipping into extra virgin olive oil and balsamic vinegar. Before baking, you can also scatter over small tender sprigs of fresh rosemary, stoned olives, thin strips of pancetta or chorizo, or sun-dried tomatoes in oil, drained. And don't neglect any left-over bread – split and grill it to make bruschetta.

Makes 2 large loaves

500g strong white bread flour
10g sea salt flakes, crushed
2 x 7g sachets fast-action dried yeast OR 18g fresh yeast
2 tablespoons olive oil, plus extra for drizzling
fine sea salt, for sprinkling

2 baking trays (baking sheets with slightly raised rims), about 30 x 20cm, lined with baking paper

✳ This is a very wet dough and handling it is messy. Because it is so wet, the introduction of the water has to be very gradual – 300ml is added first, to make a normal dough, and then the remainder of the measured water is worked in slowly. It's almost like drip-feeding, and each addition should be fully incorporated into the dough before more water is added.

✳ Cool water is used for the mixing, which means the yeast will work more slowly. But the slower a bread dough rises, the better it will taste.

✳ The bowl you use needs to big enough to accommodate the dough – it will increase 3 to 4 fold in the first rising – to be sure the dough doesn't touch the lid. I use a 2-litre square plastic bowl with a lid.

✳ Focaccia can be served hot, straight from the oven, or kept for another day. Once cooled, wrap in clingfilm and keep for 24 hours (or freeze). Just before serving, sprinkle with olive oil and reheat in a 220°C/425°F/gas 7 oven for 5 minutes (if you've frozen the bread, thaw it before warming in the oven).

1 Put the flour and salt into a large mixing bowl and stir in the dried yeast. Make a well in the centre and add the olive oil and 300ml cool water. (If using fresh yeast, crumble it into the water and mix together, then make a well in the flour and pour in the yeast liquid and oil.)

2 Gradually mix the flour into the liquid using a wooden spoon or your hand to form a rough dough. Gently massage the dough in the bowl for 5 minutes, very slowly mixing in about 100ml more cool water. The dough will have a wet consistency.

3 Work the dough in the bowl for about 5 minutes: first stretch the dough by pulling on one side using the fingers and palms of your hands.

4 Then fold the stretched dough into the centre. Turn the bowl 80 degrees and repeat the stretching and folding process.

5 When the 5 minutes is up, tip the dough onto a well-oiled worktop. Knead using your knuckles and palms for 5 minutes, pushing the dough away from you and then folding it back on itself.

6 Oil the bowl and return the dough to it. Cover with a snap-on lid or with clingfilm. Leave to rise at room temperature for about 1½ hours or until increased to about 4 times its original size.

7 Gently tip the dough onto a lightly floured worktop, trying to keep as much air in the dough as possible. Divide the dough in half. Put one half in each baking tray and press out gently, pushing the dough into the corners of the tray.

8 Leave the shaped dough to rise, uncovered, at room temperature for about 1 hour or until at least doubled in size. Towards the end of the rising time, preheat the oven to 220°C/425°F/gas 8. Drizzle a little olive oil evenly over the dough.

9 Sprinkle with fine sea salt, then bake for 20 to 25 minutes: check that the focaccia is cooked by tipping it out of the tray – the underside should be browned. Sprinkle the focaccia with a little more olive oil and serve hot, or allow to cool and serve the next day.

BEST OF THE BAKE-OFF
Picnic Loaf

Makes 1 medium loaf

30g unsalted butter
125ml full-fat milk
about 250g strong white
    bread flour
1 teaspoon fast-action
    dried yeast
1 teaspoon salt
20g caster sugar
1 large egg, at room
    temperature, beaten
egg wash (egg beaten
    with a pinch of salt)

For the sweet filling
50ml full-fat milk
1 tablespoons skimmed
    milk powder
pinch of salt
35g dark chocolate
    (70% cocoa solids),
    broken into pieces
25g blanched hazelnuts

For the savoury filling
10g unsalted butter
1½ tablespoons vegetable
    or olive oil
pinch of salt
1 medium onion, cut into
    1cm pieces
25g Parma ham, fat
    removed, cut into
    shreds

1 baking sheet, lined with
    baking paper

Gently warm the butter with the milk in a small pan until melted. Cool to lukewarm. Combine the flour, yeast, salt, sugar and egg in a large, free-standing electric mixer. Add the milk mixture and beat with the dough hook on low speed to make a soft but not sticky dough, adding more flour as necessary. Knead on high speed for about 1 minute or until smooth. (The dough can also be made by hand in the usual way.) Cover with clingfilm and leave to rise in a warm place for about 1 hour or until doubled in size.

Meanwhile, make the sweet filling. Put the milk, milk powder and salt into a milk pan and heat on medium heat, whisking to combine. As soon as the milk just comes to the boil remove from the heat.

Melt the chocolate in a heatproof bowl set over a pan of steaming hot but not boiling water (don't let the base of the bowl touch the water.) Stir until smooth, then set aside to cool slightly.

Put the nuts into a mini chopper or food-processor and grind until very fine; stop the machine before a paste forms. Scrape the melted chocolate into the processor and pulse to mix. Add the warm milk and pulse again to mix. Scrape the filling into a small bowl, cover and cool to lukewarm.

To make the savoury filling, heat the butter, oil and salt in a non-stick frying pan on medium heat. Add the onion and fry for 10 to 12 minutes or until soft and caramelized. Remove from the pan with a slotted spoon and drain on kitchen paper.

Turn out the dough onto a very lightly oiled worktop (don't use too much oil or the shaped loaf will not stick together). Knead very lightly for 1 to 2 minutes, then roll and press out into a rectangle about 38 x 25cm. Lightly score a line down the centre to divide into 2 rectangles, each 19 x 25cm. Leaving a 1cm border clear on all 4 sides, lightly spread 4 tablespoons of the sweet filling over one half of the dough. Cover the other half with Parma ham shreds and then the caramelized onion, pressing the mixture onto the dough. Be careful to keep the border clear in the centre and not to allow the 2 fillings to touch.

Fold the 2 long edges of the dough rectangle into the middle until they meet. Then fold this long 'package' in half again and pinch the edges together very hard. Place the long bread roll seam side down on the prepared baking sheet. Ensure the ends are sealed. Cover with clingfilm and leave to rise in a warm place for about 45 minutes or until doubled in size. Towards the end of the rising time, preheat the oven to 220°C/425°F/gas 7.

Brush the loaf with egg wash. Using a sharp knife, gently score the top lengthways 3 times – down the middle and on either side; be careful not to slash too deeply to expose the filling. Place in the oven and bake for 2 minutes, then turn the temperature down to 200°C/400°F/gas 6 and bake for a further 20 minutes. Remove the loaf from the baking sheet and place directly on the oven shelf. Bake for a final 5 minutes or until the loaf is a very deep brown and sounds hollow when tapped underneath. Cool on a wire rack.

BEST OF THE BAKE-OFF
Sweet Coconut Rolls

Makes 12

25g desiccated coconut
1 teaspoon icing sugar
500g strong white bread
    flour
60g unsalted butter, at
    room temperature
1 x 7g sachet fast-action
    dried yeast
40g caster sugar
1½ teaspoons sea salt
    flakes, crushed
2 large eggs, at room
    temperature, beaten
about 200ml lukewarm
    milk

For the coconut filling
100g desiccated coconut
50g unsalted butter
50g light muscovado
    sugar

1 baking sheet, lined with
    baking paper

Toast the coconut in a non-stick frying pan for about 5 minutes or until golden, stirring constantly. Tip into a bowl and add the icing sugar, then leave to cool.

Sift the flour into a large bowl. Cut the butter into small pieces and rub into the flour. Add the yeast, caster sugar and salt and stir to combine. Mix in the eggs and enough milk to make a soft but not sticky dough. Turn out onto a lightly floured worktop and knead for 10 minutes or until smooth and elastic. Knead in the toasted coconut mixture until evenly distributed. Return to the bowl and cover with a tea towel. Leave to rise in a warm place for about 1 hour or until doubled in size.

Meanwhile, make the filling. Toast the coconut in the frying pan as above. Add the butter and sugar and stir over low heat until the butter and sugar have melted and combined with the coconut. Leave to cool.

Punch down the dough and turn out onto the lightly floured worktop. Divide into 12 portions and shape each into a neat ball. Roll out each ball to a disc about 5mm thick. Divide the coconut filling among the discs and spread evenly.

To shape each roll, make a cut from the centre of the disc to the edge, then roll up the disc from one cut edge to make a cone shape. Tuck the dough at the larger (open) end in on itself to make a neat base and pinch the seam to seal. Turn the cone upright on the base. Push the point of the cone down slightly into the centre to make a dimple. Set the shaped rolls well apart on the lined baking sheets, cover loosely with clingfilm and leave to rise in a warm place for 1 hour or until just doubled in size.

Towards the end of the rising time, preheat the oven to 200°C/400°F/ gas 6. Put a roasting tin half filled with water into the bottom of the oven to heat up.

Bake the rolls for 20 minutes or until a good golden brown. Cool on a wire rack. Dust with icing sugar before serving.

Black Olive and Thyme Bread

This loaf has a light, slightly open crumb – good for mopping up salad dressings – plus a crisp crust and plenty of it.

Makes 1 medium loaf

250g strong white
 bread flour
25g strong wholemeal
 or spelt bread flour
1 teaspoon sea salt
 flakes, crushed
1 teaspoon fast-action
 dried yeast (from a
 7g sachet) OR 10g
 fresh yeast
200ml lukewarm
 water
75g small pitted black
 olives, well drained
 and patted dry
1 teaspoon fresh
 thyme leaves

1 baking sheet; non-
 stick baking paper;
 a roasting tin

Put the flours and salt into a mixing bowl, or the bowl of a large, free-standing electric mixer, and mix well. If using dried yeast, mix it into the flour, then make a well in the centre and pour in the water. (If using fresh yeast, see page 105.)

With your hand, or the dough hook attachment of the mixer, work together the flours and liquid to make a soft but not sticky dough. If the dough seems stiff and dry, work in a little more water a tablespoon at a time; if the dough feels sticky, work in a little more flour.

Turn out the dough onto a floured worktop and knead thoroughly with floured hands for about 10 minutes, or for 4 minutes using the dough hook on low speed, until smooth and soft but pliable and slightly firmer. Return the dough to the bowl and cover with a snap-on lid or clingfilm. Leave to rise in a warm room for about 1 hour or until doubled in size.

Punch down the dough, then turn out onto a well-floured worktop. Flour your knuckles well – the dough will still be soft – and gently press out to make a rectangle about 40 x 20cm. Arrange the olives down the centre third of the rectangle. Scatter the thyme leaves over the olives.

Fold the 2 long sides of the dough rectangle over the olives to make an envelope with the olives under 2 layers of dough. Pinch the seam to seal, then turn the dough over, so the 2 layers of dough are underneath.

Lift the loaf onto a sheet of non-stick baking paper. Pinch the dough at each open end to seal. Cover lightly with a sheet of clingfilm or a damp tea towel and leave to rise in a warm room for 45 to 60 minutes or until doubled in size. Towards the end of the rising time, preheat the oven to 230°C/450°F/gas 8. Put in a baking sheet to heat up, plus a roasting tin in the bottom of the oven.

Uncover the risen dough and, using kitchen scissors, snip the edges of the 2 long sides at an angle, cutting about every 3cm and snipping one-third of the way in. Gently separate the cuts to expose the filling.

Transfer the dough, on the paper, onto the hot baking sheet and return it to the oven. Pour a cupful of cold water into the hot roasting tin, to create a burst of steam (this helps achieve a crunchy crust), then quickly shut the oven door.

Bake for about 20 minutes or until the loaf is a good golden brown and sounds hollow when tapped on the underside. Transfer to a wire rack and leave to cool. This bread is best eaten slightly warm.

Paul's tip

Try using green and black olives in this recipe. It alters the taste and, I think, enhances it.

Monkey Bread  EASY FOR KIDS

This is a great way for children to start making bread. Serve warm, thickly sliced, or toasted. The cheese version makes excellent sandwiches and toasted sandwiches.

Makes 1 large loaf

500g strong white bread flour
1½ teaspoons sea salt flakes, crushed
1 x 7g sachet fast-action dried yeast OR 15g fresh yeast
50g unsalted butter, melted
200ml lukewarm milk
1 large free-range egg, at room temperature
100g unsalted butter, melted, for coating

For a sweet bread
75g light muscovado sugar
1 tablespoon ground cinnamon
100g pecan or walnut pieces, chopped a little smaller

For a savoury bread
150g mature Red Leicester cheese, grated
¼–½ teaspoon dried red chilli flakes

1 x 900g loaf tin, about 26 x 12.5 x 7.5cm, greased with butter

Combine the flour and salt in a large mixing bowl or the bowl of a large, free-standing electric mixer. If using dried yeast, mix it into the flour and make a well in the centre. Mix the 50g melted butter with the milk and egg and pour into the well. If using fresh yeast, crumble the yeast into the lukewarm milk, then stir in the 50g melted butter and the egg.

Using your hand or the dough hook attachment of the mixer, mix the flour into the liquid to make a smooth, soft dough. If there are dry crumbs and the dough feels dry and hard to work, gradually add more milk a tablespoon at a time; if the dough is very sticky work in more flour a tablespoon at a time.

Turn the dough out onto a lightly floured worktop and knead thoroughly by hand for 10 minutes, or for 4 minutes using the dough hook on low speed, until the dough feels very elastic and smooth.

Return the dough to the bowl and cover with a snap-on lid or clingfilm, or slip the bowl into a large plastic bag. Leave to rise in a warm place for about 1 hour or until doubled in size.

Punch down the dough and turn it out onto a lightly floured worktop. Divide the dough into about 60 tiny pieces, each the size of a large cherry – you can snip the dough with kitchen scissors, or pull or cut off the pieces. Roll each piece into a ball (they do not have to be neat or exactly the same size).

Put the 100g melted butter into a small bowl. Combine the sugar, cinnamon and nuts (or the grated cheese and chilli flakes) in another. Dip the dough balls, one at a time, first into the butter and then into the sugar or cheese mixture and put into the prepared tin. (The pieces of dough don't have to be arranged neatly, and there can be gaps between them, but the tin should be evenly filled.)

Slip the tin into a large plastic bag and leave the dough to rise in a warm place until doubled in size – about 1 hour, depending on the room temperature. Towards the end of the rising time preheat the oven to 200°C/400°F/gas 6.

Uncover the tin and bake the bread for about 35 minutes or until a good golden brown. Run a round-bladed knife around the inside of the tin to loosen the loaf, then carefully turn it out onto a wire rack and leave to cool.

Pizza  EASY FOR KIDS

Making pizza at home is great fun and you can add your favourite toppings. Here are two to try: a traditional Margherita-style topping and an alternative for those who don't like tomatoes. The sauce for the tomato topping can also be used for pasta.

Makes 4 pizzas

For the dough
500g strong white bread flour
1 teaspoon sea salt flakes, crushed
1 x 7g sachet fast-action dried yeast OR 15g fresh yeast
300ml lukewarm water
1 tablespoon olive oil

For the tomato topping
1 tablespoon olive oil
3 garlic cloves (or to taste), thinly sliced
1 x 400g tin chopped tomatoes
12 basil leaves, roughly torn, plus extra to garnish
good pinch of sugar
2 x 125g balls mozzarella
50g black olives
salt and black pepper

For the artichoke topping
1 tablespoon pesto
4 tablespoons olive oil
350g chargrilled marinated artichoke hearts, drained
150g log-style goats' cheese, cut into chunks

2 baking sheets; non-stick baking paper

Mix the flour with the salt in a large mixing bowl or the bowl of a large, free-standing electric mixer. If using dried yeast, mix it into the flour, then make a well in the centre. Pour the water and oil into the well. If using fresh yeast, crumble it into the water and mix well, then add the oil.

Gradually work the flour into the liquid using your hand, or the dough hook attachment of the mixer on the lowest speed, to make a soft dough. If the dough is very dry, work in a little more water a tablespoon at a time; if the dough feels very sticky, work in a little more flour.

Turn out the dough onto a floured worktop and knead thoroughly by hand for 10 minutes, or for 4 minutes using the dough hook on low speed, until the dough is very supple and elastic. Return the dough to the bowl and cover with a snap-on lid, a damp tea towel or clingfilm. Leave to rise in a warm place for about 1 hour or until doubled in size.

Meanwhile, if using the tomato topping, make the sauce. Spoon the oil into a heavy-based medium pan and warm gently, then add the garlic and cook over low heat for a couple of minutes until it begins to smell rather good.

Recipe continues on page 134

Tip: Don't overload the pizza base with sauce and topping ingredients or you'll end up with a soggy pizza and sauce running over the rim, spoiling the crunchy crust.

Add the tomatoes, torn basil and sugar and bring to the boil. Reduce the heat and simmer gently, uncovered, for about 40 minutes or until very thick; give the pan a shake from time to time during cooking to prevent the sauce from catching on the base. Taste and add a little salt and pepper, then leave to cool. (The sauce can be kept in the fridge, tightly covered, for up to 5 days.)

If using the artichoke topping, mix the pesto with the olive oil. Halve the artichoke hearts if they are large.

Punch down the dough, then turn it out onto a lightly floured worktop. Divide into 4. Using lightly oiled hands, pat, press and pull each piece of dough into a thin circle about 25cm in diameter.

Use your thumbs to make the edges slightly thicker and higher so each pizza has a 1.5cm rim all around [1]. Transfer each pizza base to a piece of non-stick baking paper and cover lightly with clingfilm or a damp tea towel. Leave to rise while you preheat the oven to its hottest setting. Put the baking sheets into the oven to heat up.

When the oven has come up to temperature, uncover the pizzas and add the chosen toppings, leaving the rims clear.

For the tomato topping, stir the sauce well, then quickly spread about 3 tablespoons over each pizza base up to the rim [2]. Tear the mozzarella into rough chunks and scatter over the pizzas along with the olives [3].

For the artichoke topping, quickly spread the pesto mixture over the pizza bases up to the rim, then add the artichokes and cheese.

Transfer the pizzas, on the paper, to the hot baking sheets and bake for about 10 minutes or until the edges are crisp and golden brown. The pizzas are best eaten immediately. Add some extra basil leaves to the tomato pizzas just before serving.

Paul's tip

Try baking your pizza base separately for 5 minutes in a very hot oven before adding the toppings and baking further. This will give you a beautiful crispy base.

Rum Babas GOOD FOR *Celebrations*

A baba looks and tastes like a rich, light cake soaked in a rum syrup. Yet it is made from a yeast dough made by mixing the dough with eggs and beating in soft butter. Babas are a challenge, but are really worth the effort. A lemon-flavoured variation follows if you don't want to use rum.

Makes 12

250g strong white bread flour
½ teaspoon sea salt flakes, crushed
1 tablespoon caster sugar
1 x 7g sachet fast-action dried yeast OR 15g fresh yeast
3 large eggs, at room temperature
4 tablespoons lukewarm milk
50g currants
2 tablespoons dark rum
2 tablespoons very hot water
100g unsalted butter, softened

For the soaking syrup
450g caster sugar
6 tablespoons dark rum

12 x 125ml small baba or dariole moulds, double-buttered (see recipe)

Combine the flour, salt and sugar in a large mixing bowl. If using dried yeast, add to the bowl and mix thoroughly, then make a well in the centre of the mixture; beat the eggs with the milk and pour into the well. If using fresh yeast, crumble it into the lukewarm milk and mix thoroughly, then mix in the eggs.

Set the bowl on a damp tea towel, to prevent it from wobbling. Work the flour into the egg mixture with your hand to make a smooth, very thick and sticky batter-like dough. Knead the dough in the bowl by beating it with your hand, lifting and slapping the dough up and down in the bowl, for about 5 minutes or until very smooth and elastic.

Cover the bowl with a snap-on lid, clingfilm or a damp tea towel and leave to rise in a warm place for 45 to 60 minutes or until the dough has doubled in size. Meanwhile, put the currants in a small heatproof bowl. Pour over the rum and hot water and leave to soak until needed.

Next prepare the baba or dariole moulds. For delicate doughs like this one, and for brioches, the best way to prepare the moulds is to double butter them; this prevents the fragile crusts from sticking and makes unmoulding easy. Wipe the insides of the moulds dry with kitchen paper, then brush with melted butter.

Chill the moulds in the freezer for 10 minutes. Brush with butter again, not forgetting the rims, then chill again. The butter sets firm, so won't be absorbed by the dough as it rises. In hot weather, keep the prepared moulds in the fridge until ready to fill.

Mash the butter with a round-bladed knife – it should be soft and creamy, but not oily or runny. Punch down the dough, then gradually work in the butter with your hand, slapping the dough up and down, and squeezing it between your fingers. Take your time. When thoroughly beaten in there will be no visible streaks of butter. The thick, sticky batter-like dough should be very smooth, glossy and elastic, looking rather similar to a rich sponge cake mixture.

Recipe continues on page 136

Thoroughly drain the currants, reserving the liquid, then work them into the dough. Using a metal spoon, drop the dough into the prepared moulds (use another spoon to scrape the dough from the spoon), taking care not to dislodge the butter coating. The moulds should be slightly less than half-filled.

Set the moulds on a baking sheet, then cover them with a sheet of clingfilm. Leave to rise in a warm room for 30 to 45 minutes or until the dough has almost reached the top of the moulds. Check frequently to be sure that the dough isn't sticking to the clingfilm. Towards the end of the rising time preheat the oven to 200°C/400°F/gas 6.

Uncover the moulds and bake for 18 to 20 minutes or until the tops are domed and a good golden brown and the babas are starting to shrink from the sides of the moulds. Turn them out carefully onto a wire rack and leave to cool.

Meanwhile, make the soaking syrup. Put the sugar and 750ml water into a medium pan and stir over low heat until the sugar has completely dissolved. Bring to the boil and boil gently for about 3 minutes to make a thin syrup. Add the reserved currant soaking liquid and remove from the heat.

Using a slotted spoon, add 2 of the babas to the hot syrup, turning them carefully so they absorb as much syrup as possible. After a couple of minutes lift them out of the pan with the slotted spoon and set on a serving plate. Soak the remaining babas in the same way. Save any remaining syrup.

Sprinkle the rum over the babas and serve immediately. Or cover tightly and keep at room temperature for up to 24 hours; reheat the reserved syrup and spoon a little over each baba just before serving.

Lemon Babas
Omit the currants and instead work the grated zest of 1 unwaxed lemon into the dough. Make up the sugar syrup, adding the finely grated zest and juice of 1 large unwaxed lemon when the syrup is removed from the heat. Just before serving, split the babas in half from top to bottom, then decorate with sliced strawberries and serve with whipped cream.

Tip: The keys for success are taking care to beat the batter-like dough well, and accurate rising – not enough rising time and the dough will be heavy; too much and the dough will run over the top of the moulds in the oven.

Hazelnut, Apricot and Honey Wholemeal Loaf

A fine-looking plaited loaf, packed with flavour, this tastes nice simply buttered yet is not too sweet to enjoy with cheese.

Makes 1 large loaf

100g blanched hazelnuts (hazelnuts with their skins removed)
500g strong wholemeal bread flour
1½ teaspoons sea salt flakes, crushed
1 x 7g sachet fast-action dried yeast OR 15g fresh yeast
1 rounded tablespoon honey
300ml lukewarm milk
100g soft-dried apricots, quartered (see TIP)
2 tablespoons milk, for brushing

1 baking sheet, lined with baking paper

Tip: An easy way to chop up dried apricots or figs is to use kitchen scissors.

Preheat the oven to 180°C/350°F/gas 4. Put the hazelnuts in a baking dish or small tin and toast in the oven for 5 to 10 minutes or until lightly golden. Cool, then halve with a sharp knife. Set aside. Turn off the oven.

Combine the flour and salt in a large mixing bowl or the bowl of a large, free-standing electric mixer. If using dried yeast, mix it into the flour and make a well in the centre; stir the honey into the milk, then pour it into the well. If using fresh yeast, crumble it into the lukewarm milk and mix well, then stir in the honey.

Using your hand or the dough hook attachment of the mixer on low speed, mix the flour into the liquid to make a soft but not sticky dough. If there are dry crumbs and the dough feels stiff, work in a little more milk a tablespoon at a time; if the dough feels sticky and won't hold its shape, work in a little more flour.

Turn out the dough onto a lightly floured worktop and knead thoroughly by hand for 10 minutes, or for 4 minutes using the dough hook attachment on low speed, until the dough feels very elastic – wholemeal flour doughs tend to firm up as they are worked. Add the halved nuts and quartered apricots to the dough and gently work in until evenly distributed.

Return the dough to the bowl and cover with a snap-on lid or clingfilm, or slip the bowl into a large plastic bag. Leave to rise in a warm place for about 1 hour or until doubled in size; allow longer if leaving to rise in a cool spot.

Punch down the dough, then turn out onto a lightly floured worktop. Divide into 3 equal portions and, using your hands, roll each into a neat sausage about 40cm long. Take one end of each strand and pinch them together, then plait the 3 strands neatly. Tuck the ends under and set the plait on the lined baking sheet.

Slip into a large plastic bag and leave to rise as before for about 1 hour or until almost doubled in size. Take care not to let the loaf get too big or it will lose its shape. Towards the end of the rising time, preheat the oven to 200°C/400°F/gas 6.

Uncover the loaf and brush it lightly with milk. Bake for about 30 minutes or until a good golden brown and the loaf sounds hollow when tapped on the underside. Cool on a wire rack.

Sticky Buns

These buns, made with butter and an egg, filled and rolled, then baked on a mixture of butter, muscovado sugar, maple syrup and chopped nuts are hard to resist.

Makes 12

200ml milk
75g unsalted butter
500g strong white bread
    flour
1 teaspoon sea salt flakes,
    crushed
2 tablespoons caster sugar
1 large free-range egg, at
    room temperature
1 x 7g sachet fast-action
    dried yeast OR 15g
    fresh yeast

For the filling
50g unsalted butter,
    melted
75g light brown
    muscovado sugar
1 teaspoon ground
    cinnamon

For the topping
100g unsalted butter,
    softened
75g light brown
    muscovado sugar
2 tablespoons maple syrup
100g walnut or pecan
    pieces

1 x 25.5 x 20.5cm baking
    sheet with rim or
    roasting tin, greased

Gently heat the milk and butter until the butter just melts, then remove from the heat and leave to cool until lukewarm. Mix the flour with the salt and sugar in a large mixing bowl or the bowl of a large, free-standing electric mixer. Beat the egg into the lukewarm milk mixture. If using dried yeast, mix into the flour and make a well in the centre; pour the milk mixture into the well. If using fresh yeast, crumble it into the milk mixture and mix together.

Using your hand, or the dough hook attachment of the mixer on low speed, work the flour into the liquid to make a soft but not sticky dough. Turn out the dough onto a lightly floured worktop and knead thoroughly for 10 minutes by hand, or for 4 minutes using the dough hook on low speed, until very smooth and pliable. Return the dough to the bowl and cover with a snap-on lid, clingfilm or a damp tea towel. Leave to rise in a warm place for about 1 hour or until doubled in size.

Punch down the dough, then turn out onto a lightly floured worktop. Roll or press out the dough to a rectangle about 24 x 48cm. Brush the melted butter over the dough. Mix the sugar with the cinnamon and sprinkle over the top. Starting from one long edge, lightly roll up the dough like a swiss roll. Using a sharp knife cut across into 12 slices. Slightly flatten each slice gently with your palm.

For the topping, beat the butter with the sugar and maple syrup until thoroughly combined. Spread the mixture evenly over the base of the prepared tin. Scatter over the nuts and gently press in. Arrange the buns cut side up in the tin, in 3 rows of 4, spaced evenly apart. Slip the tin into a large plastic bag, or cover with a damp tea towel, and leave to rise as before for 30 to 45 minutes or until almost doubled in size. Towards the end of the time, preheat the oven to 180°C/350°F/gas 4.

Uncover the tin and bake for 20 to 25 minutes or until the buns are a good golden brown and the caramel topping is bubbling around the sides. Remove from the oven and run a round-bladed knife around the inside of the tin to loosen the buns. Leave for 4 to 5 minutes – no longer – for the bubbling to subside, then very carefully invert the tin onto a baking sheet with a rim (take care because the caramel topping will be extremely hot). Lift off the tin – the topping will be sticking to the buns. Leave until cool enough to pull apart before eating while still warm.

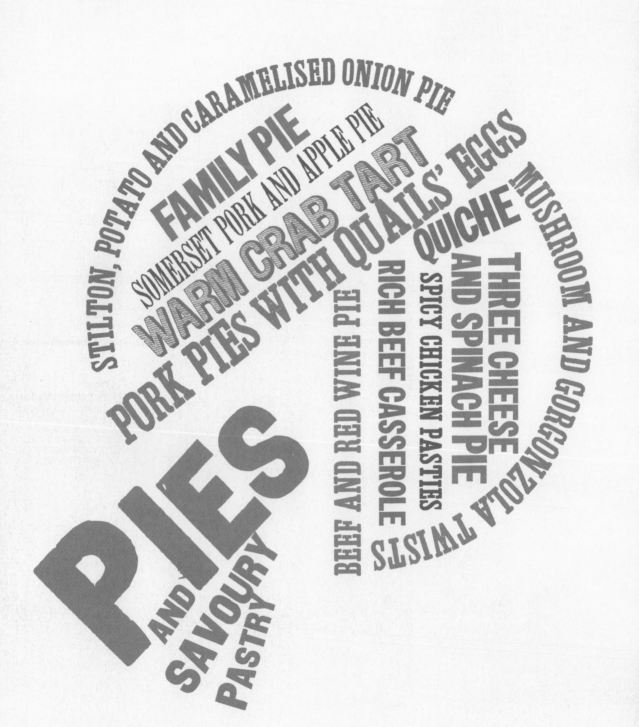

Getting the balance right

Pies and savoury pastries with bold flavours make really hard-to-beat meals, whatever the season or the occasion. The key to success is achieving a balance between crisp, buttery pastry and a delicious filling: the pastry needs to be a star in its own right, and the contents of the pie or tart perfectly seasoned and equally memorable.

As easy as pie? Maybe not. The challenges with pies and savoury tarts are to make the pastry sturdy enough to hold the filling without collapsing, but to make sure that it isn't tough, and to have a filling that is well-flavoured and cooked through by the time the pastry is done. If the filling is too wet the pastry will be soggy; if the filling is too dry or badly seasoned then the pie loses its appeal. Above all, the pastry must be crisp and browned or why bother with it at all?

There are many types of pastry you can use for pies and savoury pastries, from plain shortcrust and rich shortcrust (with egg yolk added) to rough puff, flaky and puff pastry, as well as ready-made filo pastry. Hot water crust pastry, one of our oldest surviving recipes, is unusual as it's made with hot melted fat and is used while still warm, which seems like breaking all the rules of pastry-making. It is used for 'raised pies' – often called 'hand-raised' – including the much-loved pork pie; Paul's technical challenge for *The Great British Bake Off* contestants – Pork Pies with Quails' Eggs (see page 157) – is an individual version. Here, Paul's test is to make pies that stand proud when unmoulded – no sagging walls or lopsided lids – with plenty of filling plus jelly so there are no gaps when the pie is cut.

Pastry is made primarily from flour and fat. The flour is usually plain and white, although light wholemeal or light brown adds a nice nuttiness. Unsalted butter gives pastry the best flavour; salted butter can make it taste oversalted and tends to make it a bit greasy. Using a mixture of butter and lard, or white vegetable fat, will give pastry a lighter texture than using all butter, but the flavour won't be quite as good (and not everyone wants to eat lard or vegetable fat). Beef or vegetable suet, bought ready-shredded, can be combined with self-raising flour to make very light and flaky pastry for warm pies and for fluffy dumplings to add to stews. Water is used to bind almost every dough, and since flour varies from miller to miller it's hard to predict just how much will be needed. Therefore, it is best to mix in water a little at a time. An egg yolk or two adds richness and colour to shortcrust pastry for special recipes.

There are a few tricks that make pastry easier. As with breadmaking, temperature is crucial. But here, with the exception of hot water crust pastry, it's vital to keep everything as cool as possible (including using a cold filling) for a good result – you don't want the fat in the pastry to start to melt until it's inside the oven. So, chill the fat until it is firm, and use ice-cold water. If the weather is really hot then make pastry early in the day while the kitchen is at its coolest. It's also vital to handle the dough as little as possible so the heat from your hands isn't transferred.

Mix the dough as quickly as you can, so the gluten in the flour isn't developed. The process of rubbing the fat into the flour is the major key to success (a food-processor is very useful for this). If over-worked, the crust of your pie will be hard and likely to shrink.

Before rolling out (and again before baking), chill the pastry thoroughly to help keep its shape and texture; wrap well to prevent the pastry from drying out and cracking. Then very lightly dust the work surface with flour: you don't want the pastry to start to stick, but at the same time you shouldn't incorporate any more flour into the dough because it will make it heavy and dry. If the weather is hot or the pastry butter-rich, the easiest way to roll out is between two sheets of clingfilm or non-stick baking paper.

Roll out with short, brief movements so the pastry is extended rather than stretched: you are not after a flattened, steam-rollered effect. Don't make the mistake of rolling the pastry quite thick in an attempt to avoid making holes, because it won't cook through.

If you are making a pie with a top and bottom crust – such as the technical challenge Shortcrust Pie (see page 146) – it's important to make sure the crusts are well sealed together so the pie doesn't fall apart and the contents escape, either in the oven or as the pie is unmoulded, and that the top doesn't collapse onto the filling. Moisten the pastry edges with beaten egg – sometimes called egg wash or egg glaze – or cold water and press them firmly together before 'knocking up' and 'fluting' (see page 151 for explanations of these terms). A small hole in the centre of the pastry lid will let out the steam from the hot filling during baking and help keep the crust from becoming soggy.

When you are ready to put the pie or tart into the oven, make sure it is up to temperature so the fat doesn't melt before the flour has time to set. Placing the dish or tin on a hot baking sheet will give the base of the pastry a quick boost of heat, which helps it start cooking. And be sure the pie is thoroughly cooked before you remove it from the oven – with a rich golden pastry that smells wonderfully toasty plus the enticing aromas of a tasty filling.

A good pie is a wonderful thing – so make more, and more often.

THE GREAT BRITISH

HOW TO MAKE THE PERFECT
SHORTCRUST PIE

A pale gold colour, crisp texture and a vital melt-in the-mouth deliciousness are the hallmarks of good shortcrust. It's our most popular pastry, the easiest to make and the one most used for pies, flans, tarts and quiches, both hot and cold. Here it provides the case for a double-crust beef pie.

Serves 6

For the shortcrust
300g plain flour
¼ teaspoon salt
150g unsalted butter,
    chilled and diced, OR
    75g each butter and lard
    (or white vegetable fat),
    chilled and diced
3½–4 tablespoons icy
    water

For the filling
Beef and Red Wine Pie
    Filling (see page 152)
beaten egg, to glaze

1 x 23cm round fluted or
    oval pie dish; a baking
    sheet

✳ Shortcrust pastry has a 'short' texture – crumbly, light and tender. It is made from plain flour (the type used for cakes and pastries, rather than the higher gluten strong bread flour) and cold fat (usually unsalted butter for its taste, or equal amounts of butter and lard or white vegetable fat to give an even shorter texture), plus a pinch of salt and just enough cold water to bind the ingredients together. The usual proportions are one part fat to two parts flour – as in the recipe here – but for a richer pastry more fat is used (up to three-quarters fat to flour in some ultra-rich recipes).

✳ It's important to use ice-cold water and to add it gradually. You only need enough water to bind the mixture together. If there are dry crumbs at the bottom of the bowl, add a little more water a teaspoon at a time; if the dough feels soft and sticky, work in a little more flour. Pastry that is too dry will fall apart as you try to roll it out, but if it is too wet it will stick to the work surface and rolling pin and the baked pastry will be tough and hard.

✳ Making shortcrust in a food-processor is extremely quick and efficient, and gives an excellent result. Put the flour and salt (plus any spices) into the processor bowl and 'pulse' a couple of times, just to combine. Add the cold diced fat and process until the mixture looks like fine crumbs. With the machine running, pour in the very cold water (plus egg yolk for a richer shortcrust) through the feed tube – the dough should come together in a clump. If this doesn't happen add a little more water, a teaspoon at time, through the feed tube. Remove the ball of dough from the machine, wrap in clingfilm and chill.

1 Sift the flour and salt into a mixing bowl. Add the cold fat and toss lightly so that all the pieces are well coated in flour.

2 Using a round-bladed knife, cut the fat into much smaller pieces, coating them all with flour as you go.

3 Put both hands into the bowl and pick up a little of the mixture between the fingertips and thumb of each hand. Lift your hands up to the rim of the bowl and rub the flour and fat together between your fingertips. Continue this rubbing-in until the mixture looks like fine crumbs with no visible lumps of fat.

4 Gradually pour in the icy water while you stir with the knife, mixing until the dough just comes together. Gather the dough together and knead it for a couple of seconds only so it forms a ball – if you handle it too much the fat will start to melt and the pastry will be oily. Wrap in clingfilm and chill for 15 to 20 minutes or until firm but hard before rolling out.

5 To line the pie dish: cut off one-third of the pastry for the lid; wrap and keep chilled. Lightly dust the work surface with flour and lightly flour the rolling pin. Roll out the pastry to a neat round that is the diameter of the pie dish plus twice its height including the rim (it's easiest to measure this with a tape measure or a piece of string).

6 Lightly flour the rolling pin, then gently roll the pastry around it and lift over the top of the dish. Carefully unroll the pastry so it drapes over the dish.

7 Flour your fingers, then gently press the pastry onto the base and up the sides of the dish, so there are no air pockets.

8 If there are any holes patch with a small piece of pastry saved for the lid, or pastry trimmings, pressing the patch in to seal.

9 Dampen the rim of the dish with a little water and gently press the pastry onto it. Leave the excess pastry hanging over the rim (it will be trimmed off later). Chill the pastry case for 20 minutes, if possible. Preheat the oven to 190°C/375°F/ gas 5; put a baking sheet into the oven to heat up.

10 To cover the pie: spoon the cold filling into the dish, mounding it slightly in the centre. Roll out the remaining pastry to a round about 1cm wider than the top of the dish. Dampen the pastry rim with a little water or beaten egg glaze.

11 Roll the pastry around the rolling pin and lift it over the dish. Gently unroll, as before, so the pastry lid covers the pie and the rim. Press the pastry edges together on the rim to seal firmly.

12 Using a small sharp knife, trim off any overhanging pastry to make a neat edge – if possible hold the knife at an angle to the dish, rather than vertically, so the pastry is cut just slightly larger than the rim – if the pastry shrinks during baking it won't be so obvious.

13 Use the back of the knife to 'knock up' the side of the edge – that is, make lots of small horizontal cuts into the pastry edge so it looks like the leaves of a book.

14 The rim can be decorated by 'fluting' – pinching the dough between your fingers; by pressing with the back of a fork; or by drawing a small knife between 2 fingers pressed down on the rim. Make a 2cm slit in the centre of the lid to allow the steam to escape – this is important to prevent the pastry from becoming soggy.

15 Brush with beaten egg glaze for a shiny finish. Set the pie dish on the heated baking sheet and bake for about 35 minutes or until the pastry is crisp and a good golden brown. Serve hot with plenty of green vegetables. (See page 143 for the finished bake.)

Beef and Red Wine Pie Filling

The challenge with double-crust meaty pies is to achieve pastry – crust and base – that is crisp and thoroughly cooked, with a filling of beautifully tender meat, moist with sufficient gravy and packed with flavour. If possible, cook the meat filling the day before baking the pie so it has time to mature.

Fills a 23cm pie dish

750g lean stewing steak (preferably skirt), cut into 2.5cm dice
1½ tablespoons plain flour
3 tablespoons vegetable oil
2 medium onions, finely chopped
2 garlic cloves (or to taste), finely chopped or crushed
350ml red wine
about 250ml good beef stock
large sprig of fresh thyme
125g small button mushrooms
salt and black pepper

Toss the beef in the flour, seasoned with a little salt and pepper, to coat thoroughly. Heat the oil in a large, heavy-based flameproof casserole or pan with a lid. Add the pieces of meat, a few at a time, and fry for about 2 minutes on each side or until nicely browned [1]. Remove with a slotted spoon to a plate.

When all the meat has been browned, turn the heat right down and add the onions and garlic to the pot, stirring well to dislodge any bits stuck to the base. Cover the pot and cook very gently, stirring occasionally, for about 12 minutes or until the onions are very soft and lightly golden.

Meanwhile, simmer the red wine in a small pan until reduced by about one-third. Pour into a measuring jug and make up to 500ml with beef stock. Uncover the onions and stir in the wine and stock mixture followed by the beef (plus any juices on the plate) and the leaves from the sprig of thyme. Bring to the boil, then lower the heat, cover the pot and cook gently for 1 hour, stirring from time to time.

Add the mushrooms and stir well. Simmer, uncovered, for another hour or until the meat is tender and the gravy is very thick and coats the meat [2]. If the meat is cooked but the gravy is still too thin, turn up the heat slightly and cook, stirring frequently, until the gravy is well reduced (don't let the mixture boil too rapidly or the meat will become tough and the gravy may catch on the base of the pan). Taste, and add more salt and pepper as needed. Leave to cool, then cover and chill (overnight if possible) until you are ready to fill the pie.

BEST OF THE BAKE-OFF
Stilton, Potato and Caramelised Onion Pie

Serves 6

For the pastry
200g plain flour
½ teaspoon salt
75g unsalted butter, at
    room temperature
75g lard, at room
    temperature
1½ teaspoons white wine
    vinegar
about 150ml icy water
1 egg, beaten with a
    pinch of salt

For the filling
2 medium onions, thinly
    sliced
30g butter
½ teaspoon salt
2 tablespoons caster
    sugar
1kg waxy/salad potatoes,
    peeled and thinly
    sliced
100g Stilton, crumbled
100g Gruyère cheese,
    grated
140ml crème fraîche
60ml double cream
100g mature Cheddar,
    grated
freshly grated nutmeg
black pepper

1 large deep pie
    dish (about 20cm
    diameter); a baking
    tray with a lip

First make the pastry. Sift the flour and salt into a mixing bowl. In another bowl, combine the butter and lard, using a fork to mix them together until soft, creamy and completely blended. Spread the fat evenly on the bottom of the bowl and use a knife to mark into quarters.

Take one-quarter of the fat, cut into small pieces and rub into the flour. Mixing with a table knife, add the vinegar and enough of the cold water to bind together into a soft but not sticky dough. Shape into a ball, wrap and chill for 15 minutes.

Turn out onto a well-floured worktop and use your hands to press the pastry into a rectangular shape with defined corners. Then use a rolling pin to roll out the pastry to a rectangle about 30 x 11cm and about 1cm thick. Tease the corners back into place if they have disappeared. Put your hands under the pastry and allow it to shrink back a little from where it was stretched when it was rolled.

Using a palette knife dot another quarter of the butter/lard mixture over the pastry rectangle, being careful not to get too close to the edges. The dots should be about 1cm across and about 1.5cm apart. Leave one short edge 3cm free of fat mixture. Fold the pastry into thirds like a business letter, rubbing off any excess flour as you do so. Wrap in clingfilm and chill for 15 minutes.

Meanwhile, put the onions in a frying pan with the butter, salt and sugar and fry on low heat, stirring occasionally, for about 15 minutes or until lightly caramelised. Remove from the heat and set aside.

Take the pastry from the fridge and place it on the well-floured worktop so the folds are top and bottom. Roll out using a well-floured rolling pin to 1cm thickness (use your weight rather than a dragging motion to roll the pastry). If any fat shows through, re-flour. Put your fingers under the pastry to release any stretching that has occurred, letting it shrink back a little. Dot with another quarter of the fat mixture as before and fold into thirds. Wrap and chill for 15 minutes.

Meanwhile, cook the potatoes in boiling water for 8 minutes. Drain carefully and set aside.

Recipe continues on page 154

Repeat the rolling out of the pastry, dotting with fat and folding. Chill for 30 minutes.

Combine the Stilton and Gruyère in a bowl. In another bowl mix together the crème fraîche, double cream and Cheddar.

Layer the filling in the pie dish, working from the outside of the dish into the middle to achieve a domed effect. For the first layer use one-quarter of the potato slices, one-third of the onions and one-third of the Stilton mixture, seasoning with nutmeg and pepper. Then make 2 more layers, each using one-quarter of the potato slices, one-third of the onions, one-third of the Stilton mixture, half of the cream/Cheddar mixture, and nutmeg and pepper to season. Top with the rest of the potato slices and season with nutmeg and pepper. Ensure that none of the cream mixture is visible from the top.

Cut a thin strip from each side of the pastry square. Roll out the remaining pastry on a well-floured worktop, then turn 45 degrees and roll again until you have a round that is just larger than the pie dish. Put your fingers under the pastry to release tension and allow it a little 'shrink back'.

Brush a little egg wash on the rim of the pie dish and stick the pastry strips to it. Then apply egg wash to the top of the strips. With the help of the rolling pin, lift the pastry lid and lay it over the pie dish; it should not be tightly stretched over the dome. Press the edges to the strips on the rim to seal. Using scissors cut off excess pastry around the pie, leaving about a 5mm overhang.

Knock up the edges (see page 151), then use a fork to press the rim of the pie all the way around. Brush the whole pie with egg wash. If you wish, cut a decorative shape from the pastry trimmings and stick to the pastry lid with egg wash; brush the shape with egg wash. Cut a good-sized cross into the top of the pastry lid to let steam escape during baking. Chill for 15 minutes.

Meanwhile, preheat the oven to 220°C/425°F/gas 7. Set the pie dish on the baking tray and bake for 30 minutes. Then turn the oven down to 180°C/350°F/gas 4 and bake for a further 25 to 30 minutes or until the pastry is crisp and golden. Serve hot.

TECHNICAL CHALLENGE
PAUL'S PORK PIES WITH QUAILS' EGGS

Just perfect for a picnic or a party, these little pies have a secret centre. As with all pies it's important to take care when assembling, to be sure that the pastry is well sealed so all the tasty juices can't escape during baking.

Makes 6

For the pastry
200g plain flour
40g strong white bread
    flour
50g unsalted butter
60g lard
1 teaspoon salt
100ml boiling water
1 egg, beaten, to glaze

For the filling
1 large onion
300g boneless pork loin
100g unsmoked back
    bacon
small bunch of parsley
6 quails' eggs
salt and black pepper
1 chicken stock cube
100ml boiling water
1 x sheet 7g leaf gelatine

1 x 15cm and 1 x 20cm
    round cutter; a 6-hole
    muffin tray

✳ For the hot water crust pastry here, two fats are used: butter for flavour and lard to give the pastry its unique crisp texture. It is made mainly from plain flour but with the addition of a small quantity of strong bread flour to boost the gluten content just enough to help the moulding and shaping, without making the finished pastry tough.

✳ It's vital to use the pastry while it is still warm and pliable because once it cools the fats begin to harden and the pastry is likely to crack.

✳ To soft-boil quails' eggs, gently put them into a pan of boiling water and simmer for 2 minutes. Remove the pan from the heat and put the eggs under cold running water for 1 minute. Drain the eggs and peel immediately.

✳ When you've made the pork filling mixture (before you add the eggs) take a teaspoon of the mix, shape into a mini burger and fry for a couple of minutes on each side until cooked through. Then taste and add more seasoning if needed.

1 Preheat the oven to 190°C/375°F/gas 5. Sift the flours into a mixing bowl. Add the butter and rub into the flour with the tips of your fingers until the mixture looks like fine crumbs. Make a well in the centre.

2 Put the lard in a pan and heat until it melts; remove from the heat. Add the salt to the boiling water and stir to dissolve, then add to the lard and stir to combine. Pour the hot lard mixture into the well in the flour. Using a wooden spoon gradually mix the flour into the liquid. Keep mixing until a dough has formed.

3 When the dough is cool enough to handle, tip it onto a lightly floured surface and work together quickly into a ball. If the dough is still a bit lumpy, leave it to cool slightly and then work it for 1 to 2 minutes longer.

4 The dough should be glossy and still warm to touch. Roll it out to 3mm thickness. Using the 20cm cutter, cut out 6 rounds for the pie cases. Cut out 6 rounds with the 15cm cutter for the lids.

5 Line the holes in the muffin tray with the 20cm rounds, pressing them gently over the base and up the sides without stretching the dough. There will be an overhang. Chill the lined muffin tray and pie lids while you make the filling.

6 To make the filling, finely chop the onion, pork, bacon and parsley. Mix together and add some salt and pepper. Soft-boil and peel the quails' eggs (see page 157). Spoon about half of the meat mixture into the pie cases, dividing it evenly. Place an egg in the middle of each and top with the rest of the meat mixture.

7 Brush the edge of each pastry case with beaten egg. Place the lids on top and press the edges together to seal. Trim the edges, if necessary. The easiest way to decorate the edge of the pies is with the back of a fork, as shown. You can also crimp the edges with your fingers (see page 24).

8 Using a piping nozzle, make a steam hole in the lid of each pie, then brush with beaten egg. Bake in the preheated oven for 40 minutes. When the pies are cooked, remove them from their tin and allow to cool. Dissolve the stock cube in the boiling water. Soak the gelatine sheet in a little water, gently squeeze out the excess water then whisk into the hot stock. Pour a little of the stock mixture into the hole of each pie. Leave to cool overnight or in the fridge for a couple of hours before serving.

JASON

Spicy Chicken Pasties

Often used for spicy Jamaican beef patties and some fried doughs, turmeric pastry makes a colourful change from regular shortcrust for pasties. The filling for these is tender chicken marinated in a zingy yoghurt mix and then grilled, with ready-made mango chutney (hot and spicy or mild, to taste) to add moisture.

Makes 6

For the pastry
225g plain flour
good pinch of salt
½ teaspoon ground
    turmeric
125g unsalted butter,
    chilled and diced
about 4 tablespoons icy
    water

For the filling
175g skinless boneless
    chicken breast, cut
    into 1.5cm cubes
3 tablespoons natural
    yoghurt
2 garlic cloves (or to
    taste), crushed
2cm piece root ginger,
    peeled and grated
⅛–¼ teaspoon cayenne
    pepper
¼ teaspoon each ground
    cumin and coriander
good pinch of salt
2 tablespoons mango
    chutney
beaten egg, to glaze

1 x 12cm round cutter or
    saucer; a baking sheet,
    lined with baking paper

To make the pastry, sift the flour, salt and turmeric into a mixing bowl. Add the diced butter and rub into the flour using the tips of your fingers until the mixture looks line fine crumbs.

Using a round-bladed knife, gradually stir in enough cold water to bring the mixture together to form a ball of soft but not sticky dough. The pastry can also be made in a food-processor (see page 182). Wrap in clingfilm and keep chilled until needed.

To make the filling, combine the chicken, yoghurt, garlic, ginger, cayenne, cumin, coriander and salt in a bowl. Mix thoroughly. If you have the time, cover and marinate for a couple of hours in the fridge.

Preheat the grill to its hottest setting and line the grill pan with oiled foil. Spoon the chicken mixture onto the foil and spread evenly in one layer. Grill for 5 to 6 minutes or until the chicken is just firm and starting to colour. Remove the grill pan from the heat and leave to cool.

Preheat the oven to 180°C/350°F/gas 4. Roll out the pastry on a lightly floured worktop to a 24 x 36cm rectangle. Cut out 6 rounds with the cutter, or by cutting around the saucer. Divide the chicken mixture into 6 equal portions, draining off any watery liquid that has collected. Spoon a portion of chicken onto one half of each pastry round, leaving a 1cm border clear.

Top each with a teaspoonful of mango chutney. Dampen the pastry edges with beaten egg, then fold the pastry over the filling to make a semi-circle and press the edges together firmly to seal. Press down on the edges with the back of a fork's tines to decorate.

Place on the lined baking sheet. Brush lightly with beaten egg to glaze, then make a small steam hole in the centre of each pastie with the tip of a knife. Bake for about 30 minutes or until the pastry is golden and crisp. Serve warm with extra chutney.

Somerset Pork and Apple Pie

Here's a pie for early autumn, when there's a slight chill in the air. It's made with rough puff pastry – simpler and faster to make, and less rich, than puff pastry but still with plenty of crisp and flaky layers. You can use any tart-sweet apples: they'll keep their shape and add a sharpness to balance the richness of the filling.

Serves 4–6

For the pastry
225g plain flour
¼ teaspoon salt
125g unsalted butter, chilled
about 125ml icy water
½ teaspoon lemon juice

For the filling
800g boneless leg of pork, diced
2 tablespoons plain flour
2–4 tablespoons vegetable oil
2 medium onions, halved and thinly sliced
3 celery sticks, sliced
2 garlic cloves, chopped
400ml dry cider
finely grated zest of 1 unwaxed orange
3 eating apples, peeled and thickly sliced
beaten egg, to glaze
salt and black pepper

1 large, oval 1.25–1.5 litre pie dish; a pie raiser (see TIP); a baking sheet

To make the pastry, sift the flour and salt into a mixing bowl. Cut the cold butter into fine dice and gently stir into the flour using a round-bladed knife until they are thoroughly coated in flour but not broken up. Combine the icy water and lemon juice, and stir in enough to bind the dough – it should be lumpy, soft and moist but not sticky or wet.

Turn out the dough onto a lightly floured worktop and shape it into a brick by gently patting with floured fingers. Using a floured rolling pin, roll out the dough – rolling away from you – into a rectangle about 45 x 15cm. Fold the dough in 3 like a business letter: fold the bottom third of the dough up to cover the middle third, then fold the top third down to cover the other 2 layers. Gently but firmly seal the edges by pressing down with a rolling pin. This is the first 'turn'. Wrap the dough in clingfilm and chill for 15 minutes.

Unwrap the dough and place it on the worktop so the folded edges are now to the left and right. Roll out and fold in 3 again, then wrap and chill as before – this is the second 'turn'. Do this 2 more times so the dough has been rolled out, folded up and chilled 4 times in all. Wrap in clingfilm and keep chilled until needed.

Preheat the oven to 170°C/325°F/gas 3. Put the pork into a bowl, sprinkle with the flour and a little salt and pepper, and toss to coat the meat evenly. Heat 2 tablespoons of the oil in a large flameproof casserole. Working in batches, add the pork and quickly brown, adding more oil as needed. As each batch is browned, remove from the pan to a large plate. Keep any flour left in the bowl.

Add the onions, celery and garlic to the casserole and cook gently for about 10 minutes or until soft and golden, stirring occasionally to loosen all the bits stuck to the bottom of the pot. Stir in the remaining seasoned flour followed by the cider. Bring to the boil, stirring, then return the pork to the casserole together with the orange zest and apples and stir to mix. Season with a little salt and plenty of black pepper. Bring back to the boil, then cover and transfer to the oven. Cook for 2 to 2½ hours, stirring occasionally, until the meat is very tender.

Remove the casserole from the oven and stir gently. Taste and adjust the seasoning as needed. If the liquid seems a bit thin, simmer uncovered on top of the stove until reduced to a thick gravy that coats the meat. Spoon the mixture into the pie dish, with the raiser in place in the centre, and leave to cool. (At this point the dish can be covered and kept in the fridge overnight.)

Roll out the pastry on a floured worktop to an oval about 7cm larger all around than your pie dish. Cut off a strip from around the oval, about 1cm wide and long enough to fit all round the rim of the dish. Dampen the rim with water and press the strip of pastry onto it, joining the ends neatly. Dampen the strip. Make a small slit in the centre of the pastry oval. Roll it up around the rolling pin and gently lay it over the pie dish, without stretching; the pie raiser should fit through the slit. Press the edges of the pastry lid onto the strip on the rim to seal firmly. Trim off the excess pastry with a sharp knife (save the trimmings for decorations).

Use the back of a small knife to 'knock up' the pastry edge by making small horizontal cuts all round. The edge can then be fluted by placing 2 fingers on the pastry rim and pinching, or by drawing a small knife between them to give a scalloped effect. If you like, cut the pastry trimmings into shapes and stick them onto the pastry lid with a little water. Chill the pie while preheating the oven to 200°C/400°F/gas 6.

Set the pie dish on the baking sheet and brush the pastry with beaten egg to glaze. Bake for 15 minutes, then reduce the temperature to 180°C/350°F/gas 4 and bake for a further 20 to 25 minutes or until the pastry is puffed up, crisp and a good golden brown. Serve hot with creamy mashed potatoes and celeriac.

Tip: If you don't have a pie raiser you can use an upturned egg cup. Do be sure to keep to the chilling times for the pastry to minimise any shrinkage during baking.

BEST OF THE BAKE-OFF
Stilton, Spinach and New Potato Quiche

Serves 6

For the pastry
200g plain flour, sifted
100g unsalted butter, chilled
good pinch of salt
50g walnuts, finely chopped to breadcrumb size
1 teaspoon paprika
2 large eggs

For the filling
250g baby spinach leaves
7 small (5cm) new potatoes, about 200g in total (unpeeled)
3 large eggs
250ml double cream
grated zest of ½ lemon
pinch of freshly grated nutmeg
pinch of cayenne pepper
25g Parmesan, freshly grated
small bunch of fresh thyme sprigs, large stalks discarded
150g rindless Stilton, crumbled
salt and pepper

1 x 23cm deep, loose-based flan tin; a baking sheet

To make the pastry, combine the flour, butter and salt in a bowl and rub the butter into the flour until the mixture resembles fine breadcrumbs. Add the walnuts and paprika and mix in thoroughly. Beat one egg and mix in with a knife. Then beat the other egg and add a teaspoon at a time until the mixture just comes together (you may not need all of it). Gather the dough into a rough ball, place on a lightly floured worktop and flatten with a rolling pin to a disc about 2cm thick. Wrap in clingfilm and chill for 30 minutes.

Roll out the pastry between 2 sheets of clingfilm and use to line the flan tin. Prick the base well and chill for 20 minutes.

Preheat the oven to 180°C/350°F/gas 4. Line the pastry case with non-stick baking paper or foil and baking beans. Bake blind for 10 to 15 minutes (see page 184). Remove the paper and beans, and lightly brush the pastry case with some of the remaining beaten egg. Bake for a further 5 minutes. Leave to cool. Put the baking sheet into the oven to heat up.

Wash and drain the spinach, then cook in a medium saucepan over low heat until it wilts (or follow the microwave instructions on the packet). Cool a little, then squeeze out all the excess moisture with your hands; it's important to do this thoroughly or the filling will be soggy. Chop the spinach finely.

Cook the potatoes in boiling water for about 10 minutes or until just tender. Drain and cool, then cut into 5mm slices.

Whisk the eggs to mix in a bowl, then whisk in the cream, lemon zest, nutmeg, cayenne and Parmesan. Season with a little salt (the cheese is quite salty) and some pepper. Add the spinach and half of the thyme.

Spread the potato slices in a single layer over the base of the pastry case and dot with the crumbled Stilton (reserve a few slices of each to place on the top, if you wish). Gently spoon over most of the spinach-cream mixture. Place the flan tin on the hot baking sheet in the oven, and spoon over the remaining spinach-cream mixture. Sprinkle the rest of the thyme on top.

Bake for 35 to 40 minutes or until the filling is golden brown and just set in the centre. Remove from the oven and allow to cool for about 10 minutes before serving.

BEST OF THE BAKE-OFF
Salmon and Pak Choi Quiche

Serves 6

For the pastry
250g plain flour, sifted
½ teaspoon salt
1 tablespoon toasted
   sesame seeds
150g unsalted butter,
   softened
1 large egg, plus extra
   beaten egg for sealing
   the pastry

For the filling
400g skinless salmon
   fillets
1 tablespoon soy sauce
3 medium eggs
300ml double cream
2 small pak choi,
   trimmed and cut in
   half lengthways
salt and pepper

1 baking sheet; 1 x 23cm
   deep, loose-based
   flan tin

To make the pastry, mix the flour, salt and sesame seeds in a medium-sized bowl. Make a well in the centre. In a small bowl beat the butter with the egg, then pour into the well. Gradually incorporate the dry ingredients into the butter mixture to form a soft but not sticky dough. Knead gently until smooth. Wrap in clingfilm and chill for at least 20 minutes.

Preheat the oven to 180°C/350°F/gas 4. Roll out the pastry on a lightly floured worktop and use to line the flan tin. Prick the base of the pastry case, then chill for about 20 minutes.

Meanwhile, set the salmon on a large square of oiled foil; season and wrap tightly. Set on the baking sheet and bake for about 20 minutes or until just cooked and easy to flake. Allow to cool, then flake into small pieces. Turn the oven temperature up to 190°C/375°F/gas 5.

Line the pastry case with non-stick baking paper or foil and fill with baking beans. Bake blind for 15 minutes (see page 184). Remove the paper and beans. Brush the pastry case with beaten egg and bake for a further 5 minutes. Remove from the oven. Turn the temperature back down to 180°C/350°F/gas 4 and put in the baking sheet to heat up.

Arrange the salmon pieces over the base of the pastry case and drizzle with the soy sauce. Mix the eggs with the cream in a jug and pour half of this over the salmon pieces. Arrange the pak choi cut-side up on top. Pour over the remaining egg and cream mixture and push the pak choi under the surface. Set the flan tin on the hot baking sheet and bake for 40 to 45 minutes or until the filling is golden and just set. If the top is browning too quickly, cover lightly with foil. Leave to stand for 10 minutes before unmoulding.

BEST OF THE BAKE-OFF
Smoked Haddock and Watercress Quiche

Serves 6

For the pastry
200g plain flour
good pinch of salt
100g unsalted butter,
   chilled and diced
about 3 tablespoons icy
   water

For the filling
350g smoked haddock
   (undyed)
300ml full-fat milk
30g butter
1 small onion, finely
   chopped
1 celery stick, finely
   chopped
30g plain flour
freshly grated nutmeg
2 large eggs, beaten
1 x 75g bag watercress
   sprigs or 1 bunch of
   watercress, chopped to
   the size of 20p pieces
2 tablespoons freshly
   grated Parmesan
pepper

1 x 23cm deep, loose-
   based flan tin; a baking
   sheet

Sift the flour and salt into a large bowl. Rub in the butter until you have a soft breadcrumb texture. Add enough icy water to make the crumb mixture come together to form a firm dough. Wrap and chill for 30 minutes.

Roll out the pastry on a lightly floured surface and use to line the flan tin. Don't cut off the overhanging edges yet. Chill again for 30 minutes.

Preheat the oven to 190°C/375°F/gas 5. Line the pastry case with non-stick baking paper or foil and fill it with baking beans. Bake blind for 15 minutes (see page 184). Remove from the oven and carefully trim off the overhanging pastry using a sharp knife, holding the knife at a sharp angle and slicing away from you. Lift out the paper and beans and bake for a further 5 minutes to cook the base. Remove from the oven and set aside. Put the baking sheet into the oven to heat up.

While the pastry case is baking, put the haddock and milk in a pan (don't break up the fish). Bring just to the boil, then reduce the heat and gently poach for 10 minutes. Remove the pan from the heat and allow to cool.

Remove the haddock (reserve the milk). Flake the fish into a bowl, discarding the skin and any bones. Set aside.

Melt the butter in a medium pan. Add the onion and celery and cook gently until softened. Sprinkle over the flour and stir in. Cook for a few more minutes before adding the reserved cooking milk a little at a time, stirring well. Cook, stirring, until the sauce has boiled and thickened, then simmer for 1 minute. Season with freshly ground pepper and nutmeg to taste. Remove from the heat.

Add the eggs to the sauce and mix well, then fold in the flaked fish and watercress. Pour into the pastry case and sprinkle the Parmesan over the top.

Set the tin on the heated baking sheet and bake for about 35 minutes or until the filling is puffed and golden. Allow to cool a little before unmoulding to serve.

Warm Crab Tart

For the perfect spring or summer meal, serve this tart of fresh crab and crumbly pastry with a green salad and buttered new potatoes. As it is quite rich, the pastry is best made in a food-processor, but you can make it by hand if you prefer.

Serves 6

For the pastry
200g plain flour
¼ teaspoon salt
2 good pinches of
  smoked hot paprika or
  cayenne pepper
150g unsalted butter,
  chilled and diced
1 large free-range egg
  yolk
about 2 tablespoons icy
  water

For the filling
350g fresh white
  crabmeat
3 large free-range eggs
1 tablespoon brandy
1 teaspoon lemon juice
¼ teaspoon smoked hot
  paprika or cayenne
  pepper (or to taste)
125ml double cream
salt and black pepper

1 x 23cm loose-based,
  deep flan tin;
  a baking sheet

To make the pastry, put the flour, salt and paprika into the bowl of a food-processor and 'pulse' a couple of times just to combine. Add the pieces of butter and process until the mixture resembles fine crumbs.

With the machine running, add the egg yolk, then gradually add the cold water until the mixture comes together to make a soft but not sticky dough. Shape the dough into a ball, wrap in clingfilm and chill for about 20 minutes.

Roll out the dough on a lightly floured worktop to a round about 29cm in diameter. Roll the pastry around the rolling pin and lift it over the tin. Unroll the pastry so it drapes over the tin, then gently press it onto the base and sides to line completely.

Trim off the excess, then use your thumbs to ease the pastry up so it stands slightly above the rim. Prick the base well with a fork. Chill for 20 minutes. Meanwhile, preheat the oven to 190°C/375°F/gas 5.

Line the pastry case with greaseproof paper, fill with making beans (ceramic or dried) and bake blind for 15 minutes (see page 184). Remove the paper and beans and bake the empty pastry case for a further 4 to 5 minutes or until the pastry is cooked and lightly coloured. Remove from the oven. Put a baking sheet into the oven to heat up.

Flake the crab into a mixing bowl, discarding any pieces of shell or cartilage. In another bowl whisk the eggs with the brandy, lemon juice, paprika, a little salt and black pepper and the cream. When thoroughly combined, add to the crab and mix well. Spoon the mixture into the pastry case and spread evenly.

Set the tin on the heated baking sheet and carefully slide back into the oven. Bake for 25 to 30 minutes or until the filling is just set and lightly coloured. Carefully unmould the tart and serve warm or at room temperature the same day.

Rich Beef Casserole with Dumplings

Here is a hearty and warming combination of meltingly tender beef, rich gravy, plenty of root vegetables and proper, old-fashioned, light and fluffy suet dumplings. Skirt of beef is the best cut to choose for flavour; the long cooking turns the texture silky and moist. A slightly sweet stout adds body and flavour to the gravy, although you can replace it with extra stock. The quickly made dumplings are seasoned with a little mustard powder – just enough to boost the final dish to British treat status.

Serves 4–6

750g diced lean stewing steak (preferably skirt)
2 tablespoons plain flour
¼ teaspoon each mustard powder, salt and black pepper
3 tablespoons vegetable oil or beef dripping
2 medium onions, finely sliced
300ml good beef stock
300ml stout
1 fresh bay leaf
2 medium carrots, peeled
2 medium parsnips, peeled

For the dumplings
100g self-raising flour
good pinch of salt
½ teaspoon mustard powder
50g beef or vegetable suet
1 tablespoon chopped parsley

1 large flameproof casserole dish (with lid)

Preheat the oven to 170°C/325°F/gas 3. Toss the meat in a bowl with the flour, mustard powder, salt and pepper until thoroughly coated. Heat the oil or dripping in the casserole.

Add the meat, a few pieces at a time, and fry until lightly browned. Take care not to overcrowd the pan or the meat will start to boil and steam instead of browning. Use a slotted spoon, remove the meat from the pan to a plate.

When all the meat is browned, turn the heat right down and add the sliced onions to the casserole, stirring well to dislodge any bits and pieces stuck to the base. Cover and cook very gently, stirring frequently, for 10 to 12 minutes or until soft and tender.

Return the meat to the pan along with any juices on the plate. Stir in the stock, stout and bay leaf, plus a little more pepper, and bring to the boil. Stir well, then cover and transfer to the oven to cook for 1½ hours.

Meanwhile, cut the carrots and parsnips into chunks the same size as the beef. Remove the casserole from the oven and stir in the carrots and parsnips. Cover again and return to the oven to cook for a further 30 minutes or until the meat is very tender.

Towards the end of this cooking time, make up the dumplings. Sift the flour, salt and mustard powder into a mixing bowl. Mix in the suet and parsley with a round-bladed knife, then stir in 4 to 5 tablespoons cold water to make a slightly soft but not sticky dough. Flour your hands, then divide the mixture into 8 and roll into balls.

When the meat is tender, give the contents of the casserole a stir and taste, then add more seasoning as needed. Gently drop the dumplings on top of the beef mixture, spacing them evenly. Cover the casserole, return to the oven and cook for 25 to 30 minutes or until the dumplings are firm. Serve piping hot with plenty of green vegetables.

Three Cheese and Spinach Pie

Young leaf spinach and three very different cheeses – salty feta, creamy soft ricotta and mellow Parmesan – plus plenty of herbs and onions make a delicious filling for this filo-topped pie. Keep the pastry wrapped until needed or it will dry out.

Serves 8

1kg fresh young spinach leaves, washed and drained
2 tablespoons olive oil
1 medium onion, finely chopped
4 large garlic cloves, finely chopped or crushed
4 spring onions, finely chopped
small bunch each of parsley and dill, stalks removed, chopped
¼ teaspoon freshly grated nutmeg
2 teaspoons fresh lemon juice
3 large free-range eggs, beaten
250g ricotta
400g feta, crumbled
500g filo pastry, thawed if frozen
about 75g unsalted butter, melted
50g Parmesan, finely grated
salt and black pepper

1 large baking tin or roasting tin about 30 x 22 x 7cm, greased with butter

Pack the spinach into a very large pan and set over medium heat. Cover and cook for a few minutes, stirring occasionally, until the spinach wilts. Tip into a colander and leave to drain. (If using microwaveable packs, follow the pack instructions, then drain.)

Add the olive oil to the warm, dry spinach pan and set over low heat. Add the onion and cook gently for about 10 minutes or until soft but not coloured. Meanwhile, squeeze out all the excess liquid from the spinach and roughly chop. Add to the onions together with the garlic, spring onions and herbs. Season with the nutmeg, lemon juice, a little salt and plenty of pepper. Stir well over the heat for a minute, then tip the mixture into a large bowl and leave to cool completely.

Combine the beaten eggs with the ricotta and feta. Work into the spinach mixture until thoroughly mixed. Taste and add more nutmeg or pepper if needed.

Preheat the oven to 180°C/350°F/gas 4. Unwrap the pastry and count the sheets. Cover with a damp tea towel or sheet of clingfilm. You will need 6 layers of pastry for the base, 6 more to cover the filling and 3 or 4 for the crumpled topping (although you can use up any torn sheets and scraps). Depending on the size of the pastry sheets, arrange a single layer in the buttered tin, over the base and up the sides but not over the edges; trim or overlap as needed. Brush lightly with melted butter, then add another layer of pastry and brush with butter. Continue until there are 6 layers.

Spoon the filling into the tin, spreading it evenly. Fold the pastry edges from the sides of the tin over the filling and lightly brush them with melted butter. Cover with a layer of pastry, tucking the pastry edges down the sides. Brush lightly with butter and sprinkle with a little Parmesan. Repeat until the filling is covered with 6 layers of pastry.

Tear up (or cut up with kitchen scissors) the rest of the pastry into long strips, then crumple up each piece like a chiffon scarf and gently arrange on top of the pie to cover completely. Lightly brush or drizzle the remaining butter over the top. Bake for about 50 minutes or until a good golden brown. Serve warm.

Mushroom and Gorgonzola Twists

There's no pastry to make or roll, and very little actual cooking involved here: saucer-sized portobello mushrooms filled with herbs and tangy blue cheese are wrapped in twists of filo and quickly baked. Just add some peppery watercress for an easy but special first course or light lunch.

Makes 4

300g filo pastry, thawed
   if frozen
4 very large, open cap
   portobello mushrooms
2–3 tablespoons olive oil
small bunch of parsley
few sprigs of rosemary
1 large garlic clove,
   peeled
100g Gorgonzola
   Piccante
50g unsalted butter,
   melted
black pepper

1 baking sheet, lined
   with baking paper

Preheat the oven to 190°C/375°F/gas 5. Keep the pastry wrapped until needed or it will dry out.

Wipe the mushrooms with kitchen paper; remove the stalks and put on one side. Heat 2 tablespoons of the oil in a frying pan (preferably non-stick) and add the mushroom caps, rounded side down. Cook gently for 5 minutes on each side, adding a little more oil as needed. Remove the mushrooms from the pan and leave to drain and cool on kitchen paper.

Pick the parsley and rosemary leaves from the stalks and chop finely with the garlic and the mushroom stalks. Season with black pepper. Divide the Gorgonzola into 4 portions and form each into a cube that will fit inside a mushroom.

Unwrap the pastry. Each 'twist' is made from 3 layers of pastry squares. Using kitchen scissors, cut the pastry into 12 squares with 30cm sides. The size of filo sheets varies from brand to brand so you may have to improvise: if your pastry measures 40 x 30cm cut 6 sheets in half to measure 20 x 30cm, then layer 3 sheets with the centre layer at right angles to the other 2, to make a cross shape.

Layer the pastry on the worktop to make the 4 pastry squares. Set a mushroom, rounded side down, in the centre of each square. Spoon the chopped herb mixture into the mushrooms and top with the Gorgonzola cubes. Lightly brush the edges of each pastry square with melted butter, then gather up the edges and twist together at the top to resemble a money bag.

Arrange on the lined baking sheet, spaced well apart, and brush lightly with the remaining butter. Bake for 20 minutes or until a good golden brown. Serve hot, with watercress.

Mary's tip

Do not keep filo pastry out in a hot kitchen for too long, otherwise it will become dry and brittle. Store it in the fridge, wrapped well in clingfilm, and just remove the layers as you need them.

TARTS AND SWEET PASTRY

SIMPLY GOOD APPLE PIE

Strawberry and Pistachio Tart

MERINGUE PIE MUD PIE STICKY WALNUT PIE

WARM CHERRY CRUMBLE PIE TARTE TATIN

APPLE BEEHIVES

Just Showing Off

Good looking and so refined, the perfect tart is a crisp pastry shell – or biscuit crust – containing a stellar filling. More elegant and sophisticated than a pie, a tart is served unmoulded, so the pastry sides are as visible as the contents. The rich buttery pastry can also be baked on top of a sweet filling or used to make a pie with a top and bottom crust.

Mary's pastry technical challenge for *The Great British Bake Off* contestants is a Tarte au Citron (see page 181). The test she set here is to make a pastry case that's not only a delicious container to complement the filling but to make it look neat, with just the right thickness and consistency. The lemon filling has to taste as good as it looks: neither too sweet nor too bland nor too tart, a perfect consistency and just the right amount for the pastry case.

The pastry used for tarts and sweet pastries is usually richer and sweeter than that for savoury pies. For example, shortcrust is enriched with more butter, egg yolks and sugar. A higher percentage of butter doesn't just add to the taste, it makes the texture shorter and more biscuit-like. Egg yolks add a rich gold colour and flavour, while sugar enhances the texture as well as providing a touch of sweetness (caster sugar will make the pastry slightly more crumbly; icing sugar will give a fine-textured, crisper pastry).

Rich shortcrust can be made by hand, but a food-processor will make light work of it, keeping any contact with warm hands to the minimum. The importance of chilling with a richer pastry can't be overstated – not only for preventing the butter in the dough from melting before it reaches the oven, but also for preventing the lovely, rich pastry from shrinking as it is baked. Once made, give rich shortcrust pastry plenty of chilling time in the fridge to firm up and relax before it is rolled out.

To roll out pastry into a neat round for lining a tin you need to keep turning it slightly to the right after every time you roll, so you are not just rolling up and down the same stretch of pastry (it helps to think of it as a clock: keep rotating the pastry 'clock face' rather than the 'hands', or pin). Rolling the pastry to the correct thickness is essential: too thin and the case will collapse when it is filled, too thick and the base is likely to be doughy and damp. Aim for the thickness of a pound coin, unless the recipe says otherwise. If the pastry starts to feel sticky or soft while you are rolling out, transfer it to a baking sheet lined with clingfilm, cover and chill for 15 to 20 minutes.

Be sure you have a tin or dish that is the right size and depth for the recipe; for tarts to be unmoulded, use a loose-based or springclip tin. A heavy duty tin won't buckle in the oven (avoid the very thin and flimsy sort) and is less likely to become rusty or dented in normal use. There's usually no need to grease good tins because the rich pastry has enough fat in it to prevent sticking (biscuit crusts and recipes with a lot of sugar have their own instructions).

When lining a tin with pastry, take care with the 90 degree angle between the base and sides: the pastry must fit snugly into the angle so the sides of the case are completely straight, rather than curved, but don't press too hard or make the pastry so thin that cracks appear. (If you find there's a hole or crack, just brush it very lightly with water, or egg, and patch it with a small piece of pastry.) Prick the base well with a fork to stop the pastry bubbling up in the oven, because if the sides shrink and the base rises up, there will be less room for your filling and it may overflow. Thoroughly chill before baking unless the recipe directs otherwise.

Pastry cases for sweet tarts are usually prebaked, or 'baked blind', before the filling is added, to prevent a soggy bottom. This involves covering the pastry case with either foil or baking paper and then filling the tin with baking beans. (Uncooked dried pasta also works well, if you don't have baking beans.) Setting the filled tart on a hot baking sheet is also a very good idea. Another tip is to brush the hot pastry base very lightly with beaten egg (whole egg, white or yolk, depending on the recipe), or the cooled cooked base with melted chocolate or a warm jam glaze, before adding the filling: this helps to stop the pastry from absorbing the moist filling.

A tart case will be quite fragile when it comes out of the oven so leave it to cool and firm up before attempting to unmould it. If the pastry has sprung a leak and the filling is stuck to the tin, it is better to serve the tart in the tin rather than risk it falling apart. The easiest way to remove the tart from the tin is to set the tin on an upturned jam jar or bean tin – being sure that the jar or tin is right under the centre of the tart tin – and let the tin ring fall to the worktop. Then gently slide the tart off the tin base onto the serving plate.

The decoration is up to you. Neat circles of fruit or a heap of jumbled berries? Piped meringue or craggy spoonsful? A burnished sugar crust? It should be strikingly attractive, and just slightly frivolous after all.

Mary's tip

To get the most flavour from lemon zest, grate it finely using a microplane grater.
To make lemons easier to squeeze and get the most juice, after removing the zest, cut
the lemons in half, place them in a small china bowl and microwave for a few seconds.

BAKE OFF

TECHNICAL CHALLENGE
MARY'S TARTE AU CITRON

This much-loved favourite can be left beautifully simple, with just a sprinkling of icing sugar or given the professional finish of a chef by caramelising a generous dredging of icing sugar using a blowtorch. Serve the tart on the day you make it, warm or cooled to room temperature.

Serves 8

For the pastry
175g plain flour
100g cold butter, cut
   into small cubes
25g icing sugar, sifted
1 large free-range egg
   yolk
1 tablespoon cold water

For the filling
5 large free-range eggs
125ml double cream
225g caster sugar
finely grated zest and
   juice of 3 medium
   lemons (you need
   150ml juice)

To finish
icing sugar, for dusting

1 x 23cm fluted, deep,
   loose-based tart tin;
   non-stick baking
   paper; a baking sheet

✱ Line the tart tin with pastry following the step-by-step photographs, or using this alternative method – choose the one that works best for you. Roll out the chilled pastry on a lightly floured worktop to a neat round that is the diameter of the pie dish plus twice its height including the rim (it's easiest to measure this with a tape measure or a piece of string).

Gently roll the pastry around the pin and lift over the top of the tin, then carefully unroll the pastry so it drapes over the tin. With floured fingers, delicately press the dough onto the base and up the sides, into the flutes, so there are no air pockets or wrinkles. Avoid stretching the pastry. Roll the pin over the top of the tin to cut off the excess dough.

The side of the pastry case should stand just slightly higher than the rim of the tin in case the pastry shrinks during baking, so use your thumbs to gently ease the pastry upwards to make a neat edge about 5mm higher than the rim of the tin. Curve your forefinger inside this new rim and gently press the pastry edge over your finger so it curves slightly inwards – this will make unmoulding easy. Prick the base of the pastry case well and chill before baking.

✱ If you pour all of the filling into the pastry case before it goes into the oven, there is a danger of it spilling over the side as you manoeuvre the baking sheet onto the oven shelf. Instead, pour in most of the filling so it almost fills the pastry case, then carefully set the baking sheet with the tart tin on the oven shelf. Top up with the rest of the filling to completely fill the case and close the oven door.

1 To make the pastry, put the flour, butter and icing sugar into a food-processor. 'Pulse' briefly until the mixture looks like breadcrumbs. Add the egg yolk and water and process until the ingredients stick together in clumps.

2 Tip the mixture onto a lightly floured worktop and gather it into a ball with your hands. Knead the pastry just 2 or 3 times to make it smooth. (If your butter was a bit soft, the pastry might be too. If so, wrap it in greaseproof or non-stick baking paper and chill for 15 minutes before proceeding.)

3 Lay a piece of non-stick baking paper on the worktop. Remove the base from the tart tin and lay it on the paper. Using a pencil, draw a circle on the paper, 5cm bigger than the tin base or twice the rim height. Dust the base of the tin with flour.

4 Place the pastry ball in the centre of the tin base. Flatten out the ball of pastry slightly, then roll it out, on the base, until it meets the edge of the pencilled circle all around. As you are rolling out, turn the pastry by turning the paper.

5 Gently fold the pastry surrounding the tin base inwards so it is on the base. Carefully lift the tin base off the paper and drop gently into the tin. Ease the folded-over pastry into the corners and up the sides of the tin, pressing the overhang lightly over the rim of the tin.

6 Press the pastry evenly into the flutes so that there are no air pockets or wrinkles. If there are any cracks in the pastry case, simply press them together to seal. Lightly prick the pastry base with a fork, but not quite all the way through. Place the tin on a baking sheet, cover loosely with clingfilm and chill for 30 minutes.

7 Preheat the oven to 200°C/400°F/gas 6. Remove the clingfilm, then line the pastry case with non-stick baking paper or foil and fill with baking beans. Bake blind for 12 to 15 minutes or until the pastry is set, then lift out the paper or foil and beans. Carefully trim the excess pastry from the sides using a sharp knife, holding the knife at a sharp angle and slicing away from you.

8 Return the empty pastry case to the oven to bake for a further 10 to 12 minutes or until it is a pale gold colour and completely dry. Leave to cool on a wire rack while you make the filling. Reduce the oven temperature to 160°C/325°F/gas 3.

9 Break the eggs for the filling into a large bowl and whisk together with a wire whisk. Add the rest of the filling ingredients and whisk until well combined. Transfer the filling mixture to a jug. Pour into the cooled baked pastry case and bake for 30 to 35 minutes or until the filling is just set but with a slight wobble in the centre. Leave to cool slightly, until the pastry seems firm enough, then remove the tart from the tin and transfer to a serving plate. Dust with sifted icing sugar before serving.

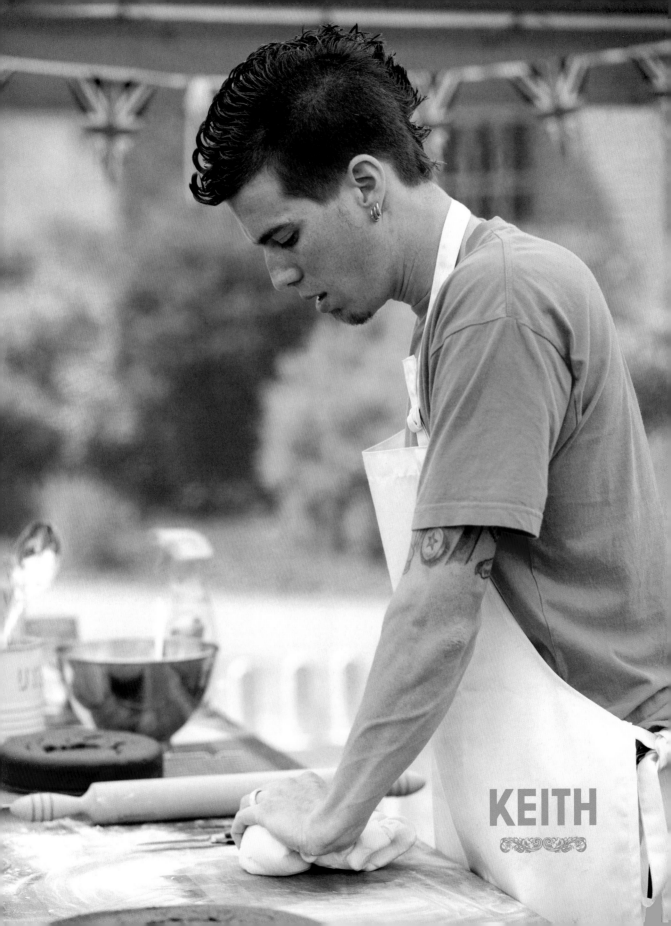

BEST OF THE BAKE-OFF
Blueberry Bakewell Tarts

Makes 12

For the blueberry jam
125g blueberries (fresh
    or frozen)
1 tablespoon caster sugar
squeeze of lemon juice
OR 2 tablespoons wild
    blueberry conserve
    or jam

For the pastry
200g plain flour
100g unsalted butter,
    chilled and cubed
40g icing sugar, sifted
1 large egg, beaten

For the frangipane
55g unsalted butter,
    softened
55g caster sugar
1 large egg, beaten
40g ground almonds
15g plain flour

To decorate
50g icing sugar, sifted
fresh blueberries

1 x 5cm round cutter;
    a 12-hole muffin tray
    (preferably non-stick),
    greased

Combine the ingredients for the jam in a small saucepan and heat gently until the berries start to burst. Cook for a few minutes until the mixture is very thick and has lost its watery appearance. Press through a sieve to remove the skins, then allow to cool completely.

To make the pastry, sift the flour into a medium-sized bowl and rub in the butter until the mixture resembles fine breadcrumbs. Stir in the sugar. Using a palette knife, cut in the beaten egg, then press together to form a ball of dough. Wrap in clingfilm and chill for at least 30 minutes.

Roll out the pastry between a sheet of greaseproof paper and the clingfilm to 3mm thickness. Use the cutter to cut out 12 discs and use to line the bases in the muffin tray. Cut 12 strips 1cm wide and 20cm long from the remaining pastry; use these to line the sides in the muffin tray, carefully pressing the pastry together at the seams to seal (make sure there aren't any holes). Chill for 15 minutes.

Preheat the oven to 170°C/325°F/gas 3. Place the ingredients for the frangipane in a bowl and beat with an electric mixer until smooth and thoroughly combined.

Carefully prick the bases of the pastry cases with a fork, then divide the cooled jam among them, placing ½ teaspoon in each. Top with the frangipane. Bake for about 25 minutes or until the frangipane is risen and golden. Cool in the tray for a few minutes, then transfer to a wire rack to cool completely.

Mix the icing sugar with a little water to form a runny paste and use to decorate the cooled tarts. Top each with one or two fresh blueberries.

Quick Apple Tarts  EASY FOR KIDS

These easy tarts are fun to make, and look and taste like those from a top pâtisserie. They're fabulous eaten warm from the oven with vanilla ice cream. Instead of apples you could use peeled and thickly sliced pears, peaches, mangoes or bananas.

Makes 6

½ quantity Puff Pastry (see page 210) or 375g ready-made butter puff pastry, chilled
3 medium eating apples
40g unsalted butter, melted
6 teaspoons caster sugar
4 tablespoons apricot jam
1 teaspoon lemon juice

2 baking sheets, lined with baking paper

Roll out the pastry thinly on a lightly floured worktop to a rectangle about 25 x 40cm. Using a 12cm biscuit cutter or saucer as a guide, cut out 6 rounds. Set them, well apart, on the lined baking sheets. Prick the centre of the pastry rounds in several places with a fork, then chill while preparing the topping.

Preheat the oven to 220°C/425°F/gas 7. Rinse the apples but don't peel. Quarter them and cut out the cores, then slice thickly.

Remove the chilled pastry from the fridge. Arrange the apple slices on the pastry rounds, leaving a 5mm border clear. Brush the fruit and pastry rim with melted butter, then sprinkle each tart with a teaspoon of sugar. Bake for 15 to 20 minutes or until the pastry is well puffed, a good golden brown and crisp.

Meanwhile, heat the apricot jam with the lemon juice and 1 tablespoon water in a small pan until melted. Push through a sieve, then reheat until just boiling.

Remove the tarts from the oven and brush immediately with the hot jam glaze. Transfer to a wire rack and leave to cool. These tarts are best eaten warm the same day.

BEST OF THE BAKE-OFF
Chocolate, Fennel and Ginger Tarts

Makes 12 little tarts

For the pastry
180g plain flour
100g unsalted butter,
  chilled and diced
1 large egg yolk

For the filling
100g unsalted butter
100g soft light brown
  sugar
100ml double cream
100g dark chocolate
  (70% cocoa solids),
  broken up
pinch of fennel seeds
15g finely chopped glacé
  ginger

1 x 7.5cm round cutter;
  12 x 6.5cm tartlet tins
  or 1 x 12-hole bun tray
  (mince pie/jam tart
  tray)

To make the pastry, sift the flour into a bowl and add the butter. Cut the butter into the flour using 2 knives until the butter is in pea-sized lumps. Then rub the butter into the flour with your fingertips until the mixture looks like fine crumbs. Beat the egg yolk with 1 tablespoon cold water. Add to the bowl and stir just to bring the rubbed-in mixture together; you may need to add a little more liquid. Turn out onto a lightly floured worktop and gather together into a ball of dough, without kneading. Wrap in clingfilm and chill for 20 minutes.

Roll out the pastry on the floured worktop to about 3mm thickness. Cut out 12 discs with the round cutter, re-rolling the trimmings as necessary. Use to line the tartlet tins. Prick the bases and chill for 20 minutes.

Preheat the oven to 180°C/350°F/gas 4. Line each pastry case with non-stick baking paper or foil and fill with baking beans. Bake blind for 12 minutes (see page 184). Remove the paper and beans and bake for a further 4 to 5 minutes or until the pastry is firm and lightly coloured. Leave to cool.

For the filling, melt the butter with the sugar in a medium pan over medium heat, then bring to the boil and boil for 2 minutes, stirring frequently. Add the cream, bring back to the boil and boil for 3 minutes. Remove from the heat and allow to cool for 8 to 10 minutes. Add the chocolate together with the fennel and ginger and whisk until the mixture is smooth and glossy.

Quickly pour the filling into the tart cases (to ensure that the tarts have a smooth finish). Leave to cool and set for at least 4 hours before serving.

Strawberry and Pistachio Tart GOOD FOR *Celebrations*

This glamorous tart is surprisingly easy to make. The crisp, buttery pastry base is made with plenty of pistachios. The whole berries that top it are finished with a professional jam glaze and shards of caramelised nuts. Serve with whipped cream.

Serves 8

For the pastry
200g plain flour
50g shelled unsalted pistachios
pinch of salt
75g icing sugar
175g unsalted butter, chilled and diced
2 large free-range egg yolks

For the glaze
500g small, just ripe strawberries
200g seedless raspberry jam or redcurrant jelly

For the topping
25g unsalted pistachios
50g caster sugar

1 baking sheet; non-stick baking paper

For the pastry, put the flour, nuts and salt into the bowl of a food-processor and run the machine until the mixture looks like coarse sand. Add the icing sugar and process just until combined. Add the butter and process until the mixture resembles crumbs.

With the machine running, add the egg yolks through the feed tube. Stop the machine as soon as the mixture comes together. Shape the dough into a thick disc, wrap in clingfilm and chill for about 30 minutes or until firm.

Unwrap the dough and set it in the middle of a sheet of non-stick baking paper. Using a floured rolling pin, roll out the dough to a thick round about 26cm in diameter. Give the edge a fluted decoration by pinching the dough between your fingers.

Transfer the pastry base, on the paper, to the baking sheet and prick all over with a fork, avoiding the fluted edge. Chill for 15 minutes or until very firm.

Meanwhile, preheat the oven to 180°C/350°F/gas 4. Bake the pastry base for about 20 minutes or until firm and lightly coloured. Remove from the oven, but leave on the baking sheet to cool and firm up for about 30 minutes before transferring, on the lining paper, to a wire rack to cool completely. Set the pastry base on a serving platter. (It can be wrapped and kept at room temperature for 24 hours.)

Wipe the berries (avoid washing if possible) and hull. Halve medium-sized berries and quarter any huge ones. Heat the jam in a small pan, stirring until smooth and melted. Bring to the boil, then remove from the heat.

Arrange the berries, pointed ends up, on the pastry base, starting from the centre and working round and round in a neat spiral. Fill in any gaps with quartered berries. (If necessary, stick any cut berries in place with a blob of hot jam glaze.)

Recipe continues on page 192

Bring the glaze to the boil once more, then brush it all over the fruit to coat completely. If the glaze becomes too thick to brush on easily, reheat it with a little water.

Put the pistachios and sugar in a small, heavy frying pan (preferably non-stick) and set over medium heat. Cook gently, frequently shaking the pan until the sugar melts and turns into a golden brown caramel. Tip onto a sheet of non-stick baking paper set on a heatproof surface, spread out evenly and leave to cool.

Just before serving, roughly break up the pistachio caramel into large shards. Use to decorate the top of the tart. This is best eaten within 3 hours of assembling.

JOANNE

BEST OF THE BAKE-OFF
Elderflower and Honeycomb Tarts

Makes 12

For the pastry
200g plain flour
2 tablespoons icing
  sugar, sifted
¼ teaspoon salt
100g unsalted butter,
  chilled and diced
1 egg
1 teaspoon elderflower
  cordial

For the honeycomb
200g caster sugar
50ml mild-flavoured
  runny honey
1 tbsp liquid glucose
¾ teaspoon bicarbonate
  of soda

For the filling
100g caster sugar
2 large eggs plus 2 egg
  yolks
2 tablespoons cornflour
200ml full-fat milk
100ml double cream
5–6 tablespoons
  elderflower cordial
small edible flowers, to
  decorate

1 x 7.5cm round cutter;
  12 x 6.5cm tartlet tins
  or 1 x 12-hole bun tray
  (mince pie/jam tart
  tray); 1 baking sheet,
  lined with baking paper

Put the flour, icing sugar, salt and butter into a food-processor and blitz until the mixture resembles fine breadcrumbs. Beat the egg and elderflower cordial together in a small jug. With the processor running, gradually add the egg mixture through the feed tube, using just enough to bind to a dough. Turn out onto a lightly floured worktop and knead briefly until smooth. Wrap in clingfilm and chill for about 30 minutes.

Roll out the pastry on the floured worktop to about 3mm thickness. Cut out 12 discs with the round cutter, re-rolling the trimmings as necessary. Use to line the tins. Prick the bases and chill for 20 minutes.

Preheat the oven to 180°C/350°F/gas 4. Line each pastry case with non-stick baking paper or foil and fill with baking beans. Bake blind for 12 minutes (see page 184). Remove the paper and beans and bake for a further 4 to 5 minutes or until the pastry is firm and lightly coloured. Leave to cool.

To make the honeycomb, put the sugar, honey, glucose and 3½ tablespoons water into a pan and boil until the temperature reaches 150°C/300°F on a sugar thermometer – it should be a light caramel colour. Remove from the heat and quickly add the bicarbonate of soda, whisking it in. Pour the mixture onto the lined baking sheet and leave to cool and set.

Next, make the filling. Mix the sugar, eggs, egg yolks and cornflour in a large bowl. Put the milk and cream into a pan and heat gently until steaming hot. Whisk the hot milk and cream into the egg and sugar mixture until smooth. Pour back into the pan and cook over low heat, whisking constantly, until the mixture starts to thicken. Cook for a minute, whisking. Remove from the heat and whisk in the cordial to taste. Leave to cool, then cover closely with clingfilm to prevent a skin from forming and chill until firm.

Using a star tube, pipe the filling (or spoon it) into the cooled tartlet cases. Place a broken piece of honeycomb on top and decorate with small purple violas or violets (or other edible flowers, or berries). If you like, dip the leftover pieces of honeycomb into melted chocolate for an extra teatime treat.)

Mud Pie

It is fair to say that this is not the most glamorous chocolate tart recipe, but it will disappear before your eyes because it's hard to have just one slice. The texture is surprisingly light and fluffy given its dark and slightly gooey appearance, and it isn't oversweet.

Serves 8–12

For the base
250g dark chocolate digestive biscuits (about 16)
50g unsalted butter, melted

For the filling
200g dark chocolate (70% cocoa solids), chopped or broken up
200g unsalted butter, diced
4 large free-range eggs, at room temperature
100g light muscovado sugar
100g dark muscovado sugar
200ml double cream, at room temperature

1 x 23cm springclip tin, greased

Preheat the oven to 180°C/350°F/gas 4. Crush the biscuits to a fine powder in a food-processor, or put them into a plastic bag and bash with a rolling pin. Tip into a mixing bowl and stir in the butter until thoroughly combined. Transfer to the prepared tin and press over the base and halfway up the sides using the back of a spoon. Chill while making the filling.

Put the chocolate and butter into a heatproof bowl and set over a pan of steaming hot but not boiling water (don't let the base of the bowl touch the hot water). Melt gently, stirring occasionally, then remove the bowl from the pan and leave to cool until needed.

Put the eggs into a large mixing bowl and whisk with an electric mixer until frothy. Make sure the sugars are lump-free, then add to the eggs and continue whisking until the mixture is very thick and mousse-like. Whisk in the cooled chocolate followed by the cream. When completely combined, pour the filling into the biscuit case.

Bake for about 50 minutes or until just firm; the filling will have puffed up but will sink as it cools, and may crack a little. Remove from the oven and leave to cool for a few minutes, then run a round-bladed knife around the inside of the tin to loosen the pie (this will prevent any major cracks from appearing). Leave to cool before unclipping and removing the tin side. Serve at room temperature. Any leftover pie will be even better the next day.

Tip: Remove the cream from the fridge well ahead because if it is chilled it will set the filling mixture and make it lumpy.

BEST OF THE BAKE-OFF
Rhubarb Meringue Pie

Serves 8

For the pastry
200g plain flour
125g unsalted butter,
  chilled and diced
50g icing sugar
½ teaspoon ground
  ginger
1 large egg, beaten

For the filling
1kg trimmed rhubarb,
  cut into 4cm lengths
125g caster sugar
finely grated zest of
  1 orange

For the meringue
4 large egg whites, at
  room temperature
200g golden caster
  sugar
2 teaspoons cornflour

1 large ovenproof dish; 1
  x 23cm deep, loose-
  based flan tin; a baking
  sheet; a piping bag
  and plain 1cm tube
  (optional)

To make the pastry, sift the flour into a bowl and add the butter. Rub in until the mixture resembles fine crumbs. Add the icing sugar and ginger and combine thoroughly. Add the egg and mix to bring together. Turn out onto a lightly floured worktop and gather into a smooth ball of dough. Wrap in clingfilm and chill for 20 minutes or until firm but not hard.

Roll out the pastry on a lightly floured worktop and use to line the flan tin. Prick the base of the pastry case, then chill for 30 minutes.

Meanwhile, make the filling. Preheat the oven to 150°C/300°F/gas 2. Put the rhubarb into a mixing bowl, sprinkle with the sugar and orange zest and toss until well mixed. Transfer to a large ovenproof dish, spreading evenly. Cook in the oven for about 20 minutes or until barely tender when pierced with the tip of a knife. Remove from the oven and leave to cool, then drain thoroughly. Turn the oven temperature up to 180°C/350°F/gas 4.

While the rhubarb is cooling, line the pastry case with non-stick baking paper or foil and fill with baking beans. Bake for 15 minutes. Remove the paper and beans, then bake for a further 8 minutes or until light gold. Remove from the oven. Put the baking sheet into the oven to heat up.

To make the meringue, put the egg whites in a large bowl and whisk to soft peaks. Gradually add half the sugar, whisking. Whisk in the cornflour, then gradually whisk in the remaining sugar. The mixture should be smooth, thick and glossy.

Fill the pastry case with the drained rhubarb, standing the pieces on end like little soldiers. Pile most of the meringue over the rhubarb, then pipe the rest in pointy peaks all over the surface. Set the flan tin on the hot baking sheet and bake for about 30 minutes or until the meringue is crisp and very pale gold. Allow to cool before removing from the tin (use a sturdy palette knife for this).

Sticky Walnut Tart

The slight bitterness of good walnuts works well with the rich and sticky-sweet toffee mixture and crumbly pastry of this tart. A mild set honey, such as a light Acacia, is a good choice for the filling. Serve the pie in thin slices with vanilla ice cream.

Serves 8

For the pastry
175g plain flour
pinch of salt
1 tablespoon caster sugar
100g unsalted butter, chilled and diced
1 large free-range egg yolk
1 tablespoon icy water

For the filling
300g walnut pieces
150g unsalted butter
100g caster sugar
¼ teaspoon sea salt flakes
100g honey
250ml double cream

1 x 23cm loose-based deep flan tin; a baking sheet

Tip: Don't throw away the spare egg white – use it to make meringues. It can be frozen for up to 3 months.

To make the pastry in a food-processor, put the flour, salt and sugar into the processor bowl and briefly 'pulse' to combine. Add the diced butter and process until the mixture looks like sand. With the machine running, add the yolk and water through the feed tube and process until the mixture comes together to make a ball of firm dough. Flatten into a thick disc, wrap in clingfilm and chill for about 15 minutes or until firm.

To make the pastry by hand, sift the flour, salt and sugar into a mixing bowl. Add the diced butter and rub into the flour between the tips of your fingers until the butter disappears and the mixture looks sandy. Using a round-bladed knife stir in the egg yolk and water, then gently work the mixture with your hands until it comes together to make a firm dough. Wrap and chill as above.

Roll out the dough on a lightly floured worktop to a round about 28cm in diameter. Roll the pastry around the pin, lift it over the flan tin and unroll to drape over the tin. Gently press the dough onto the base and sides of the tin. Run the rolling pin across the top of the tin to cut off the excess pastry, then neaten the rim with your fingers. Prick the base with a fork. Chill the pastry case for 20 minutes. Meanwhile, preheat the oven to 190°C/375°F/gas 5.

Line the pastry case with non-stick baking paper or foil and fill with baking beans. Bake blind for 12 to 15 minutes or until lightly golden and just firm (see page 184). Carefully remove the paper and beans, then bake the empty pastry case for a further 5 minutes or until crisp and golden. Remove from the oven and leave to cool while making the filling – do not unmould. Leave the oven on and put the baking sheet in to heat up.

Combine the walnuts, butter, sugar, salt flakes and honey in a large, heavy frying pan (preferably non-stick). Set over low heat and cook gently, stirring constantly with a wooden spoon, until the mixture turns a pale straw-gold. Stir in the cream and cook for another minute until bubbling.

Set the pastry case, still in its tin, on the hot baking sheet and carefully pour in the very hot filling, making sure the case is evenly filled. Return to the oven and bake for about 15 minutes or until the nuts are a deep golden brown. Leave to cool for at least 20 minutes before unmoulding. Serve warm or at room temperature.

Apple Beehives

Along with the similar puff pastry cream horns, this once very popular dessert deserves to be baked regularly as it looks and tastes sublime. The name comes from the shape of the pastries and honey in the filling. Eating apples with plenty of flavour work best, rather than Bramley cooking apples because they keep their shape and texture during baking. Serve straight from the oven with plenty of custard.

Makes 4

½ quantity Puff Pastry (see page 210) or 375g ready-made butter puff pastry, chilled
4 large eating apples
25g unsalted butter, softened
1 tablespoon honey
50g chopped mixed nuts
1–2 tablespoons milk, to glaze
caster sugar, for sprinkling

1 x 7cm round pastry cutter (or upturned glass); a baking sheet, lined with baking paper

Roll out the pastry very thinly on a lightly floured worktop to a rectangle about 15 x 60cm. Cut out 4 rounds from one end of the rectangle, using the pastry cutter or glass. Cut the rest of the pastry into long strips 1.5cm wide. Stack the trimmings on top of each other and re-roll to cut more strips, if needed.

Peel and core the apples. Mix the soft butter with the honey and nuts. Turn the apples upside down and place a pastry round over what was the base of each apple, moulding it with your hand so it makes a shallow cup shape. Set the apples, pastry base down, on the lined baking sheet. Pack the honey and nut filling into the cavities in the apples.

Lightly brush the strips of pastry with water. To make each beehive, start at the pastry base and wind strips around and up the apple in a spiral so they overlap slightly and completely cover the fruit.

Gently press the pastry to seal it around the top so each apple is completely enclosed – you can cut a small disc from the reserved pastry if you need to cover the gap. Chill for 15 to 20 minutes while preheating the oven to 220°C/425°F/gas 7.

Lightly brush the pastry with milk to glaze and sprinkle with sugar. Bake for 20 minutes, then reduce the temperature to 180°C/350°F/gas 4 and bake for a further 15 to 20 minutes or until the pastry is well puffed, crisp and golden brown, and the apples are just soft (test by poking with a skewer). Serve hot.

Simply Good Apple Pie

A good apple pie only needs two things: juicy fruit that is packed with tart-sweet flavour and melt-in-the-mouth tender pastry, crisp rather than soggy, that tastes of butter. You can serve this pie warm or cold, with custard or thick cream, and be pleased with your work.

Serves 6

4 large Bramley cooking apples (about 900g in total)
100g caster sugar, plus extra for sprinkling
finely grated zest and juice of ½ unwaxed lemon
½ quantity Puff Pastry (see page 210) or 375g ready-made butter puff pastry
2 tablespoons milk, to glaze

1 x 23cm round fluted pie dish; a baking sheet

Peel, quarter and core the apples. Thinly slice them into a mixing bowl. Add the sugar and lemon zest and juice, and toss gently until thoroughly combined.

Roll out two-thirds of the pastry on a lightly floured worktop to a round large enough to line the pie dish. Roll the pastry around the pin and lift it over the dish, then unroll the pastry so it drapes over the dish. Gently press the pastry onto the base and sides. Leave any excess pastry hanging over the rim – it will be cut off later.

Pile the apple mixture into the pastry case, packing it fairly firmly – the apples will cook down. Roll out the remaining pastry to a thin round that is big enough to cover the top of the pie. Dampen the pastry on the rim of the dish with a little water.

Roll the pastry top around the pin, lift it and unroll over the dish to cover the apples. Press the pastry edges firmly together to seal, but don't trim yet. Chill for 20 minutes.

Meanwhile, preheat the oven to 200°C/400°F/gas 6. Put the baking sheet into the oven to heat up.

Using a sharp knife trim off the excess pastry, then knock up the edges with the back of the knife: hold it horizontally and make tiny cuts in the pastry edge. Pinch the pastry edge between your fingers to flute. Brush the top with milk and sprinkle with sugar, then make a couple of small slits in the centre to let out the steam.

Set the pie dish on the heated baking sheet and bake for 15 minutes. Reduce the oven temperature to 180°C/350°F/gas 4 and bake for a further 25 minutes or until the pastry is a good golden brown and crisp. Serve warm or at room temperature.

Warm Cherry Crumble Pie

Enjoy this pie when English cherries are in season and good value in the markets. The dough is quickly made in a food-processor, then grated into the tin and pressed in place – it's too rich to roll out. The cherries are added and the rest of the dough is grated on top to make a crunchy crumble topping.

Serves 8

For the dough
250g plain flour
50g ground almonds
175g unsalted butter,
   chilled and diced
100g caster sugar
2 large free-range egg
   yolks
3 tablespoons single,
   whipping or double
   cream
1 tablespoon icy water

For the filling
600g cherries, stoned
2 teaspoons caster sugar
1 teaspoon cornflour
icing sugar, for dusting

1 x 23cm round fluted
   pie dish; a baking sheet

To make the dough, put the flour, almonds, butter and sugar into the bowl of a food-processor and 'pulse' briefly to combine. Mix together the egg yolks, cream and water and add to the bowl. Process just until the dough comes together in a ball. Wrap in clingfilm and chill for 30 minutes.

Meanwhile, preheat the oven to 180°C/350°F/gas 4. Put a baking sheet into the oven to heat up. Mix the cherries with the sugar and cornflour in a mixing bowl.

Cut off half the chilled dough, re-wrap and return to the fridge. Coarsely grate the other half into the pie dish. Flour your fingers, then press the dough onto the base and up the sides to make an even case of dough about 5mm thick. Pile the cherry mixture in the dish. Grate the rest of the dough over the cherries in an even layer – don't compress the mixture.

Set the pie dish on the heated baking sheet and bake for 45 to 50 minutes or until golden brown. Dust with icing sugar and serve warm or at room temperature.

Tarte Tatin

This upside-down apple tart is traditionally made in a cast-iron frying pan, but specially designed Tatin tins are now readily available (the tin needs to have a heavy base as it's set over heat on the hob to cook and caramelise the filling). Some recipes use puff pastry, but a rich, crisp shortcrust also provides a good contrast to the apples.

Serves 6–8

For the pastry
175g plain flour
pinch of salt
25g caster sugar
100g unsalted butter,
    chilled and diced
1 large free-range egg
    yolk
1 tablespoon icy water

For the filling
100g unsalted butter
175g caster sugar
10 eating apples (about
    1.25kg in total)

1 x 20.5cm Tatin tin; a
    baking sheet

Sift the flour, salt and sugar into a mixing bowl. Add the diced butter and rub in using the tips of your fingers until the mixture looks sandy. Using a round-bladed knife, stir in the egg yolk and water, then gently work the mixture with your hands until it comes together to make a firm dough. Wrap and chill as above. To make the pastry in a food-processor see page 198.

Cut the butter into thin slices and arrange on the base of the tin to cover completely. Sprinkle over the sugar evenly. Peel, halve and core the apples. Arrange the halves, standing on end, in the tin, packing them in tightly so the tart doesn't collapse as the fruit cooks.

Set the tin over moderate heat on the hob. Cook and bubble for 20 to 30 minutes or until the butter and sugar have turned into a richly coloured caramel and all the excess moisture from the apples has evaporated. While the apples are cooking, preheat the oven to 220°C/425°F/gas 7.

Roll out the dough on a lightly floured worktop to a fairly thick round to fit the top of the tin. Roll up the dough around the rolling pin. Remove the tin from the hob and set on a heatproof surface. Gently unroll the dough over the tin so it drapes over the apples to cover them completely. Quickly tuck the edges of the dough lid down inside the pan, then prick the lid all over with a fork.

Set the tin on the baking sheet. Bake for 20 to 30 minutes or until the pastry is golden brown and crisp. Leave to cool for about 5 minutes, then run a round-bladed knife around the inside of the tin to loosen the edges of the pastry. Set an upturned large platter over the tin and invert to turn out the tart – the pastry will end up under the caramelized apples. Eat warm or at room temperature with crème fraîche.

Tip: Golden Delicious apples are most often used for this French classic, but other well-flavoured, tart eating apples also work well.

Choux Pastry Eclairs and Profiteroles

CROQUEMBOUCHE Millefeuilles

PATISSERIE

ALMOND CROISSANTS ICED FINGERS

DANISH PASTRIES Palm Leaves and Almond Straws

The Professional Touch

A quick glance will show that the recipes in this chapter are a bit more special than those in other chapters. What a satisfying achievement to produce patisserie worthy of a pastry shop window! These glories are combinations of rich, buttery, light pastry, crisp choux pastry or enriched yeasted dough with carefully made fillings, plus exquisite toppings or decorations – sheer indulgence, really.

Choux pastry is fairly simple and quick to make yet the results look really impressive. Unlike other pastries, choux is made in a saucepan on top of the stove: flour is added to just-boiling water and butter; this is cooled before eggs are beaten in to make a thick and shiny paste. The paste is piped or spooned onto a baking sheet (rather than rolled out) to make finger-like éclairs, small round profiteroles or larger choux buns or puffs. In the oven the dough puffs up to many times its original size to make a crisp, golden case for a sweet filling: pastry cream, chocolate mousse, whipped cream or ice cream.

The keys to success are making the dough the correct consistency – it must hold its shape rather than be sloppy – and ensuring the pastry is thoroughly cooked because under-cooked pastry will collapse when it comes out of the oven and quickly turn soggy. To help with this, towards the end of the baking time make a small hole in each pastry to let the steam out, then return to the oven to finish baking.

Mastering the technique of making a layered or laminated dough – that is, one made up of many layers of a basic dough and lots of butter – is more of a challenge. Puff Pastry (see page 210) is created by rolling out and folding the dough and butter many times so that in the heat of the oven the moisture trapped between the layers produces steam which pushes them apart and puffs them up, resulting in layer upon layer of pastry flakes. If this technique seems rather daunting, don't worry.

Even if your first attempts don't look perfect, they will most certainly taste far better than anything you can buy ready-made in a supermarket.

You will need to invest in a decent rolling pin, one that feels comfortable in your hands but isn't too light; a couple of heavy-duty baking sheets that won't buckle in a hot oven or rust after use; a couple of pastry brushes – one to dust off excess flour when you're rolling the pastry, the other for brushing on beaten egg glaze before baking or a sweet glaze afterwards; and a large wire cooling rack. For professional-looking pastries, measure accurately with a ruler and use a large, sharp knife (or a pizza cutter or wheel) for trimming dead-straight sides.

Making a layered dough is time-consuming and it's vital not to cut corners if you want a good result. The butter must stay cool enough so it doesn't start to melt and ooze out of the dough, so keep to the chilling times (make sure the dough is well wrapped in clingfilm so it doesn't start to dry out and crack); chill for slightly longer if the dough still feels soft.

When rolling out, only use enough flour on the worktop to stop the pastry from sticking. Roll out smoothly and evenly to a neat rectangle with straight edges and sharp corners so when the dough is folded in three it forms a perfect sandwich (if the dough gets out of shape, it won't rise evenly in the oven and will look lopsided).

Preheat the oven so the pastry gets a blast of high heat as it goes in (if the temperature is too low the butter will melt before the dough has had time to set and it will then become soggy and dense), and be sure that the pastry is thoroughly baked for the best taste and texture. Slight over-baking is better than under-cooking.

The method of making puff pastry is used to turn a yeast-raised dough into croissants and Danish pastries, which call upon both bread- and pastry-making skills. While the yeasted dough needs to be thoroughly kneaded and properly risen, adding butter and 'laminating' by repeatedly rolling out and folding up the dough means that it must also be kept cool and treated with care so the butter doesn't melt. And the dough should not be so over-worked that it becomes tough. In fact, keeping these yeasted doughs cool is more important than giving the yeast a hand with a little warmth. Shaping and decorating the pastries is the fun part – the more you practice the better they will look.

Paul's patisserie technical challenge for *The Great British Bake Off* contestants is Iced Fingers (see page 240), made with a rich, sweet yeasted dough. The test here is to pay particular attention to details: the dough must be well made, to bake to a fine and even crumb (with no holes) and each finger must be the same size and colour. The filling of jam and cream must be judged right to look attractive and in proportion.

Patisserie is a combination of craft and art – everything should taste as good as it looks.

THE GREAT BRITISH BAKE OFF

HOW TO MAKE PERFECT
PUFF PASTRY

This is the lightest, richest, flakiest and trickiest of all pastries. What makes it so delicious is its butteriness – it is made with as much butter as flour – and what makes it so flaky is the way the butter is rolled into the flour and water dough to make literally hundreds and hundreds of layers. The lightness is the result of the water in the dough turning to steam in the oven and puffing up the fragile layers.

Makes about 750g

300g plain flour
½ teaspoon salt
300g unsalted butter,
   cold but not rock-hard
1 teaspoon lemon juice
about 140ml icy water

* Don't let the butter get warm or it will start to ooze out of the dough, which will then be hard to handle, and the pastry will end up greasy and heavy. If the butter becomes soft while it is being pounded, chill it briefly.

* Keep a dry pastry brush next to the rolling pin and brush off the excess flour before folding the dough. Too much flour could make the pastry dry and heavy.

* It's difficult to make puff pastry in small quantities, but once it has had 4 'turns' it can be kept in the fridge for 4 days or frozen (thaw before using). Complete the last 2 'turns' when you want to use the dough.

* Save the pastry trimmings. Just stack them on top of each other and re-roll – don't knead them together as for shortcrust pastry. Chill thoroughly, then use to make some Palm Leaves and Almond Straws (see page 216).

1 Put the flour and salt into the bowl. Rub the butter into the flour with your fingertips. Mix the lemon juice with the water, then stir the liquid into the flour mix with a round-bladed knife to form a ball of slightly moist dough.

2 To make with a food-processor, 'pulse' the flour and salt a few times just to combine and aerate the flour. Cut 50g of the cold butter into small pieces and add to the bowl, then process until the mixture looks like fine crumbs. With the machine running, pour the liquid through the feed tube to make the dough. Turn out the dough ball onto a lightly floured worktop and cut a deep cross in the top. Wrap and chill for 15 minutes.

3 Sprinkle a little flour over the remaining piece of butter, then place it between 2 sheets of clingfilm or greaseproof paper. Pound it with a rolling pin until it is half its original thickness. Remove the film and fold the butter in half, then cover with film and pound again. Keep doing this until the butter is pliable but still very cold (the butter should be about the same temperature as the dough when they are combined). Beat it into a square with sides about 13cm.

4 Put the unwrapped ball of dough, cross-cut up, on a floured worktop and roll out in 4 directions (lifting the dough and making a quarter turn after each rolling), to make a shape like a cross with 4 flaps and a thicker square in the centre. Lightly dust the butter square with flour, then place in the centre of the dough and fold the flaps over to enclose it. Gently press the seams with the rolling pin to seal the butter in. Make sure the butter is completely enclosed so it won't ooze out during the rolling and folding processes.

5 Turn the dough upside down and lightly press with the rolling pin to flatten it. Taking care not to squeeze the butter out, gently roll out the dough away from you into a rectangle about 54 x 18cm. Then fold the dough in 3 like a business letter: fold the bottom third up to cover the centre third, then fold the top third down to cover the other 2 layers and make a neat square.

6 Lightly press the open edges with the rolling pin to seal. This completes your first 'turn'. Lift up the dough and give it a quarter turn anti-clockwise so that the folded, rounded edge that was at the bottom is now on the left side. Roll out the dough to a rectangle and fold it in 3 again, just as before. Seal the edges. This completes the second 'turn'. Wrap and chill the dough for 15 minutes, then give it 2 more 'turns'. Wrap and chill the dough as before (at this point the dough can be kept in the fridge for 4 days or frozen). Before using, give the dough 2 more 'turns' to make a total of 6.

Millefeuilles with Raspberries

This is the sweet puff pastry of 'a thousand leaves' – each layer is made up of 729 leaves (3 to the power of 6, as you'll see if you make it yourself). The pastry is rolled to a thin sheet, sliced in three after baking and then layered with a rich orange pastry cream and fresh raspberries. It is served with raspberry sauce.

Serves 6

½ quantity Puff Pastry
    (see page 210) or 375g
    ready-made butter
    puff pastry, well chilled
½ teaspoon caster sugar
icing sugar, for dusting
Raspberry Sauce (see
    page 272), to serve

For the filling
250ml full-fat milk
finely grated zest of
    1 unwaxed orange
3 large free-range eggs,
    at room temperature
50g caster sugar
1½ tablespoons cornflour
100ml double cream,
    well chilled
1 teaspoon orange
    liqueur (or to taste)
200g small raspberries

1 large baking sheet,
    lightly greased

Roll out the pastry on a lightly floured worktop to a square with sides about 31cm. Neatly trim the edges with a large sharp knife, taking care not to drag the knife or the pastry because this will distort the shape.

Roll the pastry around the rolling pin and lift it over the baking sheet, then gently unroll the pastry so it is upside down on the sheet. Brush off the excess flour with a dry pastry brush, then sprinkle the surface with the sugar. Prick well with a fork. Chill for 20 minutes.

Preheat the oven to 220°C/425°F/gas 7. Bake the pastry sheet for about 15 minutes or until well risen, golden and very crisp. It must not be undercooked or the middle will be flabby and soggy – it is better to slightly overcook if in doubt. Transfer to a wire rack and leave to cool.

Meanwhile, make the pastry cream for the filling. Heat the milk with the orange zest in a medium pan (preferably non-stick). In a heatproof bowl, whisk the egg yolks with the caster sugar and cornflour for a couple of minutes until thick and light. Whisk in the hot milk, then tip the mixture back into the pan and stir over medium heat until the custard boils and thickens.

Remove the pan from the heat and stir well to make sure the custard is very smooth. Pour and scrape into a bowl. Press a piece of clingfilm onto the surface of the custard to prevent a skin from forming. Cool, then chill for about 2 hours or until firm.

Whip the cream until firm. Uncover the custard and mix in the liqueur, stirring well until smooth. Fold in the whipped cream. Cover the bowl and chill the pastry cream for about 4 hours or until firm enough to spread.

When ready to assemble, use a sharp knife to cut the pastry square into 3 equal strips, each about 10 x 30cm, then cut each strip across into 6 pieces. Layer 3 pastry pieces with pastry cream and raspberries, then repeat to make 6 individual millefeuilles. Dust with icing sugar and serve with a jug of raspberry sauce.

Palm Leaves and Almond Straws

Use puff pastry – freshly made or trimmings – to make these crisp sweet pastries.

Makes 20

½ quantity Puff Pastry
(see page 210) or 375g
ready-made butter
puff pastry, well chilled

For Palm Leaves
about 150g caster sugar

For Almond Straws
about 50g caster sugar
50g flaked almonds

2 baking sheets, lined
with baking paper

*Tip: For spicy,
sweet Palm Leaves
add ½ teaspoon
ground cinnamon to
the caster sugar. You
can also add a
couple of pinches of
ground cardamom
to the sugar for the
Almond Straws.*

For Palm Leaves
Sprinkle a worktop generously with sugar and roll out the pastry to make
a rectangle about 50 x 20cm. Position it so the long sides are top and
bottom. Generously sprinkle the pastry with sugar and gently run the rolling
pin over it. With a lightly floured, sharp knife, trim the edges to neaten.

Using a ruler, note the centre point along one long side, then fold in
the short sides to meet in the centre at this point. Sprinkle the pastry
with more sugar. Fold in the short sides once more so they meet in the
centre. Sprinkle with sugar again, then fold one short side over on top of
the other piece of folded pastry. Gently press together. Wrap and chill
for about 15 minutes or until firm.

With a floured, sharp knife, cut the roll into 1cm slices. Place them flat, well
apart, on the prepared baking sheets. Gently separate the two rounded
ends of each pastry so it can expand during baking. Chill for 15 minutes.
Meanwhile, preheat the oven to 200°C/400°F/gas 6.

Bake for about 12 minutes or until lightly golden. Remove from the oven
and carefully turn each pastry over (they will still be soft), then return to
the oven. Bake for a further 7 to 10 minutes or until both sides are a shiny
golden brown. Transfer to a wire rack and leave to cool.

For Almond Straws
Roll out the pastry on a sugared worktop to make a rectangle about
44 x 20cm. Sprinkle the pastry generously with sugar. With a ruler, mark
the centre point along both long sides. Scatter the almonds over one half
of the pastry. Gently roll the rolling pin over the pastry, then fold over the
half without almonds, like closing a book, so the almonds are sandwiched
between the 2 pastry layers. Gently press the layers together.

The pastry will now measure 22 x 20cm. Using a floured, sharp knife cut
the pastry into 20 strips, each 1cm wide and 22cm long. Hold one end of
each strip in each hand and gently twist in opposite directions. Arrange
the twists well apart on the prepared baking sheets and scatter over all the
almonds that have fallen out. Chill for 15 minutes.

Meanwhile, preheat the oven to 200°C/400°F/gas 6. Bake the pastries
for about 15 minutes or until golden brown. Transfer to a wire rack and
leave to cool completely.

Home-made Buttery Croissants

A croissant dough is a luxurious combination of light, soft bread dough and crisp, flaky, butter-rich puff pastry. This is one of those recipes that takes a bit of practice and you need to start the day before serving, but once you've tasted home-made croissants you will be hooked. Having mastered the technique, you can make filled croissants and there are ideas for these at the end of this recipe. So, clear the decks – you'll need plenty of space – and get out the rolling pin.

Makes 20–24

500g strong white
   bread flour (regular,
   not extra-strong for
   breadmaking)
1 x 7g sachet fast-action
   dried yeast OR 15g
   fresh yeast
3 tablespoons caster
   sugar
1 tablespoon sea salt
   flakes, crushed
325ml cool skimmed
   milk
250g unsalted butter in
   a block, chilled
1 free-range egg yolk
   beaten with
   1 tablespoon milk,
   to glaze

2 baking sheets, lined
   with baking paper

Put the flour into a large mixing bowl or the bowl of a large, free-standing electric mixer. If using dried yeast, mix it into the flour and make a well in the centre. Add the sugar and salt to the milk and stir until completely dissolved, then add the milk to the well in the flour. If using fresh yeast, crumble it into half of the cool milk and mix well; add the sugar and salt to the remaining milk and stir until dissolved. Make a well in the flour and add the sugared milk and the yeast liquid.

Beat by hand, or with the dough hook of the mixer at the lowest speed, for about 1 minute or just until the ingredients are thoroughly combined to make a soft, slightly sticky and shaggy-looking dough that comes away from the sides of the bowl. Do not knead or overwork the dough at this point. Cover the bowl with a snap-on lid, or put it into a large plastic bag, and leave in a warm spot for 30 to 45 minutes or until the dough has doubled in size.

Gently punch down the dough, then re-cover and put into the fridge. Leave for at least 6 hours or overnight to firm up.

Next day, take the block of butter out of the fridge, place it between 2 sheets of clingfilm or greaseproof paper and pound it with a rolling pin to flatten it to about half its original thickness. Fold the butter over into a brick shape and pound again. Repeat the process a few times until the butter is pliable but still very cold and quite firm. Finally, shape the butter into a square with sides about 12cm.

Turn out the chilled dough onto a lightly floured worktop. Punch down, then shape the dough into a ball. Cut a deep cross in the top. Using a floured rolling pin, roll out the dough in 4 directions (lifting the dough and making a quarter turn after each rolling), to make a shape like a cross with 4 flaps and a thick rough square of dough in the centre. Place the butter on top of the central square of dough, then fold the flaps of dough over the butter, tucking in the edges and making sure the butter is completely enclosed so it won't ooze out during the rolling and folding processes. (For step-by-step photographs, turn to page 211).

Recipe continues on page 218

Turn the dough square over, then roll out away from you into a rectangle about 30 x 60cm. Brush off any excess flour from the surface of the dough, then fold in 3 like a business letter: fold the bottom third up to cover the centre third, then fold the top third down to cover the other 2 layers and make a neat square. Use the rolling pin to seal the open edges. Set the dough on a plate, cover tightly and chill for 30 minutes. This completes the first 'turn'.

Repeat to give the dough 2 more 'turns', each time – before you roll out – placing the dough on the worktop so the folded sides are to the right and left.

After chilling following the third 'turn', roll out the dough thinly to a rectangle about 40 x 75cm. With a floured sharp knife, trim the edges to neaten. Cut the rectangle in half lengthways into 2 equal strips. Flour the knife and cut each strip into triangles with 20cm sides and a 12cm base. Stack the trimmings, gently re-roll and cut another 1 or 2 triangles (these won't look so good but they'll taste just as nice). Arrange the triangles on the prepared baking sheets, cover with clingfilm and chill for 10 to 15 minutes to firm up the dough.

To shape each croissant, place a triangle in front of you on the floured worktop with the long point nearest you. Gently stretch out the two shorter points. Then, starting from the wide base, roll up the dough triangle towards you: use one hand to roll the dough and the other to gently pull down the long point [1]. Make sure you have the pointed end neatly in the centre of the shaped dough and underneath it, so it will keep its shape in the oven. Arrange the croissants on the lined baking sheets, spacing them well apart, and gently shaping them so the pointed ends curve inwards to make a crescent shape.

Lightly brush the croissants with egg glaze, taking care not to 'glue' the dough to the paper and working from the inside outwards so the layers of dough don't stick together and prevent the dough from rising properly. Leave to rise in a warm but not hot place (you don't want to melt the butter) for about 1 hour or until doubled in size.

Towards the end of the rising time, preheat the oven to 230°C/450°F/gas 8. Brush the croissants very lightly with the egg glaze and bake for 10 minutes, then lower the temperature to 200°C/400°F/gas 6. Bake for a further 5 to 7 minutes or until well risen, crisp and a good dark golden brown, underneath as well as on top. Be sure that the croissants are fully cooked or they will be heavy and soggy. Transfer to a wire rack and leave to cool.

Tip: Croissants are baked in a very hot oven to help the layers puff up before the butter has time to melt. If the oven temperature is too low, or the croissant dough gets too warm before baking, the butter will ooze out and the croissants will be tough rather than tender.

Ham and Cheese Croissants

You can use other thinly sliced ham and mature Cheddar, if you prefer.

1 quantity Croissant dough (see page 217), cut into triangles ready to shape
6 thin slices Parma ham (about 100g in total), quartered
150g Emmenthal cheese, grated
1 free-range egg yolk, beaten with 1 tablespoon milk, to glaze

To make each croissant, fold a piece of ham into a shape to fit just inside the dough triangle, then set on the dough. Using about two-thirds of the cheese in total, put a heaped teaspoon on the ham near to the base of each dough triangle. Roll up and shape the croissants as in the main recipe. Set on the lined baking sheets, glaze and leave to rise. Just before baking, brush with glaze and sprinkle with the reserved grated cheese. Bake as in the main recipe.

Almond Croissants

These are filled with a rich, but not too sweet mixture.

1 quantity Croissant dough (see page 217), cut into triangles ready to shape
1 quantity Almond Filling (see page 234)
1 free-range egg yolk, beaten with 1 tablespoon milk, to glaze
50g flaked almonds
icing sugar, for dusting

To make each croissant, put a heaped teaspoon of almond filling near the centre of the base of the triangle, and slightly flatten it. Roll up, shape, glaze and leave to rise as in the main recipe. Just before baking, lightly brush with egg glaze and scatter the flaked almonds over the croissants. Bake as in the main recipe. Before serving, dust with icing sugar.

Chocolate Croissants

Fill croissants with your favourite dark chocolate, and drizzle over more after baking.

1 quantity Croissant dough (see page 217), cut into triangles ready to shape
100g dark chocolate (70% cocoa solids), broken into 24 squares or roughly chopped
1 free-range egg yolk, beaten with 1 tablespoon milk, to glaze
50g dark chocolate, melted

Divide the squares of chocolate among the triangles, placing the chocolate near the centre of the base of the triangle. Roll up, shape and finish as described in the main recipe. When the baked croissants are cool, spoon the melted chocolate into a piping bag and drizzle over them. Leave to set before serving.

Danish Pastries GOOD FOR *Celebrations*

These crisp yet tender filled pastries are made in much the same way as croissants (a yeast dough rolled and folded to incorporate a fair amount of butter), with the addition of eggs to give a slightly softer and more cake-like texture. Once you've made the dough you can use it to fashion a variety of individual pastry shapes or a large braid, with a choice of fillings.

Makes 20 windmills
or envelopes, or
48 pinwheels or twists,
or 2 braids

500g strong white
  bread flour (regular,
  not extra-strong for
  breadmaking)
1 teaspoon sea salt flakes,
  crushed
¼ teaspoon ground
  cardamom
50g unsalted butter,
  chilled and diced
1 x 7g sachet fast-action
  dried yeast OR 15g
  fresh yeast
2 large free-range eggs,
  at room temperature
200ml lukewarm water
300g unsalted butter in
  a block, cold and firm
  but not hard
beaten egg, to glaze

For the apricot filling
175g soft-dried apricots,
  chopped
100ml fresh orange juice
1 tablespoon caster sugar
  (or to taste)

Mix the flour with the salt and ground cardamom in a large mixing bowl. Using the tips of your fingers, rub the diced butter into the flour until the mixture resembles fine crumbs. If using dried yeast, mix it into the flour, then make a well in the centre; beat the eggs into the lukewarm water and pour into the well in the flour. If using fresh yeast, crumble it into the lukewarm water and mix well, then beat in the eggs. Make a well in the flour and pour in the yeast liquid.

Using your hand, work the ingredients together to make a soft but not sticky dough. If there are dry crumbs in the base of the bowl, or the dough feels hard and dry, work in extra water a tablespoon at a time.

Turn out onto a lightly floured worktop and knead gently for 2 minutes only. Return to the bowl and cover with a damp tea towel, or slip the bowl into a large plastic bag. Leave to rise at room temperature for about 1 hour or until doubled in size.

Punch down the dough, then cover with clingfilm, or return the bowl to the plastic bag, and chill for 2 to 4 hours (no longer) until firmer but not hard.

Place the block of butter between 2 sheets of clingfilm or greaseproof paper and pound it with a rolling pin to flatten it to about half its original thickness. Fold over into a brick shape and pound again.

Repeat the process a few times until the butter is pliable but still very cold and quite firm (the butter should be about the same temperature as the dough when they are combined). Finally, shape the butter into a square with sides about 12cm.

Turn out the chilled dough onto a lightly floured worktop and shape into a ball. Using a sharp knife, cut a deep cross in the top. Using a lightly floured rolling pin, roll out the dough in 4 directions (lifting the dough and making a quarter turn after each rolling), to make a shape that looks like a cross with 4 flaps and a thick rough square of dough in the centre.

For the sweet cheese filling

200g full-fat cream cheese

3 tablespoons caster sugar

1 large free-range egg yolk

1 tablespoon plain flour

finely grated zest of ½ unwaxed lemon

For Almond Filling see page 234

For the sweet icing glaze

175g icing sugar, sifted

1 teaspoon lemon juice

5 tablespoons milk

flaked almonds, to decorate (optional)

For the glacé icing (optional)

100g icing sugar, sifted

2 tablespoons milk

2 baking sheets, lined with baking paper

Put the square of butter on top of the central square of dough. Fold the 4 dough flaps over the butter, tucking in the edges and making sure the butter is completely enclosed so it won't ooze out during the rolling and folding process. (For step-by-step photographs see from page 211.)

Turn the dough square over, then roll out away from you into a rectangle about 45 x 15cm. Brush off any excess flour from the surface of the dough, then fold in 3 like a business letter: fold the bottom third up to cover the centre third, then fold the top third down to cover the other 2 layers to make a neat square. Use the rolling pin to seal the open edges. Set the dough on a plate, cover tightly and chill for 30 minutes. This completes the first 'turn'.

Repeat to give the dough 2 more 'turns', each time – before you roll out – placing the dough on the worktop so the folded sides are to the right and left. Wrap tightly and chill for at least 1 hour and up to 24 hours.

While the dough is chilling, make the filling. To make the apricot filling, put the apricots and orange juice into a small pan. Bring to the boil, then leave to stand for 10 to 15 minutes or until lukewarm. Transfer to a food-processor and process to make a thick purée. Add the sugar. Transfer the mixture to a bowl, cover tightly and chill until needed (it can be kept in the fridge for up to 4 days).

To make a sweet cheese filling, beat the cream cheese with the sugar until creamy, then beat in the egg yolk, followed by the flour and lemon zest. Cover and chill until needed (it can be kept in the fridge for up to 4 days).

Recipe continues on page 224

Tip: The dough and fillings can all be prepared and stored in the fridge overnight. Shaped pastries can also be open-frozen before rising, then kept in the freezer for up to a month; thaw at room temperature and leave to rise before baking.

For windmills

Roll out one-quarter of the dough (keep the remaining dough chilled) to a 10 x 50cm rectangle. With a lightly floured, large, sharp knife cut across into 5 squares. Put a teaspoonful of filling – almond, cheese or apricot – into the centre of each. To shape each pastry use the floured knife to make a 4cm cut from each corner in towards the centre. Brush the edges of the square with egg glaze, then fold alternate corners into the centre and squeeze them firmly together, to make a pastry that resembles a child's plastic windmill. Arrange them, well apart, on a lined baking sheet. Cover lightly with clingfilm and leave to rise at warm room temperature for about 45 minutes or until almost doubled in size. Repeat to make more windmills or other shapes.

For pinwheels

Roll out one-quarter of the dough (keep the remaining dough chilled) to a 16 x 30cm rectangle. Spread over one-quarter of the almond filling, then roll up loosely from one long side like a swiss roll. Using a floured, large, sharp knife cut the roll into 12 even slices. Arrange, well apart, on a lined baking sheet. Gently flatten slightly with the palm of your hand, then leave to rise as above. Repeat with the rest of the dough or make a different shape.

For twists

Roll out one-quarter of the dough (keep the remaining dough chilled) to an 18 x 28cm rectangle. Spread over one-quarter of the apricot filling, then fold in half lengthways to make a thin 9 x 28cm rectangle. Press the open long edges together to seal. Using a lightly floured, large, sharp knife, cut across the folded dough into 12 strips. To shape each pastry, hold the 2 ends of a strip and twist it firmly, slightly stretching the dough. Arrange the twisted strips on the lined baking sheet, spacing them well apart, and leave to rise as above. Repeat with the rest of the dough or make another shape.

For envelopes

Roll out one-quarter of the dough (keep the remaining dough chilled) to a 10 x 50cm rectangle. With a lightly floured, large, sharp knife cut across into 5 squares. Put a teaspoonful of filling – almond, cheese or apricot – into the centre of each square. To shape each pastry, brush the corners of the square with egg glaze, then bring them up over the filling to meet in the centre and pinch them firmly together. Arrange the pastries, spaced well apart, on a lined baking sheet and leave to rise as above. Repeat with the rest of the dough or make a different shape.

For a large braided pastry

Roll out half the dough to a 35cm square (keep the remaining dough chilled). Spread half the almond or apricot filling down the middle third of the dough, leaving an even strip of dough uncovered on either side. Using a floured sharp knife make diagonal cuts, 2cm apart, from the edges of the dough to the filling. Alternating sides from left to right, fold the dough strips over the filling, criss-crossing the strips to cover it. Pinch the ends to seal neatly. Transfer to a lined baking sheet and leave to rise for about 1 hour as above. Repeat with the remaining dough or use to make individual shapes.

To finish

Leave the shaped dough to rise, then chill for about 15 minutes while heating the oven.

Preheat the oven to 200°C/400°F/gas 6. Lightly brush the pastries with the beaten egg glaze, taking care not to 'glue' them to the paper. Bake for 12 to 15 minutes, or 25 to 30 minutes for a braid, until well risen, crisp and golden.

While the pastries bake, make the sweet icing glaze by mixing the icing sugar with the lemon juice and milk until smooth. Transfer the hot pastries to a wire rack and immediately brush with the icing glaze. Decorate with flaked almonds, if using, then leave to cool.

The pastries can be left plain or decorated with a drizzle of glacé icing. For this, mix the icing sugar with the milk to make a smooth, runny icing. Spoon into a small plastic bag, snip off the end and zig-zag the icing over the pastries.

BEST OF THE BAKE-OFF
Raisin, Banana and Chocolate Pastries

Makes 34

For the pastry
650g strong white bread
flour
1 ½ teaspoons salt
1 x 7g sachet fast-action
dried yeast
85g caster sugar
about 425ml lukewarm
water
500g unsalted butter,
cold but not hard

For the pains au raisin
20g plain flour
20g cornflour
60g caster sugar
2 large egg yolks
300ml full-fat milk
finely grated zest of ½
unwaxed orange
3 tablespoons large
raisins

**For the banana and
raisin pastries**
40g soft light brown
sugar
40g unsalted butter
2 firm medium bananas
1 tablespoon raisins
good pinch of ground
cinnamon

For the chocolate twists
24 chocolate cigarellos

To make the pastry, sift the flour and salt into a mixing bowl, or the bowl of a large, freestanding electric mixer fitted with the dough hook, and stir in the yeast and sugar. Work in enough water to make a soft but not sticky dough. Turn onto a floured worktop and knead by hand for about 5 minutes (or in the mixer using the dough hook) or until pliable. Return to the bowl, cover and leave to rise for about 1 hour or until doubled in size.

Punch down to deflate, then cover tightly and chill for 1 hour.

Turn out onto a floured worktop and roll out into a rectangle about 20 x 60cm. Place the butter between 2 sheets of clingfilm. With the rolling pin, flatten to a rectangle about 20 x 40cm. Lay the butter on the dough rectangle to cover two-thirds of it. Fold the remaining third over, then fold over again so the butter is sandwiched between layers of dough. Press the open edges to seal. Cover and chill for 30 minutes.

Place on the worktop with the folded edges to the side. Roll out, fold into 3 and seal the edges as before, then cover and chill for 15 minutes. Repeat 2 more times.

For the Pains au Raisin
Mix the flour, cornflour, sugar, egg yolks and one-third of the milk to a smooth paste in a heatproof bowl. Heat the rest of the milk in a pan and stir into the yolk mixture, then return to the pan and stir rapidly until the mixture boils and thickens. Cook for 1 minute, stirring, then remove from the heat. Add the orange zest. Press a sheet of clingfilm onto the surface of the crème pâtissière and leave to cool.

Roll out one-third of the dough to a rectangle about 26 x 30cm. Spread a thick layer of crème pâtissière over the dough (you won't need it all), then sprinkle on the raisins. Roll up from a long end and cut across into 12. Place cut side up on a baking sheet and press lightly with a floured hand to flatten. Cover with oiled clingflim and leave in a warm place to rise for 20 minutes

For the Banana and Raisin Pastries
Heat the sugar and butter in a non-stick frying pan until melted, then bubble for a couple of minutes to make a thick, sticky caramel. Remove from the heat. Slice each banana into 10 and stir into the caramel with

To bake and finish
beaten egg, to glaze
icing sugar OR Sweet
  Icing Glaze OR Glacé
  Icing (see page 223)

2 or more baking sheets,
  lined with baking paper

the raisins and cinnamon. Leave to cool. Roll out one-third of the dough to a rectangle about 20 x 50cm and cut into 10 squares with 10cm sides. Shape into envelopes (see page 225), filling with the banana caramel mixture. Leave to rise as for Pains au Raisin above.

For the Chocolate Twists

Roll out one-third of the dough to a rectangle about 36 x 24cm and cut into 12 strips, each 2cm wide. To fill and shape each twist, place the top of 2 chocolate cigarellos on one end of a dough strip and twist the dough around to the end of the cigarellos. Leave to rise as for Pains au Raisin above.

To bake and finish

Towards the end of the rising time, preheat the oven to 200°C/400°F/gas 6. Lightly brush the pastries with egg glaze, then bake for 20 to 25 minutes or until golden brown and crisp. Cool on wire racks. Dust with icing sugar, brush with sweet icing glaze or add glacé icing to finish.

MARY ANNE

Choux Pastry

It's rather amazing that a lump of thick, sticky paste made in a saucepan can be transformed in the heat of the oven to a crisp and light ball of air – choux is, in fact, a double-cooked pastry. When cooled, the crisp, hollow containers – in the shape of éclairs, profiteroles and choux or cream puffs – can be filled with pastry cream, Chantilly cream or ice cream.

Makes about 12 éclairs, or 48 profiteroles

100g plain flour
¼ teaspoon salt
75g unsalted butter, diced
3 free-range eggs, at room temperature, beaten

Sift the flour onto a sheet of greaseproof paper. Put the salt, butter and 175ml water into a medium-sized pan and heat gently until the butter has completely melted – don't let the water boil and begin to evaporate. Quickly bring the mixture just to the boil, then tip in the flour all in one go.

Remove the pan from the heat and beat furiously with a wooden spoon. The mixture will look a mess at first, but don't worry – as you beat it will turn into smooth, heavy dough. Put the pan back on low heat and beat for about 2 minutes to slightly cook the dough until it comes away from the sides of the pan in a smooth, glossy ball [1].

Tip the dough into a large mixing bowl and leave to cool until barely warm. Using an electric mixer (a wooden spoon won't give the same result) gradually beat the eggs into the dough, beating well after each addition.

Add enough egg to make a very shiny and paste-like dough that just falls from a spoon when lightly shaken [2]. You may not need the last tablespoon or so of egg because the dough must be stiff enough to pipe or spoon into shapes; if the dough is too wet it will spread out rather than puff up in the oven.

The dough is now ready to shape. Use immediately or cover tightly and keep at cool room temperature. Use within 4 hours.

Éclairs

For these popular pastries, the choux dough is piped into long fingers. Once baked, try filling them with the darkly rich, coffee pastry cream here, then topping with melted chocolate for a cappuccino flavour. Or use a thick glacé icing (see page 223) made with strong coffee rather than water. You can also fill the éclairs with sweetened whipped cream (see Chantilly cream, page 234), but eat these within an hour of assembling as the pastry will not stay crisp as long as it will if filled with pastry cream.

Makes about 12

1 quantity Choux Pastry dough (see page 229)

For the coffee pastry cream
2 large free-range egg yolks, at room temperature
5 tablespoons caster sugar
1½ tablespoons cornflour
3 tablespoons double cream
4 teaspoons instant coffee dissolved in 200ml hot water OR 200ml espresso
50g unsalted butter, at room temperature, diced

For the topping
100g dark chocolate (70% cocoa solids), broken up
2 tablespoons double cream

1 piping bag fitted with a 1.5cm plain tube; a baking sheet, lined with baking paper

Preheat the oven to 200°C/400°F/gas 6. Spoon the choux dough into the piping bag and pipe into 10cm lengths on the lined baking sheet, spacing them well apart to allow for rising and spreading.

Bake for 15 minutes, without opening the oven door, then reduce the oven temperature to 180°C/350°F/gas 4. Quickly open and close the oven door (to let out the steam), then bake for a further 15 to 20 minutes or until the choux fingers are well puffed, golden brown and crisp.

Remove from the oven and make a small hole in one end of each finger to allow the steam to escape. Return them to the oven to bake for a final 5 minutes, to ensure there's no soggy uncooked dough inside, which would cause the pastry to collapse as it cools: the pastry will look cooked long before the insides are fully dried out. Cool on a wire rack.

Meanwhile, make the filling. Using a wooden spoon, beat the yolks with the sugar, cornflour and cream in a heatproof bowl until very smooth. Stand the bowl on a damp cloth so it won't wobble, then pour in the hot coffee, in a thin steady stream, stirring constantly. Tip the mixture into a medium-sized pan and set over medium heat.

Bring to the boil, stirring constantly until very smooth and thick. Remove from the heat and stir in the butter. Transfer the mixture to a bowl and press a sheet of clingfilm or dampened greaseproof paper onto the surface to prevent a skin from forming. Leave to cool, then chill for about 1 hour or until firm. (The mixture can be kept, tightly covered, for up to 24 hours in the fridge.)

When ready to assemble, split open the pastry fingers lengthways and spoon in the filling. To make the topping, put the chocolate and cream into a heatproof bowl and set over a pan of steaming hot but not boiling water (don't let the base of the bowl touch the hot water). Melt very gently, then remove the bowl from the pan and stir until smooth. Spread on top of the filled éclairs with a round-bladed knife. Leave to set in a cool place, then eat the same day.

Profiteroles

It's wonderful to watch small blobs of choux dough turn into ping-pong balls of light pastry in the oven. These may no longer be as fashionable as they once were, but they are still a great treat, filled with sweetened whipped cream (or small balls of vanilla ice cream) and served with a jug of hot, glossy, dark chocolate sauce.

Makes about 48

1 quantity Choux Pastry
   dough (see page 229)
1 egg, beaten with a
   pinch of salt, to glaze
1 quantity Chantilly
   Cream (page 234)

For the chocolate sauce
100g dark chocolate
   (70% cocoa solids),
   broken up
25g unsalted butter
2 tablespoons icing sugar

1 piping bag fitted with
   a 1.5cm plain tube;
   2 baking sheets, lined
   with baking paper

Preheat the oven to 200°C/400°F/gas 6. Spoon the choux dough into the piping bag and pipe mounds about 3cm wide and 2cm high on the prepared baking sheets, spacing them well apart to allow for rising and spreading.

Lightly brush with the egg glaze, taking care it doesn't drip down and glue the pastry to the paper. Bake for 15 minutes, then reduce the oven temperature to 180°C/350°F/gas 4. Quickly open and close the oven door (to get rid of the steam), then bake for a further 5 minutes or until crisp and golden.

Remove the baking sheets from the oven and make a small hole at one side of each profiterole to let out the steam. Return the sheets to the oven and bake the profiteroles for a final 3 to 4 minutes or until firm. Cool on a wire rack.

To make the chocolate sauce put all the ingredients with 100ml water into a small pan (preferably non-stick) and heat gently, stirring frequently, until melted and smooth. Keep the sauce warm until needed.

Just before serving fill the profiteroles with chilled Chantilly cream – either by piping it through the steam hole, or by splitting each profiterole horizontally and using a teaspoon. Pile them in a serving dish or individual bowls and drizzle over the hot sauce.

Mary's tip

It is essential to dry out the cooked choux buns in the oven to be sure they are firm and crisp. Set aside until stone cold, as they will go soggy if filled with the cream while still warm.

Almond Filling

This is an easy-to-make rich almond mixture for almond croissants and Danish pastries. It can be kept, in an airtight container, in the fridge for up to 5 days. Remove from the fridge about an hour before use.

Makes 350g

100g unsalted butter, softened
100g caster sugar
finely grated zest of ½ unwaxed lemon
1 large free-range egg plus 1 yolk, at room temperature
100g ground almonds
1 tablespoon plain flour

Beat the butter with a wooden spoon or electric mixer until creamy. Add the sugar and lemon zest and beat in until the mixture looks light and fluffy. Beat the egg with the yolk to mix, then gradually beat into the butter mixture. Gently fold in the ground almonds and flour using a large metal spoon.

Chantilly Cream

Makes about 350g

250ml whipping cream, well chilled
2 tablespoons icing sugar, sifted
1 teaspoon vanilla extract

For the best results, chill your mixing bowl and whisk beforehand. Whip the cream with the sugar and vanilla until just stiff enough to hold a peak. Use immediately or cover and chill for up to an hour.

Pastry Cream

Thick, rich, velvety-smooth pastry cream, which is a thickened egg custard sauce, is used in many desserts and pastries, from fruit tarts to cream horns, millefeuilles, éclairs and profiteroles. Cornflour prevents the mixture from separating and gives it a fine glossy finish. Whipped cream provides lightness. Vanilla or grated lemon or orange zest, or a dash of kirsch or orange liqueur, add a real edge to pastry cream and stop it tasting bland.

Makes about 500ml

250ml milk
1 vanilla pod, split open,
   OR finely grated zest
   of 1 medium unwaxed
   orange or lemon OR
   1 teaspoon liqueur (or
   to taste)
3 large free-range
   egg yolks, at room
   temperature
50g caster sugar
1½ tablespoons cornflour
150ml double or
   whipping cream,
   well chilled

Heat the milk with the split vanilla pod, or the zest, in a medium pan. Remove from the heat and leave to infuse for 10 minutes. If using a vanilla pod, remove it and use the tip of a knife to scrape a few seeds out of the pod back into the milk (the pod can be rinsed, dried and used again or used to make vanilla sugar).

In a heatproof bowl, whisk the egg yolks with the sugar and cornflour for 1 to 2 minutes or until smooth, thick and light. Whisk in the hot milk. When thoroughly combined, tip the mixture back into the pan and set over medium heat.

Whisk constantly until the mixture boils and thickens to make a smooth custard, taking care it doesn't scorch on the base of the pan. Pour into a bowl and press a piece of clingfilm or dampened greaseproof paper onto the surface, to prevent a skin from forming. Cool, then chill thoroughly.

Whip the cream until it holds a soft peak. Stir the pastry cream until smooth and add the liqueur, if using. Fold in the whipped cream. Use immediately or cover tightly and keep in the fridge for up to 4 hours.

ROBERT

SIMON

BEST OF THE BAKE-OFF
Limoncello and White Chocolate Croquembouche

Serves 20–30

2 recipe quantities
(about 96) Profiteroles
(see page 233)
300g caster sugar, for
the caramel
caster sugar, for the
spun sugar decoration
(optional)

For the filling
4 large egg yolks
75g caster sugar
25g plain flour
finely grated zest of
1 unwaxed lemon
250ml full-fat milk
150g white chocolate,
broken up
1 tablespoon limoncello
(or orange liqueur)
250ml double cream,
whipped
Sugar flowers to
decorate (optional)

1 piping bag fitted with
a 0.5cm plain tube; a
sugar thermometer;
a cake board or large
flat serving platter; a
croquembouche cone,
oiled (optional)

To make the filling, whisk the egg yolks in a bowl with the sugar, flour, lemon zest and one-third of the milk until smooth. Heat the rest of the milk in a medium pan until almost boiling, then pour onto the yolk mixture, stirring constantly. Return to the pan and cook, whisking constantly, until the mixture boils and thickens. Simmer for 1 minute, whisking, to cook out the flour taste. Cool until lukewarm.

Meanwhile, gently melt the chocolate in a heatproof bowl set over a pan of steaming hot but not boiling water (don't let the base of the bowl touch the hot water). Cool until lukewarm, then whisk the chocolate into the custard, followed by the limoncello. Cover and chill for at least an hour before folding in the whipped cream.

When ready to assemble the croquembouche, spoon the filling into the piping bag. Pipe into the cooled profiteroles, through the steam hole, taking care not to overfill them (to avoid leaks).

To make the caramel, dissolve the sugar in 4 tablespoons water in a medium pan, stirring occasionally (don't boil until the sugar has completely dissolved). Bring to the boil and boil rapidly to a light caramel (160°C/320°F on a sugar thermometer). Immediately plunge the base of the pan into cold water for 20 seconds to halt the cooking.

Place the cake board on the worktop. Working quickly, dip one side of each profiterole in the hot caramel (take care not to burn your fingers) and stick them together to form a pyramid with a 25cm circular base on the board. Alternatively, build them up into a neat pyramid inside the croquembouche cone. If the caramel 'glue' starts to set, gently warm it, without boiling, until it melts and softens again. Leave the croquembouche to set in a cool spot. Serve as soon as possible.

An optional decoration is spun sugar (this is quite messy and can burn you, so take care). Make another batch of caramel as above and, after dipping in the cold water for 20 seconds, leave to cool for 5 minutes. Hold a couple of forks in one hand: dip the tines in the caramel, lift them out and flick strands of caramel over the assembled croquembouche. Repeat until the spun sugar surrounds the pyramid. Stop as soon as the caramel starts to set and the strands become thick. Decorate the croquembouche with sugar flowers, if you like.

THE GREAT BRITISH
BAKE OFF

TECHNICAL CHALLENGE
PAUL'S ICED FINGERS

It's becoming increasingly difficult to find these old favourites in bakers' shops today. Don't let the recipe disappear – make them at home. Once iced and filled with cream and jam, eat as soon as possible the same day.

Makes 12

For the dough
500g strong white bread
   flour
2 x 7g packets fast-
   action dried yeast
50g caster sugar
40g unsalted butter,
   softened
2 large free-range eggs
10g sea salt flakes,
   crushed
150ml lukewarm milk
140ml water

For the icing and filling
300g icing sugar
32ml water
200ml whipping cream
1 x 400g jar strawberry
   jam, warmed and
   sieved, then cooled

2 baking sheets, lined
   with baking paper;
   a piping bag; a small
   plastic bag

✳ Use a large mixing bowl because all the ingredients for the dough are added at the same time and mixed by hand.

✳ Before the dough is kneaded it is massaged in the bowl. To do this, use your hand to gently work the dough up and down so it becomes smooth.

✳ When dividing the dough into pieces, you can weigh them to be sure they are all about the same. This is what professional bakers do. Each piece should weigh about 70g. Use a ruler to ensure all the fingers are the same length.

✳ If necessary, rotate the baking sheets towards the end of the baking time so all the fingers are evenly coloured.

✳ Be sure the icing has set before adding the cream and jam, and handle the fingers gently. Otherwise the smooth finish could be spoiled.

1 Put all the ingredients for the dough into a large mixing bowl with 100ml water. Mix together with your hands until a dough is formed. Slowly work in 40ml more water and massage the dough in the bowl for about 4 minutes.

2 Tip the dough onto a lightly floured worktop and knead well for 10 minutes or until the dough is smooth and elastic. Return to the bowl and cover with a damp tea towel or clingfilm. Leave to rise for 1 hour or until at least doubled in size.

3 Tip the dough out onto the very lightly floured worktop again and divide into 12 pieces. Roll into balls and then into 'fingers' about 12.5cm long.

4 Divide the fingers between the baking sheets, leaving plenty of space around and between them to allow for spreading. Leave to rise, uncovered, for about 40 minutes or until doubled in size. Towards the end of the rising time, preheat the oven to 220°C/425°F/gas 7. Bake the fingers for about 10 minutes. Separate the fingers and leave to cool on a wire rack.

5 For the icing, sift the icing sugar into a bowl. Gradually stir in 32ml cold water to make a thick paste. When the fingers have completely cooled, split them open lengthways, not cutting all the way through. Dip one side of each finger into the icing and smooth it with your finger. Leave to set on a wire rack.

6 Lightly whip the cream until thick and place in the piping bag. Pipe a generous line of whipped cream into each finger. Spoon the strawberry jam into a small plastic bag and snip off one corner. Pipe a delicate line of jam onto the cream in each finger. Dust with icing sugar, if you like.

BEST OF THE BAKE-OFF
Chocolate Orange Mousse Cake

Serves 12

For the paste
100g unsalted butter,
    softened
100g icing sugar, sifted
3 large egg whites, at
    room temperature
110g plain flour
orange food colouring

For the sponge
See Chocolate Raspberry
Opera Cake (page 312)

For the mousse
175g plain chocolate (70%
    cocoa solids), broken up
grated zest and juice of
    1 unwaxed orange
1 teaspoon powdered
    gelatine
2 large eggs, at room
    temperature, separated
300ml double cream,
    at room temperature,
    whipped

To decorate
1 teaspoon arrowroot
100ml strained orange
    juice
300ml double cream,
    chilled and whipped
orange peel curls

Using a large electric mixer, cream the butter with the sugar until light and fluffy. Gradually whisk in the egg whites and continue whisking for 2 minutes. Sift the flour into the bowl and fold in. Using the tip of a knife, add a little food colouring to tint the paste a light orange.

Fit the piping bag with the 0.5cm tube and fill with the paste. Draw/pipe in a swirly pattern onto each of the lined baking trays. Cover and place in the freezer to chill. Wash the mixer bowl and beaters.

Preheat the oven to 200°C/400°F/gas 6. Make the sponge mixture, bake the sponge sheets and cool following the instructions on page 312. (Make sure you divide the sponge mixture evenly between the trays, spreading it smoothly over the frozen paste and into the corners where it might get too thin.)

Measure the height of the side of the springclip tin. Cut a strip of sponge as wide as this measure from a short end of each of the sheets. Placing the patterned side against the tin, use the 2 sponge strips to line the side. When adding the second strip, trim it to be 2cm too long, then ease the ends of the sponge together to make a tight fit against the side of the tin (this will help keep the mousse inside the cake until it sets).

Cut a circle from one of the sponge sheets to fit the base of the tin. Place it, patterned side down, on the base – this will be the top of the finished cake. Reserve the remainder of the other sponge sheet.

To make the mousse, melt the chocolate in a large heatproof bowl set over a pan of steaming hot but not boiling water (don't let the base of the bowl touch the water). Leave to cool to room temperature.

Strain the orange juice through a fine mesh sieve into a small heatproof bowl. Sprinkle the gelatine over the juice and leave to 'sponge' for about 3 minutes, then warm over a pan of boiling water until the gelatine has completely dissolved. Cool to room temperature.

Mix the orange zest and egg yolks into the melted chocolate, then gradually stir in the gelatine followed by the whipped cream. (Everything needs to be at the same temperature.) Whisk the egg whites to stiff peaks and fold into chocolate mixture.

2 baking trays with rims, each about 31.5 x 25.5cm, greased and lined with baking paper; a piping bag with a 0.5cm plain tube and a star tube; 1 x 20.5cm springclip tin, oiled and lined with baking paper

Pour the mousse into the cake-lined tin. Cut a circle of sponge from the second sheet to fit over the mousse and place it on top, patterned side up. Trim the sponge sides if needed so the top is completely flat. Chill until the mousse is set.

To make the glaze, mix the arrowroot with a little orange juice, then stir into the rest of the juice in a small pan. Heat without boiling until the glaze thickens and clears. Cool.

Invert the mousse cake onto a serving plate, then remove the tin and lining paper. Brush very lightly with the orange glaze. Chill to set. To finish, use the star tube to pipe swirls of whipped cream around the outer top edge of the cake and decorate with curls of orange peel.

PUDDINGS AND DESSERTS

PAVLOVA WITH MANGO AND PASSIONFRUIT

- LEMON ICE CREAM MERINGUE PIE
- Chocolate Mousse
- CHOCOLATE ROULADE
- CHEESECAKE
- CHOCOLATE FUDGE HOT POT
- BREAD AND BUTTER PUDDING
- Peach and Ginger Cobbler
- LEMON CURD SOUFFLE
- CHOCOLATE CHEESE CAKE
- MERINGUES

What's for Afters?

Our favourite puddings evoke feelings of sheer joy – it's the most anticipated part of the meal. Food fashions may come and go, but our best-loved sweet recipes endure.

Whole eggs and egg whites are the basis for countless pudding recipes. Whisking is the key to success for fat-less sponges, roulades, cake mixtures, meringues, soufflés and mousses – all recipes relying on whole eggs or whites beaten to a voluminous, fine foam, to give a light-as-air result. Mary's Chocolate Roulade (see page 265), another of *The Great British Bake Off* technical challenges, and the Meringues step-by-step recipe (see page 250) both depend on perfect whisking.

The basic equipment for whisking egg whites and whole eggs, and for whipping cream, is an electric mixer – hand-held or a large free-standing model – or a rotary or balloon whisk, plus a couple of large bowls and a large metal spoon. Stainless steel or toughened glass or china bowls are the best choice. Plastic bowls are difficult to get them 100 per cent grease-free, but if you do want to use a plastic bowl it's a good idea to wipe it out with a slice of lemon first. Standing the bowl on a damp tea towel will stop the bowl from wobbling as you whisk.

Whisking egg whites for meringues or for adding to a mousse or cake mixture isn't hard work these days but there are a few tips for ensuring you achieve maximum volume. For the best results don't use newly laid eggs and make sure the whites are at room temperature. Put them into a dry, spotlessly clean, grease-free bowl – any spot of fat or yolk will mean less volume – and whisk on low speed for about 30 seconds so they become frothy and the structure starts to develop. Adding a pinch of cream of tartar or a drop of lemon juice or vinegar (all acidic) at this point will help the structure stiffen. Then increase the speed and continue whisking until the mixture is a mass of tiny bubbles, with a very smooth, fine texture.

Soft peak is the stage when you lift the whisk and the peak of egg whites on it slightly droops down. The next stage is **stiff peak**, when the peak stands upright and you can turn the bowl upside down without the whites falling out. This is a key stage in Mary's Chocolate Roulade method. Care must be taken not to overwhisk as the fine texture will start to look grainy, then curdled and then risks collapsing all together!

Not all meringues are the same: there are three types. **Simple meringue** is the one most often used in home baking. The egg whites are whisked to soft peak stage, half the sugar is whisked in, to reach the stiff peak stage, and then the rest of the sugar is folded in. The resulting glossy, firm meringue – suitable for shaped or piped meringues, pie toppings and pavlova as well as soufflés or mousse – must be used straight away. **Italian meringue** produces more volume and can be kept for several hours. It's made by whisking the egg whites to the soft peak stage and then slowly whisking in a hot sugar syrup; the heat slightly cooks and stabilizes the whites. This meringue is often used for more elaborately piped desserts, as well as iced soufflés, because it keeps its shape well. **Cooked meringue** – often called chef's meringue because it's very firm but still flexible and ideal for hot soufflés – is made by whisking the egg whites and sugar in a bowl over hot water to give a huge mass of meringue.

For whisked sponges, eggs must be beaten 'to the ribbon'. To achieve this, the eggs must be whisked thoroughly with sugar to build up a thick mass of tiny bubbles that form the structure of the cake. After 4 or 5 minutes of whisking on high speed, the initial volume of eggs and sugar will increase five-fold and become so thick that when the whisk is lifted out of the bowl the mixture on it falls back in a thick, ribbon-like trail. Skimping at this stage will risk a dense, heavy sponge because it's the bubbles that make the mixture puff up during baking. Invest in a good whisk and it should repay you with many years of sublime puddings and desserts.

When whipping cream it's best to chill the bowl and whisk as well as the cream before you start, to help prevent the butterfat from separating and the mixture from curdling. Whip the cream to soft peak stage if you are going to fold it into another mixture, and to a slightly firmer peak for piping. If you are not going to use it straight away, then cover and chill; it may need a little more whipping before use if it has softened in the fridge.

Folding in is an important technique for puddings. Sugar is folded into whisked egg whites; meringue or whipped cream are folded into another mixture to raise and lighten it; flour is folded into a whisked egg mixture or a creamed butter-sugar-egg mixture. In all cases, it's important to retain the volume so the airy mixture isn't deflated.

A large metal spoon is the best choice for folding. It's also much easier if both mixtures are the same consistency to begin with, which is why a quarter or so of the whisked or whipped mixture is added to the other, heavier one and stirred in to soften and loosen. Then the rest of the lighter mixture is gently folded through. To do this, use a downwards cutting motion with the metal spoon, to get right down to the base of the bowl, then lift the spoon up and flip it over so the mixture from underneath is folded on top. Give the bowl a quarter turn and repeat until there are no visible streaks – remember that overmixing is as bad as undermixing.

Many of our favourite desserts and puddings are made with chocolate and it's worth using a good-quality bar. Dark chocolate with around 70 per cent cocoa solids gives the best flavour. When melting chocolate it's a good idea to take the pan – with the bowl still over it – off the heat before the chocolate has completely melted (this is particularly important with white chocolate, which melts at a lower temperature than dark chocolate). Doing this helps prevent the chocolate from seizing (which means it forms a thick, claggy mass rather than a smooth liquid). If chocolate seizes it can't be used.

HOW TO MAKE PERFECT
MERINGUES

The type of meringue used here is often called a 'simple meringue'. There are two other types – Italian and cooked. All meringue is made from stiffly whisked egg whites and sugar, the differences between the three types being the way the whites and sugar are combined (see page 248).

Makes 12

3 large free-range
  egg whites, at room
  temperature
2 good pinches of cream
  of tartar
175g caster sugar

1 baking sheet lined with
  non-stick baking paper
  or a re-usable silicone
  sheet

* For successful meringue, the egg whites must be at room temperature: if they are too cold you won't be able to incorporate the maximum amount of air to increase their volume. When you separate the yolks from the whites, take special care because any trace of yolk will prevent the whites from being beaten to their full volume.

* The sugar for meringues is normally caster because coarser sugars, such as granulated, will make the texture gritty. Some of the caster can be replaced with light brown muscovado sugar, to add a toffee flavour and slightly chewy texture.

* Under-whisked and over-whisked meringue mixtures have a tendency to collapse and may weep beads of sugar syrup during baking. To be sure your meringue isn't under-whisked, at the stiff peak stage you should be able to turn the bowl upside down without the meringue falling out. If over-whisked the meringue will start to look grainy and then curdled.

* Meringues are notoriously difficult to shift if they become stuck during baking, which is why it is a good idea to line the baking sheets with non-stick baking paper or a silicone sheet.

* Once the meringue is made it should be shaped and baked as soon as possible or it will lose volume. Baking is long and slow to dry out the meringues rather than cook them, so they stay white or a pale creamy colour (depending on the sugar you use) and become crisp all the way through.

1 Preheat the oven to 120°C/250°F/gas ½. Put the egg whites into a large bowl that's spotlessly clean and grease-free. Whisk with an electric mixer for 20 to 30 seconds or until the whites are foamy. Add the cream of tartar and continue whisking until the mixture forms a soft peak when the whisk is lifted out.

2 Whisk in half of the sugar, a tablespoon at a time, and continue whisking for about 1 minute or until the mixture is glossy and forms a stiff peak when the whisk is lifted out.

3 Sprinkle the rest of the sugar over the mixture and fold in lightly using a large metal spoon, taking care that the sugar is fully incorporated but not over-mixed.

4 Using a soup spoon, scoop up a heaped spoonful of the mixture. With a second spoon, gently push the mixture off onto the lined baking sheet.

5 Repeat to make 12 craggy meringues, spacing them slightly apart to allow for spreading. Bake for about 2 hours or until firm. Remove the sheet from the oven and leave to cool completely before peeling the meringues away from the lining paper. If not using immediately, store in an airtight container for up to 5 days.

Tip: For an easy dessert, dust the meringues with cocoa powder before baking, and when cold sandwich pairs with Chantilly Cream (see page 234).

Pavlova with Mango and Passionfruit

This glamorous dessert was named for Anna Pavlova, the legendary Russian ballerina, when she toured Australia and New Zealand in 1926. The base is meringue, designed to look like a ballet tutu, crisp and light on the outside but soft and marshmallow-like in the centre. The pavlova should be eaten as soon as it is assembled.

Serves 8

For the meringue
3 large free-range
  egg whites, at room
  temperature
½ teaspoon cream of
  tartar
pinch of salt
175g caster sugar
½ teaspoon vanilla extract
1½ teaspoons cornflour

For the topping
300ml double cream,
  well chilled
1 or 2 mangoes
  (about 550g)
3 passionfruit
1 lime

1 baking sheet, lined with
  baking paper or a re-
  usable silicone sheet

Preheat the oven to 140°C/275°F/gas 1. Put the egg whites into a large bowl and whisk with an electric mixer on medium speed for about 20 seconds or until frothy. Add the cream of tartar and salt and whisk on full speed until the whites stand in soft peaks when the whisk is lifted out.

Whisk in half the sugar, a tablespoon at a time, plus the vanilla and continue whisking just until the whites stand in firm peaks. Scrape down the sides of the bowl, then sift the rest of the sugar and the cornflour onto the whites. Using a large metal spoon, gently but thoroughly fold in.

Spoon the mixture onto the prepared baking sheet and gently spread to a round about 23cm in diameter and 3cm high. Using the back of the spoon make a shallow dip in the centre, and swirl the outer edges attractively but not too neatly.

Bake for about 1¼ hours or until very crisp on the outside – the very centre should still be soft. If the meringue starts to colour, turn down the oven a little for the rest of the cooking time.

Turn off the oven and leave the pavlova inside, with the door closed, to cool. Remove from the cold oven, peel the pavlova off the lining paper and set it on a large serving plate (or store in an airtight container in a dry spot overnight).

Whip the cream in a chilled bowl until thick enough to form soft peaks; cover and chill. Peel the mango and cut the flesh away from the stone. Cut into 2cm cubes and put into a bowl. Halve the passionfruit and scoop the pulpy seeds into the bowl with the mango.

Finely grate the zest from the lime, then cut it in half and squeeze the juice from one half. Add ½ teaspoon of juice and half of the zest to the fruit mixture and stir well. Taste and add a little more juice if needed to bring out the flavours of the fruits. Save the remaining zest for decoration.

When ready to serve, give the cream a final whip, then pile it onto the pavlova, leaving the edge visible. Stir the fruit mixture, then spoon on top of the cream. Decorate with the reserved zest and serve, swiftly.

Warm Chocolate Mousse Cake

The light, mousse-like texture of this dessert cake comes from whipped cream and whisked egg whites; its richness is provided by mascarpone. (Check the recipe before you begin – you will need several mixing bowls to prepare all the elements of the filling.)

Serves 10

For the base
200g digestive biscuits (about 12)
2 tablespoons cocoa powder
75g unsalted butter, melted

For the filling
50g dark chocolate (70% cocoa solids), broken up
4 tablespoons cocoa powder
50g ground almonds
2 large free-range eggs, at room temperature, separated
75g caster sugar, plus 1 tablespoon for the meringue
150ml whipping cream
250g mascarpone cheese
icing sugar, for dusting

1 x 23cm springclip tin, greased

Preheat the oven to 170°C/325°F/gas 3. Crush the biscuits to a fine powder in a food-processor, or put them into a plastic bag and bash with a rolling pin. Tip the crumbs into a mixing bowl and stir in the cocoa powder, then mix in the melted butter until thoroughly combined.

Transfer the mixture to the prepared tin and press evenly over the base and halfway up the sides with the back of a spoon. Chill while making the filling.

Put the chocolate into the bowl of a food-processor and grind to pea-sized lumps. Add the cocoa and almonds and run the machine just until the mixture looks like coarse sand – don't overwork the mixture or it will start to become sticky. Set aside until needed.

Put the egg yolks into a large mixing bowl with the 75g sugar and whisk with an electric mixer until very thick and mousse-like; the whisk should leave a ribbon-like trail when lifted out.

Whip the cream until it stands in soft peaks. Stir the mascarpone in its tub until smooth, then stir into the cream. Using a large metal spoon, gently fold the cream into the yolk mixture followed by the chocolate mixture.

Whisk the egg whites until they stand in soft peaks, then add the remaining tablespoon of sugar and whisk briefly until the whites stand in stiff peaks. Fold into the chocolate mixture in 3 batches.

Spoon into the biscuit case and spread evenly. Bake for about 1 hour or until just firm. Remove from the oven and leave to cool for about 10 minutes, then carefully run a round-bladed knife around the inside of the tin to loosen the crust.

Leave to cool for another 10 minutes, then unclip the tin. Set the cake on a serving platter, dust with icing sugar and serve, with vanilla ice cream.

URVASHI

YASMIN

Double Chocolate Chip Cheesecake

A simple-to-make cheesecake that's not too rich or sweet, this contains chips of both dark and white chocolate and is finished with more white chocolate. Once it is baked and cooled, it is refrigerated overnight before finishing for serving.

Serves 10

For the base
250g digestive biscuits (about 16)
50g unsalted butter, melted

For the filling
100g dark chocolate (70% cocoa solids)
50g good-quality white chocolate
500g full-fat cream cheese
100g caster sugar
1 teaspoon vanilla extract
3 large free-range eggs, beaten
250ml soured cream

To finish
50g good-quality white chocolate, grated

1 x 23cm springclip tin, greased; a baking sheet

Preheat the oven to 150°C/300°F/gas 2. Crush the biscuits to a fine powder in a food-processor, or put them into a plastic bag and bash with a rolling pin. Tip into a mixing bowl and stir in the melted butter until thoroughly combined.

Transfer the mixture to the prepared tin and press it evenly over the base and halfway up the sides using the back of a spoon. Chill while making the filling.

Chop the dark and white chocolates fairly finely and put on one side until needed. Put the cream cheese, sugar and vanilla into a large mixing bowl and beat with a wooden spoon until smooth.

Beat in the eggs. When thoroughly combined, stir in the soured cream followed by the chopped chocolate. Transfer the mixture to the prepared biscuit base and spread evenly.

Set the tin on the baking sheet and bake for 1 hour or until just set. Turn off the oven and leave the cheesecake to cool down in the oven with the door closed (this helps to prevent the surface from cracking). Then remove from the oven and run a round-bladed knife around the inside of the tin to loosen the cheesecake crust. Cover and chill overnight.

When ready to serve, unclip the tin and set the cheesecake on a serving platter. Scatter the grated white chocolate over the top of the cheesecake just before serving.

BEST OF THE BAKE-OFF
Rum and Raisin Baked Cheesecake

Serves 6–8

10 digestive biscuits
50g unsalted butter,
   melted
600g full-fat cream
   cheese
2 tablespoons plain flour
175g caster sugar
½ teaspoon vanilla
   extract
2 large eggs plus 1 egg
   yolk
285ml soured cream
40g large raisins,
   soaked overnight in
   2 tablespoons white
   rum or orange juice,
   then drained

1 x 20.5cm springclip
   tin, greased; a baking
   sheet

Preheat the oven to 160°C/325°F/gas 3. Crush the biscuits in a food-processor, then mix with the butter. Press onto the base and halfway up the sides of the prepared tin. Bake for 5 minutes, then cool.

Using an electric mixer on low speed, beat the cream cheese with the flour, sugar, vanilla, eggs, egg yolk and half the soured cream until thoroughly combined. Don't let the mixture become frothy as this will spoil the creamy, even texture of the cheesecake. Stir in the raisins, reserving a few for decoration, if you like.

Pour the mixture into the tin on top of the biscuit base. Set the tin on the baking sheet and bake for 40 minutes. Stir the remaining soured cream, then carefully pour it over the top of the cheesecake. The top will still be fragile so if you need to spread the soured cream, do this gently. Bake for a further 15 minutes or until the cheesecake is set but still slightly wobbly in the centre.

Remove from the oven and run a round-bladed knife around the inside of the tin to loosen the cheesecake. Leave to cool in the tin, then cover and chill overnight before unmoulding for serving and scattering with the reserved raisins, if you like.

BEST OF THE BAKE-OFF
Rhubarb and Ginger Baked Cheesecake

Serves 6–8

For the rhubarb
600g trimmed young
   pink rhubarb
75g caster sugar

**For the cheesecake
   mixture**
1 x 175g packet stem
   ginger shortbread
50g unsalted butter,
   melted
250g full-fat cream
   cheese
65g caster sugar
finely grated zest of
   1 large unwaxed lemon
3 large free-range eggs,
   separated
150ml soured cream
1 tablespoon icing sugar,
   for dusting

1 large ovenproof dish;
   1 x 20.5cm springclip
   tin, greased and the
   base lined with baking
   paper; a baking sheet

Preheat the oven to 200°C/400°F/gas 6. Select the best-looking rhubarb and cut to make 6 sticks each exactly 7.5cm long (these will be used for decoration). Put them into a small ovenproof dish and sprinkle with 1 tablespoon of the caster sugar.

Cut the rest of the rhubarb into pieces about 5cm long and arrange in a single layer in a large ovenproof dish. Sprinkle with the rest of the caster sugar. Put both dishes in the oven and roast for about 15 minutes or until the rhubarb is just tender when pierced with the tip of a knife (don't overcook – the sticks and pieces must remain slightly firm and intact). Remove and leave to cool, then drain if necessary. Reduce the oven to 180°C/350°F/gas 4.

Put the biscuits in a plastic bag and crush with a rolling pin to coarse crumbs. Stir in the melted butter. Press onto the base and 2cm up the sides of the prepared tin. Chill while making the filling.

Beat the cream cheese with a wooden spoon or electric mixer until soft, then add the caster sugar and lemon zest. Mix thoroughly. Add the egg yolks and soured cream and beat until smooth. In another bowl, whisk the egg whites until stiff. Fold into the cheese mixture.

Arrange the smaller pieces of rhubarb on the biscuit base to make an even layer. Pour over the cheesecake mixture – it will almost fill the tin. Set it on the baking sheet and bake for 15 minutes or until risen, then lower the heat to 160°C/325°F/gas 3 and bake for a further 30 to 35 minutes or until firm to touch but still a little wobbly.

Remove from the oven and run a round-bladed knife around the inside of the tin to loosen the cheesecake. Leave to cool in the tin, then cover and chill overnight.

To serve, carefully remove the cheesecake from the tin. Decorate with the rhubarb sticks in a little stack, 3 over 3 pieces, and finish with a dusting of icing sugar.

THE GREAT BRITISH
BAKE OFF

TECHNICAL CHALLENGE
MARY'S CHOCOLATE ROULADE

Totally irresistible, this impressive dessert is made from just a few ingredients: chocolate, eggs, sugar and a little cocoa powder plus double cream for the filling. The joy of the sponge is that it tastes rich yet is not heavy – there's no flour or butter in the mixture, so it's rather like a baked chocolate mousse. It's made by whisking egg yolks with sugar, adding melted chocolate and cocoa, and then folding in whisked whites.

Serves 8

175g dark chocolate (39% cocoa solids), finely chopped
6 large free-range eggs, at room temperature
175g caster sugar
2 tablespoons cocoa powder

For the filling and finishing
300ml pourable double cream
icing sugar, for dusting

1 x 23 x 33cm swiss roll tin, greased with butter; non-stick baking paper

✳ If you are worried about breaking the yolks when separating the eggs, crack the whites into a cup first, then tip them into the bowl one at a time. This will ensure that you don't get any bits of yolk in the whites, which would prevent your whites from whisking to maximum volume.

✳ As you roll up the sponge, don't worry if it cracks – that is quite normal and all part of the charm of a home-baked roulade.

1 Line the base and sides of the buttered tin with non-stick baking paper. If you make a small diagonal snip in each corner of the paper, it will help fit the paper snugly into the corners of the tin.

2 Put the chocolate in a heatproof bowl and set it over a pan of steaming hot but not boiling water (don't let the base of the bowl touch the hot water). Leave to melt, stirring occasionally. Remove the bowl from the pan of water and stir until the chocolate is smooth, then leave to cool for about 15 minutes or until just warm. Preheat the oven to 180°C/350°F/gas 4.

3 Separate the eggs, putting the whites in one large mixing bowl and the yolks in another; set the yolks aside. Whisk the egg whites with an electric mixer on high speed until they stand in stiff peaks. If you turn the bowl upside down, the whites should be stiff enough not to fall out.

4 Put the sugar into the bowl with the egg yolks and whisk using the electric mixer (no need to wash it) on high speed for 2 to 3 minutes or until very thick and pale in colour, and the mixture leaves a ribbon-like trail on itself when the whisk is lifted out.

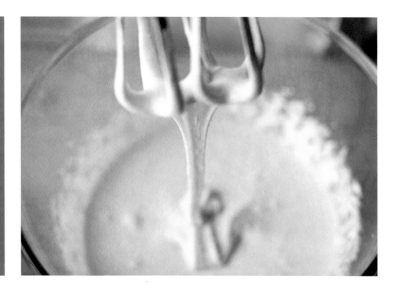

5 Pour the cooled chocolate into the yolk and sugar mixture and gently fold in with a wooden spoon to blend evenly. Add 2 large spoonfuls of the whisked egg whites to the chocolate mixture and stir in gently to loosen the mix, then fold in the remaining egg whites using a large metal spoon. Take care not to knock out the air you have just whisked in.

6 Sift the cocoa powder over the top and lightly but thoroughly fold it in with the metal spoon. Pour the mixture into the prepared tin and gently move the tin around on the worktop so the mixture finds its own level. Bake for 20 to 25 minutes or until risen and the top feels firm and slightly crisp when pressed gently with a finger. Remove from the oven and leave to cool in the tin; the sponge will fall and crack a little as it cools.

7 Lay a large piece of non-stick baking paper on the worktop and dust it lightly with icing sugar. Turn the sponge out onto the paper, then carefully peel off the lining paper. Whip the cream for the filling until it just holds its shape.

8 Spread the whipped cream over the sponge, leaving a clear edge of about 2cm on all sides. Using a sharp knife, make a shallow cut along one of the short edges.

9 Roll this cut edge over tightly to start. Use the sugar-dusted paper to help continue the tight rolling by pulling it away from you as you roll. Finish with the join underneath, then lift the roulade onto a serving plate or board using a large wide spatula or 2 fish slices.

Chocolate Mousse

Just three ingredients make this wonderfully light but intense chocolate mousse. As well as being a quick and impressive dessert, it can be used to fill a roulade (see page 265), choux buns (page 229) or Tuile biscuit baskets (page 64). Use the best dark chocolate you can find, with around 70 per cent cocoa solids: using chocolate of a higher percentage will make the mousse taste too bitter.

Serves 6–8

200g dark chocolate (70% cocoa solids), broken up
4 large free-range eggs, at room temperature, separated
1 tablespoon caster sugar

Put the chocolate into a large heatproof bowl with 100ml cold water. Set the bowl over a pan of steaming hot but not boiling water (don't let the base of the bowl touch the hot water) and melt gently, stirring occasionally. Remove the bowl from the pan and gently stir in the egg yolks one at a time.

Whisk the egg whites in a large bowl until they stand in soft peaks. Add the sugar and continue whisking until the whites are firm and stand in stiff peaks when the whisk is lifted out.

Add one-quarter of the whites to the chocolate mixture and mix in with a large metal spoon to soften the mixture. Carefully fold in the rest of the whites in 2 batches until thoroughly combined. Spoon the mousse into wine glasses or little coffee cups. Cover and chill for about 1 hour or until firm.

If using to fill a roulade, choux buns or biscuit baskets, cover the bowl and chill until the mousse is firm enough to spread. Once made, the mousse can be kept in the fridge overnight.

Tip: Replace 1 tablespoon of the water with brandy or dark rum for an extra kick.

Lemon Ice Cream Meringue Pie  EASY FOR KIDS

Harking from the days before ice-cream makers, this old-fashioned frozen dessert is very easy to make. The crunchy cornflake base is topped with a rich and creamy lemon mixture and covered with little meringues, then left to freeze overnight.

Serves 8

For the meringues
2 large free-range
    egg whites, at room
    temperature
pinch of cream of tartar
100g caster sugar

For the base
100g cornflakes
75g unsalted butter,
    melted
50g caster sugar

For the filling
1 x 379g tin sweetened
    condensed milk (full-
    fat rather than 'light')
150ml double cream
2 large free-range eggs,
    separated
finely grated zest
    and juice of 3 large
    unwaxed lemons
1 tablespoon caster sugar

1 baking sheet, lined with
    baking paper or a re-
    usable silicone sheet;
    a 23cm loose-based
    deep flan tin

Preheat the oven to 120°C/250°F/gas ½. Put the egg whites into a large mixing bowl and whisk until frothy. Add the cream of tartar and continue whisking until the whites stand in soft peaks when the whisk is lifted. Whisk in the sugar and continue whisking until the meringue mixture is thick and glossy and stands in stiff peaks.

Spoon the mixture onto the prepared baking sheet to make about 15 craggy-looking mounds about 5cm across and 6cm high. Bake for about 1½ hours or until crisp and dry. Turn off the oven and leave the meringues to cool down in the oven. Once cold they can be stored in an airtight container for a couple of days until ready to use.

To make the base, first prepare the flan tin. Set the tin on the worktop and remove the base. Lay a large piece of clingfilm over the (baseless) tin and press onto the sides and across the empty centre to line completely. Replace the base so it holds the clingfilm in place. Leave the excess clingfilm hanging over the sides.

Put the cornflakes into a mixing bowl and crush lightly with your hands. Stir in the melted butter and sugar, mixing until the cornflakes are thoroughly coated. Tip the mixture into the prepared tin and, using the back of spoon, press evenly over the metal base and up the clingfilm-lined sides. Chill while making the filling. Clear a shelf in the freezer.

Pour the condensed milk and cream into a mixing bowl. Stir in the egg yolks with a wooden spoon. When thoroughly combined stir in the lemon zest and juice, mixing well so the mixture thickens very slightly. Whisk the egg whites in another mixing bowl until they stand in soft peaks, then add the sugar and continue whisking until the mixture stands in stiff peaks. Fold into the lemon mixture in 3 batches.

Pour the lemon mixture into the cornflake case and spread evenly. Gently arrange the meringues on top, then fold over the overhanging clingfilm to cover loosely. Freeze overnight or until firm. When ready to serve unwrap and unmould the dessert. Set on a serving platter and leave in the fridge for about 15 minutes to 'come to' before serving. (For the finished bake, see page 247.)

Hot Lemon Curd Soufflé

If you can make meringues you can make a soufflé. This one is a combination of cheat's lemon curd and whisked egg whites, and it turns out extremely light and full of flavour. Serve with warm raspberry sauce (see below) and vanilla ice cream.

Serves 4–6

3 large free-range eggs
  plus 1 egg white, at
  room temperature
100g caster sugar
finely grated zest
  and juice of 2 large
  unwaxed lemons
50g unsalted butter,
  softened

1 x 1.5-litre soufflé dish,
  greased with butter
  and dusted with
  caster sugar

Preheat the oven to 200°C/400°F/gas 6. Separate the eggs, putting the 3 yolks into a large heatproof bowl and the 4 whites into another large bowl (or the bowl of a large, free-standing electric mixer). Set the whites aside. Add half of the sugar to the yolks and whisk for a couple of minutes until pale and creamy-looking. Whisk in the lemon zest and juice.

Set the bowl over a pan of simmering water (the base of the bowl should not touch the water) and whisk constantly until the mixture thickens and becomes opaque. Don't let it get too hot or the eggs will scramble. Immediately remove the bowl from the pan and whisk in the butter. As soon as the butter has melted transfer the lemon curd to a clean bowl.

Whisk the egg whites until thick enough to form soft peaks. Whisk in the remaining sugar, then continue whisking for a minute or so to make a thick, glossy meringue.

Using a large metal spoon fold the meringue into the warm lemon curd in 3 batches. Transfer the mixture to the soufflé dish. Run a finger around the inside of the rim to separate the mixture from the sides of the dish and help it to rise in the oven. Bake immediately for about 15 minutes or until well risen and golden brown but still slightly wobbly. Serve straight away.

Fresh Raspberry Sauce

A quick and easy, vibrant sauce, serve this chilled or warm with Hot Lemon Curd Soufflé as well as meringues and profiteroles, or simply with some good vanilla ice cream. It can also be made with frozen berries – remove them from the freezer 15 minutes before use.

Makes about 300ml

250g fresh raspberries
1 teaspoon lemon juice
4 tablespoons icing sugar
  (or to taste)

Put all the ingredients into a food-processor and process until the mixture becomes a smooth thick purée. Taste and add more sugar if needed. For an even smoother, seedless purée, push the mixture through a sieve into a bowl. Cover and chill until needed. Stir well before serving cold or hot.

Chocolate Bread and Butter Pudding

Easy to make and utterly luxurious, this recipe takes a family favourite to another level. Slices of brioche or challah bread replace the usual sliced white, and chopped dark chocolate is added to the rich egg custard. For an extra, rather adult treat you could also add a tablespoon of brandy or dark rum. Serve with vanilla ice cream.

Serves 6

7 slices brioche or challah loaf (not too thick)
50g unsalted butter, softened
300ml single or whipping cream
200ml full-fat or semi-skimmed milk
50g caster sugar
150g dark chocolate (70% cocoa solids), roughly chopped or broken up
3 large free-range eggs
icing sugar, for dusting

1 baking dish (about 1.25 litres), greased with butter

Cut the crusts off the slices of brioche, then spread with butter. Cut into triangles or pieces to fit your dish and arrange them, buttered side up, overlapping and standing up slightly, in the dish.

Put the cream, milk and caster sugar into a medium-sized pan (preferably non-stick). Heat gently, stirring to dissolve the sugar. Remove from the heat before the mixture comes to the boil. Add the chocolate and stir or whisk until the chocolate has melted.

Beat the eggs in a large heatproof jug or a bowl with a lip, then slowly stir in the chocolate cream (and any alcohol, if using). Pour this custard into the dish. With a fork gently press the brioche under the custard so it is completely coated (it will bob up again). Leave to soak for an hour.

Towards the end of this time, preheat the oven to 160°C/325°F/gas 3. Set the dish in a large roasting tin and pour enough warm water into the tin so it comes halfway up the sides of the dish.

Carefully slide the roasting tin into the oven and bake for about 40 minutes or until the pudding is just set. Lift the dish out of the roasting tin, dust with icing sugar and serve warm.

Peach and Ginger Cobbler

Just what you need when you're in a hurry – a quick combination of juicy fruit and a light topping with a crunchy exterior. In high summer when peaches (or nectarines) are at their sweetest and most affordable they'll just need a little lemon and no sugar. You can also make this at other times of year, with young spring rhubarb or an early autumn mixture of blackberries and apples, which won't need the lemon. For the fluffiest texture, mix the soft scone-like topping seconds before dropping it onto the hot fruit.

Serves 6

For the filling
6 medium to large peaches (about 700g in total)
finely grated zest and juice of ½ unwaxed lemon
1½ tablespoons caster sugar (or to taste)

For the topping
150g self-raising flour
¼ teaspoon bicarbonate of soda
50g caster sugar
25g chopped glacé ginger
50g unsalted butter, melted
100ml low-fat or full-fat natural yoghurt
2 teaspoons caster sugar mixed with ¼ teaspoon ground ginger, for sprinkling

1 baking dish or pie dish (about 1 litre)

Preheat the oven to 190°C/375°F/gas 5. Rinse the fruit, then halve and remove the stones. Cut each peach half into 4 thick slices. Put into a mixing bowl with the lemon zest and juice and the sugar. Toss gently, then transfer to the baking dish. Spoon over 2 tablespoons water.

Bake for 20 to 25 minutes or until the fruit is half-tender and the juices are bubbling.

Just before the end of the cooking time sift the flour, bicarbonate of soda and sugar into a mixing bowl. Using a round-bladed knife stir in the chopped ginger, followed by the melted butter and yoghurt to make a soft, sticky dough.

Remove the baking dish from the oven and turn up the heat to 220°C/425°F/gas 7. Divide the dough into 8 equal portions and drop in rough mounds, slightly apart, on top of the hot peach mixture.

Sprinkle the dough with the sugar and ginger mixture. Return to the oven and bake for about 20 minutes or until the topping is crisp and a good golden brown. Serve warm with custard, cream or ice cream.

Chocolate Fudge Hot-Pot Pudding

This is a luxury version of the classic British self-saucing pudding, which has its own sauce hidden underneath a very rich chocolate sponge. The longer the pudding stands after it comes out of the oven, the more the sauce will be absorbed by the sponge, but it will still taste good. Any leftovers can be reheated.

Serves 6

125g unsalted butter, softened
125g caster sugar
½ teaspoon vanilla extract
4 large free-range eggs, at room temperature, beaten
75g self-raising flour
4 tablespoons cocoa powder
50g dark chocolate (70% cocoa solids), finely chopped
1 tablespoon milk

For the sauce
4 tablespoons cocoa powder
125g light muscovado sugar
300ml very hot water

1 baking dish (about 1.7 litres), greased with butter

Preheat the oven to 180°C/350°F/gas 4. Put the butter into a mixing bowl and beat with a wooden spoon or electric mixer until creamy. Beat in the sugar and vanilla, then continue beating until the mixture looks paler and is fluffy in texture.

Gradually add the eggs, beating well after each addition. Add a tablespoon of the measured flour with the last portion of egg – the mixture will curdle but don't worry.

Sift the rest of the flour and the cocoa into the bowl and fold in using a large metal spoon. When thoroughly combined stir in the chopped chocolate and the milk. Transfer the soft mixture to the prepared dish and spread evenly.

To make the sauce, sift the cocoa and sugar into a heatproof bowl with a lip, or a wide-necked jug, and stir or whisk in the hot water to make a smooth, thin sauce. Pour evenly over the pudding mixture.

Bake immediately for 30 to 35 minutes or until the sponge is just firm to the touch and the sauce is bubbling. Serve straight away, with vanilla ice cream.

Queen of Sheba

A luxuriously rich, elegant chocolate and almond cake, covered and decorated with more dark chocolate, this recipe came from France via the late American cookery writer Julia Child, who said it was the first French cake she ever ate, and it remained her favourite.

Serves 8

For the sponge

100g dark chocolate (70% cocoa solids), broken up

2 tablespoons strong coffee (espresso, or ½ teaspoon instant coffee dissolved in 2 tablespoons hot water) OR dark rum

100g unsalted butter, softened

100g caster sugar, plus 2 tablespoons extra

3 large free-range eggs, at room temperature, separated

good pinch each of cream of tartar and salt

50g ground almonds

¼ teaspoon almond extract

65g plain flour

Preheat the oven to 180°C/350°F/gas 4. To make the sponge, put the chocolate into a heatproof bowl, add the coffee or rum and set over a pan of steaming hot but not boiling water (don't let the base of the bowl touch the hot water). Melt gently, stirring occasionally. Remove the bowl from the pan and leave to cool while making the rest of the mixture.

Put the soft butter into a mixing bowl and beat thoroughly with a wooden spoon or electric mixer until the butter looks creamy. Gradually beat in 100g sugar (save the 2 tablespoons for the egg whites) and continue beating until the mixture looks very pale and fluffy. Add the egg yolks one at a time, beating well after each addition.

Whisk the egg whites in a large bowl until frothy. Add the cream of tartar and salt and continue whisking until soft peaks form when the whisk is lifted out. Whisk in the 2 tablespoons sugar and continue whisking for another minute or until the mixture stands in stiff peaks.

Using a large metal spoon gently fold the chocolate mixture into the butter and sugar mixture followed by the ground almonds and almond extract. Fold in one-quarter of the egg whites.

When completely incorporated sift half the flour onto the mixture. Add half of the remaining egg whites and gently fold in – the whisked whites make the cake rise so take care not to lose too much air. Repeat with the remaining flour and egg whites.

Spoon the mixture into the prepared tin and spread evenly. Bake for 20 to 25 minutes or until a skewer inserted halfway between the side of the tin and the centre of the cake comes out clean; take care not to overcook – the centre should still be just moist.

Remove from the oven and run a round-bladed knife around the inside of the tin to loosen the cake. Cool for 5 minutes, then turn out onto a wire rack and leave to cool completely.

Recipe continues on page 280

For the icing
100g dark chocolate
   (70% cocoa solids),
   broken up
1 tablespoon strong
   coffee (espresso, or
   ¼ teaspoon instant
   coffee dissolved in
   1 tablespoon hot water)
   OR dark rum
100g unsalted butter,
   softened

For the decoration
75g dark chocolate
   (70% cocoa solids),
   broken up
cocoa powder or icing
   sugar, for dusting
   (optional)

1 x 20.5cm sandwich
   tin, greased and
   lined with baking
   paper; non-stick
   baking paper or a
   re-usable silicone sheet

To make the icing, melt the chocolate with the coffee or rum as before. Remove the bowl from the pan and stir in the butter a little at a time to make a smooth, glossy icing. Leave to cool, stirring frequently, until thick enough to spread.

Set the cake on a serving plate and spread the chocolate icing evenly over the top and around the sides. Leave until almost set.

Meanwhile, make the chocolate decoration. Melt the chocolate, without coffee or rum, as before. Remove the bowl from the pan and stir until smooth.

Pour the chocolate onto a sheet of non-stick baking paper or a re-usable silicone sheet and spread out fairly thinly (work fast so the chocolate doesn't start to set before it is evenly spread).

Leave to set in a cool place, but not the fridge (beads of moisture will appear on the chocolate when you remove it), then carefully break it up into shards.

Arrange the shards, vertically on top of the cake, pressing them gently into the soft icing. The cake looks impressive as it is but you can dust it with cocoa or icing sugar. Serve at room temperature. Store in an airtight container in a cool spot (not the fridge) and eat within 5 days.

Tip: Handle the chocolate shards as little as possible (use a small palette knife) so they don't start to melt or show fingermarks.

CELEBRATION TRIFLE

CHRISTMAS CAKE

SIMNEL CAKE

CHRISTMAS PUDDING

CELEBRATION
CAKES CUPCAKES

ICINGS AND DECORATIONS

TWELFTH NIGHT KING CAKE

Show-off Time

The milestones in our lives are marked with a celebration, a party, a special meal and often a toast. Special occasions call for celebratory food and focus on an impressive centrepiece. This usually means a cake or rich dessert to cut and share. Here's how to achieve the 'wow' factor at home.

Show-off recipes are often based around good but simple classics that taste delicious and which are exquisitely finished. Although dark, bitter chocolate sponges and cup cakes have recently become favourites, a traditional rich fruit cake is still popular for weddings, christenings and Christmas. The step-by-step recipe here, a Large Iced Fruit Cake (see page 286), can be decorated as simply or elaborately as you wish, to suit any occasion, and is a test of cake-baking as much as icing, decoration and presentation skills.

Once you've chosen the basic cake mixture, and decided the number of portions needed, you can work out what you'll need and choose the decorations. Many of these recipes take time but a lot can be prepared ahead – a rich fruit cake can, and should, be made at least a month in advance of icing for the fullest flavour, which is also true of Christmas pudding and mincemeat, while other cakes and desserts, like the Yule Log, can be made several days in advance and carefully stored. If you are catering for large numbers, beg or borrow fridge, freezer and safe storage space from friends – well away from pets and small fingers.

Before you embark on a large, important bake take time to read the recipe through and make sure you have everything you need before you start. If you're following a new recipe, or something you're not quite sure of, then try it out before the big day. Always use the right size tin: large or special-shaped cake tins can be hired from cookware shops, and cake-decorating suppliers (do check the tin fits easily into your oven). If a recipe needs a lot of whisking, beating or creaming, it's worth borrowing a large, free-standing mixer if you don't have one. Work out how many large bowls, wire cooling racks and other bits and pieces are needed – a sharp knife about 30cm long is useful for splitting sponge cakes in half – as well as storage containers. A revolving cake stand is invaluable for complex cake decorating, along with piping bags, tubes and palette knives.

Use the correct ingredients. For example, granulated sugar will not work in the same way as caster in a sponge cake, and caster sugar won't give a fruit cake as deep a flavour and colour as muscovado. Never replace cocoa powder with drinking chocolate and don't replace dark chocolate with cake covering or butter with spread because the taste will not be anywhere near as good. Make sure spices, nuts and raising agents (baking powder, bicarbonate of soda) are fresh and well within their use-by dates because spices quickly stale, nuts turn rancid and raising agents lose their power.

Allow plenty of time to prepare the tins and ingredients. Carefully lining cake tins with greaseproof or non-stick baking paper makes a big difference to the success of a baked cake, preventing hard, overcooked edges, and making turning out easy. Sift flour (with any other dry ingredients) to remove lumps and add air. Lumps can also be a problem with muscovado sugar (opened packs dry out), and sieving takes time. It's easier to tip the sugar into a large bowl, cover with a damp tea towel and leave overnight; next day the sugar will be softer and moister and the lumps will quickly break up. Take butter and eggs out of the fridge in good time so the butter is soft enough to cream thoroughly and the eggs are at room temperature. But keep cream for whipping thoroughly chilled, along with the bowl and whisk. Toast and chop nuts so they are ready when needed.

Even if it is easy to make, a special occasion cake or dessert should look spectacular. Here you can be as imaginative and inventive as you like. If you are short of time or lack confidence, go for something uncomplicated. The quickest and easiest way to make a cake look special is to use a stencil to add a design to the top. Usually made from plastic or thick card, stencils are available from cookware shops and specialist cake-decorating suppliers.

Set the stencil on top of the cake – the surface must be dry and firm – and dust with a finely sifted powder in a contrasting colour. Icing sugar works well on all but very pale surfaces. Cocoa powder varies in colour from brand to brand – some have more copper-red tones, others are slightly grey-brown – so practise first on a sheet of paper and pick the one that works best. For sheer glamour, mix cocoa powder with edible gold dust or lustre for a shimmering effect. Finely grated chocolate can also be used. Clean the stencil with a dry brush after use and store flat so it is ready to use again.

Edible gold leaf looks exotic against a dark chocolate background. Available from specialist suppliers in the form of very fine leaves or as sparkles, gold leaf needs to be handled carefully as it easily disintegrates. Use the tip of a small knife to transfer the gold leaf, in small segments, to the cake (it sticks better if the icing is still slightly soft or damp), or sprinkle gold leaf sparkles directly onto the cake. Fine gold leaf powder or lustre can be brushed onto a cake or onto sugar flower or chocolate decorations using a small, dry paint brush. Or mix a couple of drops of vodka with a similar quantity of the edible gold powder to make a gold paint, to make hand-drawn designs or to paint onto chocolate.

Ready-to-roll icing comes in many colours, as do edible colouring pastes for tinting home-made icings and frosting. If you are matching icing for a colour scheme it's worth making up a small trial batch to check before you work on the cake because it often looks different when it has dried.

And finally, you will need something suitable for presenting the cake or dessert. A cake stand looks impressive. More simply, a large tray or platter, or a board, can be disguised by covering with paper doilies or edible leaves such as vine, strawberry or banana. Don't forget a sharp knife for cutting the cake or dessert.

THE GREAT BRITISH
BAKE OFF

HOW TO MAKE A
LARGE ICED FRUIT CAKE

Traditional for celebrations, such as Christmas, weddings, and christenings, a rich fruit cake is hard to beat. Making the cake can be broken down into stages, and you can make the cake up to 3 months in advance, which will give it plenty of time for the flavours to mature.

Makes 1 large cake

100g blanched almonds
250g plain flour
750g mixed dried fruit
250g unsalted butter, softened
250g dark brown muscovado sugar
4 large free-range eggs
2 teaspoons ground mixed spice
50g ground almonds
9 tablespoons brandy

For covering the cake
2 tablespoons apricot jam, warmed
icing sugar, for dusting
800g ready-made white marzipan
1kg ready-to-roll or rolled white icing

1 x 21.5–22cm deep round cake tin or springclip tin

✱ You can use any combination of dried fruit and nuts, but a large bag of luxury dried fruit mix – including cherries, and sometimes candied pineapple, as well as the usual raisins, sultanas, currants and mixed peel – saves buying lots of bags of different ingredients. If you don't like almonds use walnuts or make up the weight with more dried fruit.

✱ It's well worth taking time to prepare the tin properly, or your lovely cake may turn out wrinkled or dry with burnt edges and an undercooked centre. Grease the tin with butter before lining it. You can buy cake liners, but they are simple enough to fashion from greaseproof or non-stick baking paper (see steps 1 and 2 opposite). For baking the cake, you'll also need a baking sheet and an old newspaper.

✱ Plan to cover and decorate the matured cake several days ahead of serving. The icing can be bought ready-rolled, but it is fairly simple to roll it out yourself. Before starting to work with the marzipan or icing, be sure your hands are spotlessly clean and dry, and remove your watch and all rings and bangles (to prevent marks and dents).

✱ The decoration is up to you – just add some pretty candles or a fancy centrepiece, or have fun with the piping or painted decorations. (See pages 292–293 for more ideas.)

Mary's tip
It's difficult to remember tin sizes, but getting the tin size right is so important in baking. Measure the base and the capacity of your tins and write the figures on the bottom of the base in permanent marker.

1 Preheat the oven to 180°C/350°F/gas 4. Cut out 2 rounds of greaseproof or baking paper just a fraction smaller than the base of your tin. For the sides, cut a double thickness strip long enough to go around the tin and stand about 5cm higher than the rim. Make a 2cm fold along one long edge, then snip diagonally up to the fold at intervals of about 1cm.

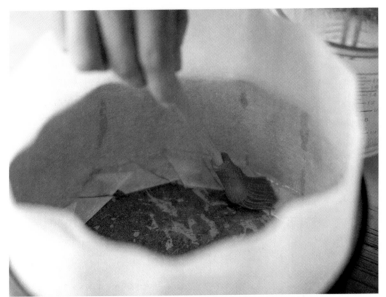

2 Put one of the paper rounds in the base of the tin, then place the long strip around the inside so that the snipped edge lies flat on the base. Lightly brush the base and the snipped edge with melted butter, then place the second round on top. Lightly brush the paper lining with melted butter.

3 Put the whole almonds into a heatproof dish or small tin and toast in the oven for about 5 minutes or until light brown. Leave to cool, then chop roughly. Lower the oven temperature to 150°C/300°F/gas 2. Put a tablespoonful of the flour and the fruit into another bowl and toss gently to separate any clumps of fruit. This will ensure the even distribution of the fruit in the cake. Mix in the chopped almonds.

4 Put the soft butter into a large mixing bowl and beat well with an electric mixer or wooden spoon for a minute until creamy. Add the sugar (if it is lumpy you may need to sieve it first) and beat thoroughly for about 4 minutes or until the mixture turns much lighter in colour and fluffy in texture. Scrape down the bowl from time to time. Beat the eggs, then add a tablespoon at a time, beating well after each addition. If the mixture looks as if it is about to curdle or separate, add a tablespoonful of the flour with the final addition of egg. Sift the remaining flour and the mixed spice onto the egg mixture. Add the ground almonds and gently but thoroughly fold in with a large metal spoon. Now add the fruit mixture, along with any flour left in the bottom of the bowl plus 5 tablespoons brandy. Gently fold into the mixture.

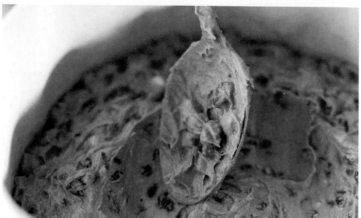

5 When thoroughly combined, spoon into the prepared tin and spread evenly. Bang the tin down on the worktop to dislodge any pockets of air, then make a shallow hollow in the centre of the cake so it will rise evenly in the oven to give a flat surface.

6 Line a baking sheet with several sheets of newspaper and set the tin on top. Fold several more sheets of newspaper into a strip slightly wider than the depth of the tin and long enough to go all around it. Wrap this strip around the tin and secure with a couple of paper clips or tie it in place with a piece of string.

7 Bake for about 3 hours or until golden brown and a skewer inserted into the centre of the cake comes out clean. If necessary rotate the cake a couple of times during baking so it cooks evenly and cover the top with a sheet of greaseproof paper if it is getting too brown. Remove from the oven, set on a wire rack and leave to cool completely before removing the tin and lining paper.

8 Prick the top and base of the cake with a skewer, then trickle about 3 tablespoons of the remaining brandy into the holes (you will need 1 tablespoon later on), first over the base and then over the top. Set the cake on a plate and leave until the brandy has soaked in, then wrap in fresh greaseproof paper and foil. Leave in a cool, dry place to mature for at least a month before finishing.

9 To cover the cake: unwrap the cake and set it on a cake board or serving platter (for a completely flat surface it's best to turn the cake upside down). Brush all over with a thin coat of apricot jam.

10 Knead the marzipan for a minute until smooth and pliable. If there is a gap between the cake and the board, press a thin roll of marzipan around the base so the sides are completely flat and straight.

11 Lightly dust the worktop with icing sugar. Roll out the rest of the marzipan to a round large enough to cover the top and sides of the cake (it's easier to use a tape measure for this than go by eye).

12 Carefully wrap the marzipan around the rolling pin and lift it over the cake. Gently unroll the marzipan so the edge just touches the cake board, then continue unrolling the marzipan over the cake so it covers the cake evenly and touches the board all around.

13 Use the palms of your hands to smooth the marzipan on the top surface and down the sides of the cake, to make sure it is well fixed and there are no pockets of air.

14 With a sharp knife, trim off the excess marzipan flush with the board, leaving no gaps or holes. If time allows leave the cake, very loosely covered, in a cool dry spot for 1 to 2 days, to allow the marzipan to firm up.

15 Brush the marzipan very lightly with the remaining brandy. Roll out the icing (if necessary) as for the marzipan and cover the cake in the same way, smoothing with your hands. Keep the icing trimmings for decorations, tightly wrapped in clingfilm.

16 To decorate the cake: while the icing is still soft, you can use shaped cutters or crimpers to press designs or patterns into the icing. Otherwise leave the cake in a cool place, uncovered, for a day to firm up the icing before adding decorations.

17 The icing trimmings can be re-rolled and cut into shapes such as stars, holly leaves, Christmas trees and reindeer using biscuit cutters or special decorative cutters and stuck onto the cake with a dab of royal icing. Leave the icing white or colour it with a very little colouring paste, kneaded in before rolling out or painted on afterwards. The shapes can also be dusted with edible gold or silver glitter or lustre.

18 For a very easy piped decoration, cover the top and sides of the cake with polka dots, either white or coloured, using Royal Icing (see page 68) in a piping bag fitted with a fine plain icing tube (No. 0 or No. 1) – or a small plastic bag (or ready-made pouch) with the tip snipped off.

19 For more elaborate decorations draw the design onto greaseproof or tracing paper, then set the paper on the cake and, holding it firmly, prick through the paper with a pin onto the icing underneath so the pattern is transferred. You can then pipe, draw or paint on your design. When you've finished, attach a ribbon around the base of the cake so it covers the join where the cake meets the board, fixing it with a dab of icing. Leave to dry, then store the cake in a large covered container in a cool, dry spot.

20 Make 5 petals from tinted sugar paste or ready-made icing, to form a simple flower. Flatten a pea-sized amount and roll it loosely. Wrap another petal around this and continue, gently curling the edges. Leave to firm up.

21 For sugared petals, beat a tablespoon of water with an egg white until just frothy, then paint onto edible petals (roses or violets) with a very fine brush. Sprinkle with very fine, white caster sugar to coat completely. Dry on a wire rack.

Simnel Cake

Traditionally, Simnel Cake was made by young girls in service in large houses to take home to their mothers on Mothering Sunday. These days it is decorated with balls of marzipan to represent the 11 disciples and is eaten on Easter Day.

Makes 1 large cake

225g plain flour
1½ teaspoons baking
    powder
good pinch of salt
100g glacé cherries
350g mixed dried fruit
175g unsalted butter,
    softened
175g light brown
    muscovado sugar
finely grated zest of
    1 large unwaxed lemon
4 large free-range eggs,
    at room temperature
50g ground almonds
2 tablespoons milk
450g marzipan
2 tablespoons apricot
    jam, warmed, or
    sherry, for brushing

1 x 20.5cm round deep
    cake tin or springclip
    tin, greased and lined
    with baking paper

Preheat the oven to 180°C/350°F/gas 4. Sift the flour, baking powder and salt onto a sheet of greaseproof paper. Halve the cherries; rinse with warm water to remove the sticky syrup, then dry thoroughly on kitchen paper. Put them into a bowl with the dried fruit and 1 tablespoon of the sifted flour. Mix well so the fruit is evenly dusted with flour.

Put the soft butter into a large mixing bowl and beat with a wooden spoon or electric mixer for a couple of minutes until light and creamy. Add the sugar (make sure there are no lumps) and lemon zest and beat for 4 to 5 minutes or until the mixture turns lighter in colour and fluffy in texture. Add the eggs a tablespoon at a time, beating well after each addition; add the ground almonds with the last portion of egg.

Sift the flour mixture again, this time straight onto the beaten mixture, and fold in with a large metal spoon. Add the fruit mix and the milk and fold in. When thoroughly combined spoon half of the mixture into the prepared tin and spread evenly.

Cut off one-third of the marzipan and roll out to a round just slightly smaller than the diameter of the tin. Gently set the marzipan round on top of the mixture in the tin. Spoon the rest of the cake mixture on top and spread evenly. Make a slight hollow in the centre so the cake rises evenly. Tap the tin on the worktop a couple of times to dislodge any pockets of air.

Bake for 30 minutes, then reduce the oven temperature to 170°C/325°F/ gas 3 and bake for a further 60 to 70 minutes or until a skewer inserted into the centre of the cake – just down to the marzipan layer – comes out clean. Set the tin on a wire rack and leave to cool completely.

Remove the cake from the tin and peel off the lining paper. Cut off one-third of the remaining marzipan and set aside. Roll out the remaining marzipan to a round to fit the top of the cake. Lightly brush the top with jam or sherry, then firmly press on the marzipan round. Pinch the edge with your fingers or icing crimpers to decorate. With the tip of a knife score the marzipan in a diamond pattern, then quickly brown under a preheated hot grill. Roll the remaining marzipan into 11 balls and arrange around the edge of the marzipan top.

Yule Log  EASY FOR KIDS

The tradition of Yule harks back to the pagan Vikings – their ceremony of the Yule Log celebrated the sun at the time of the winter solstice. This recipe is based on a classic swiss roll, filled with chocolate pastry cream and covered in rich ganache (chocolate melted with cream). It can be kept for up to 2 days, in an airtight container.

Makes 1 large cake

For the sponge
150g plain flour
pinch of salt
4 large free-range eggs, at room temperature
125g caster sugar
½ teaspoon vanilla extract
50g unsalted butter, melted and cooled

For the pastry cream
200ml full-fat milk
2 large free-range egg yolks
50g caster sugar
1½ tablespoons cornflour
½ teaspoon vanilla extract

For the ganache
200ml double cream
200g dark chocolate (70% cocoa solids)
Icing sugar, for dusting (optional)

1 swiss roll tin about 25 x 32cm, greased and lined with baking paper; a piping bag fitted with a 0.5cm plain tube; a baking sheet lined with non-stick baking paper or a re-usable silicone sheet

Preheat the oven to 220°C/425°F/gas 7. To make the sponge, sift the flour and salt onto a sheet of greaseproof paper and set aside. Put the eggs into a large bowl and whisk with an electric mixer until frothy. Add the sugar and vanilla, and whisk on high speed for about 5 minutes or until the mixture is very thick and will make a ribbon-like trail. Sift the flour and salt again, straight onto the mixture in the bowl. Very gently but thoroughly fold in the flour using a large metal spoon. Drizzle the cool but still liquid butter over the top and fold in delicately.

Transfer the mixture to the prepared tin and spread evenly. Bake for about 10 minutes or until golden brown and just firm to the touch. While the sponge is baking cover a wire rack with a tea towel and top with a sheet of non-stick baking paper. Turn out the cooked sponge onto the prepared rack, then peel off the lining paper. Using the tea towel to help you, gently roll up the still-hot sponge from one narrow end, with the baking paper inside. Leave to cool completely.

Next make the pastry cream (follow the instructions on page 235, without adding whipped cream; stir in the vanilla before cooling).

To make the ganache, heat the cream in a medium pan (preferably non-stick) until almost boiling. Remove from the heat. Break the chocolate into the hot cream and leave for a couple of minutes, then stir gently until melted and smooth. Leave at room temperature, stirring occasionally, until needed (no more than 2 hours).

When ready to assemble, unroll the sponge; peel off and discard the paper. Trim off the hard edges. Stir the ganache, then mix one-quarter of it into the pastry cream. Spread this evenly over the sponge. Roll up again, wrap tightly in foil to maintain the neat shape and chill for an hour.

Unwrap the rolled cake and set it on a cake board or serving platter. If you want to make a 'branch' for your log, cut off a slice from one end on a slight diagonal and place the cut end against the side of the log. Spread the remaining ganache over the log, leaving the ends uncovered. Run the back of a fork down the log to give a ridged bark effect. Dust the log with icing sugar for 'snow' just before serving, if you like.

Twelfth Night King Cake

The 12 days of Christmas come to an end on 6th January, Epiphany. For many centuries this involved a feast, including the King Cake. Whoever found the bean hidden inside was the Lord of Misrule until midnight. This version is made from puff pastry and filled with a rich almond and chocolate cream. Serve warm, decorated with a gold paper crown for the Lord or Lady of Misrule to wear for the night.

Makes 1 large tart

1 quantity Puff Pastry
   (see page 210) or 750g
   ready-made butter
   puff pastry, chilled

For the filling
100g dark chocolate
   (70% cocoa solids),
   chopped
100g unsalted butter,
   softened
100g caster sugar
1 large free-range egg
   plus 1 yolk, at room
   temperature
100g ground almonds
50g flaked almonds
¼ teaspoon almond
   extract
1 ceramic or dried bean
beaten egg, to glaze

1 baking sheet, lined with
   baking paper

Tip: Remember to tell guests to look out for the inedible bean.

Roll out half the pastry on a lightly floured worktop until slightly thinner than a pound coin. Cut out a round about 24cm in diameter. Set on the lined baking sheet and cover with clingfilm. Roll out the rest of the pastry in the same way and cut a second round. Set this on top of the clingfilm, then cover the whole lot with clingfilm. Chill while making the filling.

Put the chocolate into a heatproof bowl and set over a pan of steaming hot but not boiling water (don't let the base of the bowl touch the hot water). Leave to melt gently. Remove the bowl from the pan. Stir the chocolate until smooth, then leave to cool.

Beat the butter until creamy with a wooden spoon or electric mixer. Beat in the sugar, then beat thoroughly until the mixture looks pale and fluffy. Beat the egg with the yolk until just combined, then gradually add to the butter mixture a tablespoon at a time, beating well after each addition. When the mixture is very light in colour and texture gently stir in the ground almonds, flaked almonds and almond extract followed by the cooled chocolate. Cover the bowl and chill for 15 to 20 minutes.

When ready to assemble uncover the pastry, and remove the top round and clingfilm. Spoon the chocolate filling onto the pastry round on the baking sheet, mounding it slightly in the middle, and leaving a 2cm border uncovered all around the edge. Push the bean into the filling, not too close to the centre.

Brush the pastry border with beaten egg, then gently lay the second pastry round over the filling. Press the edges firmly together to seal. Holding a small knife blade at right angles to the side of the pastry, 'knock up' the edge all around by making small indentations in the pastry. Then scallop the edge by pulling the indentations in at 2cm intervals with the back of the knife. Brush the top of the pastry very lightly with beaten egg to glaze and chill for 20 minutes. Meanwhile, preheat the oven to 220°C/425°F/gas 7.

Brush the top a second time with the beaten egg glaze, then score a diamond pattern with the tip of a sharp knife. Make a couple of small steam holes in the centre. Bake for 25 to 30 minutes or until the pastry is a golden brown and crisp. Leave to cool slightly before serving.

Panettone

In recent years this tall, cylindrical loaf has become known as the 'Italian Christmas Cake', and is available from all kinds of supermarkets. It is a speciality of Milan, where true bakers vie to make the tallest, lightest and most butter-rich loaf. The real thing can be achieved at home, as long as you've got a bit of time to spare – panettone gets its fine, cake-like crumb from several risings of the yeast dough. Dark chocolate is a fairly modern addition to the traditional mix of sultanas, peel, vanilla and zests but very popular. Serve panettone in thick slices with coffee or hot chocolate for breakfast on Boxing Day – any leftovers will make a good bread and butter pudding (see page 274).

Makes 1 large loaf

1 x 7g sachet fast-action
   dried yeast OR 15g
   fresh yeast
400g strong white bread
   flour
75g caster sugar
2 large free-range eggs
   plus 2 egg yolks, at
   room temperature
3 tablespoons lukewarm
   water
½ teaspoon vanilla
   extract
finely grated zest of
   1 unwaxed orange
finely grated zest of
   1 unwaxed lemon
½ teaspoon salt
175g unsalted butter,
   softened and cut into
   small pieces
75g large sultanas

If using dried yeast: mix about 125g of the weighed flour with the yeast and sugar in a large mixing bowl or the bowl of an electric mixer, and make a well in the centre; beat the whole eggs with the water and pour into the well.

If using fresh yeast: mix 125g of the flour with the sugar in a large mixing bowl or the bowl of an electric mixer, and make a well in the centre. Beat the whole eggs until broken up, then add to the well. Crumble the yeast into the lukewarm water, mix thoroughly and pour into the well.

Using your hand or the dough hook attachment of the mixer, mix the flour into the liquid to make a thick, smooth batter. Sprinkle a little of the remaining weighed flour over the top of the batter to prevent a skin from forming, then leave in a warm spot for about 1 hour or until the batter is very bubbly.

Stir the egg yolks, vanilla and the grated zests into the batter using your hand or the dough hook (on the lowest speed). Gradually work in 175g of the remaining flour plus the salt to make a soft and very sticky dough.

Add the soft butter and work it in by squeezing the dough through your fingers, or beating on the same low speed, until the butter is thoroughly incorporated and there are no streaks.

Turn out the dough onto a floured worktop and knead thoroughly by hand for 10 minutes, or with the dough hook for 3 to 4 minutes, working in the remainder of the weighed flour to make a dough that is satiny soft and very pliable, but not sticky. Depending on the flour, you may not need it all or you may need a little more.

(Ingredients continued)
50g candied orange
  and lemon peel, finely
  chopped
50g dark chocolate
  (70% cocoa solids),
  finely chopped
about 40g unsalted
  butter, to finish

1 x panettone mould or a
  15cm round, deep cake
  tin (see TIP), greased
  with melted butter; a
  paper panettone liner
  or greaseproof paper

Tip: If you
don't have a
panettone tin or a
small, deep cake
tin, you can use a
clean large coffee
tin or a catering-
size baked bean tin,
lined as above.

Return the dough to the bowl and cover with a snap-on lid or clingfilm or slip the bowl into a large plastic bag. Leave to rise at normal, or just slightly warm, room temperature until doubled in size – 2 to 2½ hours. Don't leave in a sunny or very warm spot or the butter will begin to melt.

Uncover the dough and punch down to deflate. Cover the bowl and leave to rise as before until doubled in size again – this time it will take 1 to 1½ hours.

Meanwhile, combine the sultanas with the chopped peels and chocolate in a small bowl and toss with a teaspoon of flour (this helps prevent clumps in the dough).

Finish preparing the tin: slip a paper panettone liner into the buttered tin, or line the base and sides with a double layer of greaseproof paper; the paper should extend 5cm above the height of the tin. Wrap a strip of foil or newspaper around the outside of the tin, again 5cm above the rim, and tie in place with string.

Punch down the risen dough, then turn out onto a floured worktop. Sprinkle the fruit and chocolate mixture over the dough and work in very gently with floured hands until evenly distributed.

Shape the dough into a ball and gently drop it into the prepared tin. With the tip of a long, sharp knife cut a cross in the top of the dough. Lay a sheet of clingfilm lightly across the top of the tin – don't stretch it – and leave to rise as before for about 1 hour or until doubled in size.

Towards the end of the rising time preheat the oven to 200°C/400°F/gas 6. When ready to bake, set aside a knob (about 15g) of the butter for finishing and melt the rest. Brush half the melted butter over the risen dough and put the knob of butter in the centre of the cross.

Bake for 10 minutes or until just starting to colour, then brush again with melted butter. Reduce the temperature to 180°C/350°F/gas 4 and bake for a further 40 minutes or until a good golden brown and a skewer inserted into the centre comes out clean.

Remove from the oven and set the tin on a wire rack. Cool for 10 minutes to allow the very fragile crust of the panettone to firm up a bit, then very gently unmould the loaf. Remove the liner or greaseproof paper lining and place the panettone on its side on the rack.

Leave to cool completely before slicing. (The best way to cool a panettone – once unmoulded – is to put it in an old-fashioned, clean string bag and suspend from a hook or jelly-bag stand.

Mincemeat Lattice Tart

The pastry for this Christmas tart is made with cream cheese as well as butter, and rolled and folded up as for puff pastry (see page 210), making it slightly flaky.

Makes 1 medium tart

For the pastry
250g plain flour
125g unsalted butter, chilled and diced
125g full-fat cream cheese, chilled
1 large free-range egg, separated

For the filling
300g cranberries (fresh or frozen)
2 tablespoons caster sugar, plus extra for sprinkling
½ teaspoon ground cinnamon
400g mincemeat

1 x 23cm loose-based deep flan tin; a baking sheet

To make the pastry put the flour and butter into a food-processor and run the machine until the mixture looks like fine crumbs. Add the cream cheese and egg yolk and process until the mixture forms a ball of fairly firm dough. Wrap in clingfilm and chill for 15 minutes.

Roll out the dough on a floured worktop, rolling away from you, to make a rectangle about 15 x 45cm. Fold the dough in 3 like a business letter and seal the edges with the rolling pin. Wrap and chill for 15 minutes. Repeat the rolling out, folding and chilling 2 more times, each time starting with the folded edges to the left and right.

Cut off one-quarter of the dough for the lattice; wrap and chill until needed. Roll out the remaining dough to a round about 30cm in diameter and use to line the tin. Roll the pin over the top of the tin to cut off the excess pastry; save the trimmings. Prick the base well, then chill the pastry case for 20 minutes. Meanwhile, preheat the oven to 200°C/400°F/gas 6.

Line the pastry case with non-stick baking paper or foil, fill with baking beans and bake 'blind' for 10 to 12 minutes or until the pastry is just firm (see page 184). Remove the paper and beans, then return the empty case to the oven and bake for a further 5 minutes or until the pastry is just starting to colour. Remove the pastry case from the oven but do not unmould. Turn up the oven to 220°C/425°F/gas 7 and put in the baking sheet to heat up.

While the pastry case is baking, make the filling. Put the cranberries, sugar, cinnamon and 1 tablespoon water into a medium pan and heat gently, stirring frequently, until the juices start to run. Simmer for 5 minutes or until the berries are just tender but still hold their shape. Stir in the mincemeat. Cool.

Roll out the dough reserved for the lattice, plus the trimmings, to a 13 x 24cm rectangle that is the thickness of a pound coin. Cut 10 strips about 1.25cm wide. Spoon the filling into the pastry case. Brush the rim with a little beaten egg white. Arrange the pastry strips over the filling in a lattice pattern, 5 one way and 5 the other, pressing the ends to the rim to seal. Set the tart on the hot baking sheet and bake for 15 minutes.

Remove from the oven. Brush the lattice with egg white and sprinkle with caster sugar. Bake for a further 5 to 10 minutes or until the pastry is crisp and golden brown. Leave to cool for 5 minutes before unmoulding. Serve warm or at room temperature with crème fraîche or ice cream.

Christmas Pudding

Here's a pudding that's packed with all the traditional ingredients and flavours but with a little bit less fat and sugar.

Makes 2 medium puddings

350g luxury dried fruit mix
100g soft-dried figs
finely grated zest and juice of 1 large unwaxed lemon
3 tablespoons brandy, plus extra to serve
100g blanched almonds (almonds with their skins removed)
50g pine nuts
75g unsalted butter, softened
75g dark brown muscovado sugar
75g honey
2 large free-range eggs, at room temperature, beaten
1 medium eating apple, such as Cox
125g fresh white breadcrumbs
½ teaspoon ground mixed spice
¼ teaspoon each freshly grated nutmeg and ground cinnamon

2 x 570ml (1-pint) pudding basins, greased; greaseproof paper, foil and string

Put the dried fruit into a mixing bowl. Using kitchen scissors snip the figs into pieces the size of a half cherry and add to the bowl. Add the lemon zest and juice and the brandy. Stir well, then cover the bowl tightly and leave to soak overnight.

Next day, preheat the oven to 180°C/350°F/gas 4. Put the almonds into a small pan, add cold water to cover and bring to the boil. Drain, then slice each almond into 3 long slivers. Put the almonds into an ovenproof dish or small tin with the pine nuts and toast in the oven for about 4 minutes or until very lightly coloured. Remove and cool.

Meanwhile, put the soft butter into a large mixing bowl and beat with a wooden spoon until creamy. Add the sugar and honey and beat thoroughly until the mixture is very light and fluffy. Gradually add the eggs, beating well after each addition.

Grate the apple (no need to peel) into a mixing bowl, discarding the core. Add the breadcrumbs and all the spices, plus the almonds and pine nuts, and mix thoroughly. Add to the butter mixture with the soaked fruit mixture and mix very well.

Spoon the pudding mixture into the prepared basins so they are evenly filled. Gently tap them on the worktop to dislodge any pockets of air. Cover each with a piece of greased greaseproof paper pleated in the middle (to allow for the pudding to expand) and then with foil. Tie the paper and foil securely in place with string, then loop the string across the top of each basin to make a handle (for easy removal). Alternatively, use snap-on lids.

Stand each basin on an upturned old saucer or trivet in a large pan, then pour in boiling water from the kettle to come about two-thirds up the side of the basins. Partially cover the pans and simmer gently for 3 hours, topping up with boiling water from time to time so the pans do not boil dry. Remove the basins and leave to cool before covering with fresh greaseproof paper and foil. Store in a cool dry place or the fridge for up to a month or keep in the freezer for 3 months.

On Christmas day, boil/steam a pudding as before for 2 hours, then turn out onto a platter. Gently warm a little more brandy, ignite and pour over the pudding. Serve with brandy butter, cream or ice cream.

A Celebration Sherry Trifle GOOD FOR *Celebrations*

A trifle is, of course, anything but. It's sheer indulgence – layer upon layer of treats. It requires a fair amount of work, over 2 days, but can be made in stages well ahead.

Serves 12–16

3 large free-range eggs,
   at room temperature
75g caster sugar, plus
   extra for sprinkling
75g plain flour
good pinch of salt
6 tablespoons good
   raspberry jam
about 5 tablespoons
   sweet sherry
250g fresh raspberries
toasted almonds,
   ratafia biscuits and
   extra raspberries, to
   decorate

For the custard
425ml single cream
1 vanilla pod, split open
4 large free-range eggs,
   at room temperature
3 tablespoons caster
   sugar
1 teaspoon cornflour

For the syllabub
100ml sweet sherry
50g caster sugar
1 tablespoon lemon juice
freshly grated nutmeg
300ml double cream,
   well chilled

1 x 20 x 30cm swiss roll
   tin, greased and lined

Preheat the oven to 220°C/425°F/gas 7. Put the eggs into a large bowl and whisk with an electric mixer until frothy. Whisk in the sugar, then continue whisking until very thick and pale and the mixture leaves a ribbon-like trail when the whisk is lifted out.

Sift the flour and salt onto a sheet of greaseproof paper, then sift half of it a second time straight into the bowl. Using a large metal spoon gently fold the flour into the mixture. Sift the rest of the flour into the bowl and continue folding in until you no longer see streaks or specks of flour.

Transfer the mixture to the prepared tin and spread evenly. Bake for about 10 minutes or until golden brown and springy to touch. Turn out onto a sheet of non-stick baking paper sprinkled with caster sugar.

Peel off the lining paper. Make a shallow cut across the sponge (see page 268), then roll up with the paper inside. Cool completely. Once cold, unroll the sponge and trim off the edges. Spread with jam and re-roll. Store in an airtight container until ready to use (up to 3 days).

For the next stage, a day before serving thickly slice the swiss roll and use to line the base of a large glass bowl. Arrange the slices in a single layer, cutting pieces to fit into corners or gaps if necessary.

Sprinkle the sherry over the sponge, then add the raspberries, spreading them evenly. Cover with clingfilm and chill while making the custard.

Heat the cream with the vanilla pod until scalding hot, then remove the pan from the heat and leave to infuse for 20 minutes. Lift out the pod and use the tip of a knife to scrape a few of the vanilla seeds into the milk (wash and dry the pod to use again).

Beat the eggs with the sugar and cornflour, then stir in the hot cream. Return the mixture to the pan and cook over very low heat, stirring constantly, until thick enough to coat the back of the spoon; don't let the custard boil. Strain into a bowl and leave to cool. When cold, spoon the custard over the sponge and raspberries, then cover and chill overnight.

To make the syllabub, combine the sherry, sugar, lemon juice and several gratings of nutmeg in a jug and stir well. Leave to stand for 15 minutes, then stir again. Meanwhile, chill a mixing bowl and whisk or whisk attachment of an electric mixer. Pour the cream into the chilled bowl and begin to whisk. Gradually whisk in the sherry mixture and keep whisking until the mixture is very thick and light.

Carefully spread the syllabub over the trifle. Decorate with the toasted nuts, ratafia biscuits and/or berries. Cover tightly and chill for at least 4 hours before serving.

Celebration Cup Cakes

With their fine and light, soft texture, cup cakes are the glamorous big sisters of fairy cakes. Bake these cup cakes in a 12-hole muffin tray or deep-hole bun tray, lined with paper muffin or cup-cake cases. See page 309 for icings and decoration ideas.

Rich Vanilla Cup Cakes

Makes 12

175g self-raising flour
pinch of salt
125g unsalted butter,
 softened
175g caster sugar
2 large free-range eggs,
 at room temperature
½ teaspoon vanilla
 extract
3 tablespoons semi-
 skimmed or full-
 fat milk, at room
 temperature

Preheat the oven to 180°C/350°F/gas 4. Sift the flour and salt onto a sheet of greaseproof paper and set aside until needed.

Put the butter into a mixing bowl and beat with a wooden spoon or an electric mixer until very pale. Gradually beat in the sugar, then beat the mixture thoroughly for about 4 minutes or until light and fluffy.

Beat the eggs with the vanilla, then add to the creamed mixture a tablespoon at a time, beating well after each addition and scraping down the sides of the bowl from time to time. Using a large metal spoon, delicately fold in the sifted flour in 3 batches alternately with the milk. When thoroughly combined, spoon the mixture into the paper cases, dividing it evenly.

Bake for 20 minutes or until risen, golden brown and firm to the touch. Remove the tray from the oven and leave to cool for about 2 minutes, then carefully transfer the cup cakes to a wire rack and leave to cool completely before icing.

Chocolate Velvet Cup Cakes

Makes 12

175ml semi-skimmed or
 full-fat milk
100g dark chocolate
 (70% cocoa solids)
125g caster sugar
60g unsalted butter,
 softened
½ teaspoon vanilla
 extract

Preheat the oven to 180°C/350°F/gas 4. Pour the milk into a small, heavy-based pan (preferably non-stick). Chop the chocolate and add to the milk with one-third of the sugar. Set over the lowest possible heat and leave until melted and smooth, stirring frequently. Remove from the heat. If necessary, give the liquid a quick whisk to amalgamate, then set aside until needed.

Put the butter into a mixing bowl and beat until creamy with a wooden spoon or an electric mixer. Add the rest of the sugar and the vanilla and beat thoroughly for about 4 minutes or until the mixture is very light and fluffy.

1 large free-range egg,
  at room temperature,
  beaten
150g self-raising flour, sifted

Gradually add the egg, beating well after each addition and scraping down the sides of the bowl from time to time. Using a large metal spoon fold in the flour in 3 batches alternately with the chocolate liquid. When completely amalgamated spoon the mixture into the paper cases so they are evenly filled.

Bake for 15 to 18 minutes or until the cakes are well risen and spring back when gently pressed with a finger. Remove the tray from the oven and leave to cool for about 2 minutes, then transfer the cup cakes to a wire rack and leave to cool completely before icing.

Tip: To make American red velvet cup cakes, add a few drops of red food colouring after the flour.

Very Lemony Cup Cakes

Makes 12

125g unsalted butter,
  softened
200g caster sugar
finely grated zest of
  1 large unwaxed lemon
2 large free-range eggs,
  at room temperature,
  beaten
200g self-raising flour,
  sifted
100ml buttermilk
2 teaspoons lemon juice

Preheat the oven to 180°C/350°F/gas 4. Put the butter into a mixing bowl and beat with a wooden spoon or an electric mixer until very creamy. Beat in the sugar and lemon zest, then beat thoroughly for about 4 minutes or until the mixture is very light and fluffy.

Gradually add the eggs, a tablespoon at a time, beating well after each addition and scraping down the sides of the bowl from time to time. Using a large metal spoon fold in the flour in 3 batches alternately with the buttermilk. When the mixture is almost amalgamated add the lemon juice and mix in thoroughly.

Spoon the mixture into the paper cases, filling them evenly. Bake for about 25 minutes or until a light golden brown and just firm to the touch. Remove the tray from the oven and leave to cool for about 2 minutes, then transfer the cup cakes to a wire rack and leave to cool completely before icing.

Tip: Rotate the tray two-thirds of the way through the cooking time so the cup cakes colour evenly.

Icings and Toppings

If you want a 'mile-high' topping, just double the quantities of the three icings below. Other ideas include the chocolate butter icing for the Queen of Sheba cake (see page 278), Glacé Icing (see page 223), Buttercream and Butter Icing (see pages 54–55) and Royal Icing (see page 68).

Easy Vanilla or Lemon Frosting

Makes enough for
12 cup cakes

75g unsalted butter,
softened
250g icing sugar, sifted
4 tablespoons semi-
skimmed or full-fat
milk plus 1 teaspoon
vanilla extract OR
3 tablespoons Lemon
Curd (see page 32)
edible food colour or
paste (optional)

Beat the butter with a wooden spoon or an electric mixer until creamy. Gradually beat in the icing sugar (use low speed). When the mixture is very light and smooth beat in the flavourings and colour, if using. In warm weather, or if the mixture is very soft, cover and chill until it is firm but still spreadable.

Swirl on top of cold cup cakes using a round-bladed knife or spoon into a piping bag fitted with a star tube and pipe onto the cakes. Add any decorations and leave to firm up.

Chocolate Fudge Frosting

Makes enough for
12 cup cakes

100g dark chocolate
(70% cocoa solids),
chopped or broken up
1 rounded tablespoon
golden syrup
50g unsalted butter

Put the chocolate, golden syrup and butter into a heatproof bowl. Set over a pan of steaming hot but not boiling water (don't let the base of the bowl touch the water) and melt gently, stirring frequently. As soon as the mixture is smooth remove the bowl from the pan and cool, stirring frequently.

When very thick and on the point of setting, swirl the frosting on top of the cup cakes using a round-bladed knife. Quickly add any decorations and leave to set.

Ideas for Decorations

Supermarkets sell a wide range of icings, toppings and decorations. Specialist stores, online and on the high street, carry a vast selection of ready-made decorations, specialist tools and colours, as well as cup-cake holders, stands and displays.

The simplest decorations are coloured, chocolate or edible gold sprinkles, tiny marshmallows or jelly beans – all available from supermarkets. Paper cup-cake frills and party wrappers, to go around the outside of each finished cake, come in many colours and designs from supermarkets and specialists.

Cutters: ready-to-roll icing is sold in white and in colours, and can also be tinted to match a particular scheme using colouring pastes. Once thinly rolled out, it can be shaped with cutters and used to top iced cup cakes. To avoid fingermarks, while the icing is still in the cutter, brush the back of it with a little water, then release the shape onto the cake. The icing can be painted afterwards, or finished with piped decorations.

Piped decorations: there is a wide range of options, from home-made royal icing in a piping bag with a fine writing tube inserted (No. 1 or 2), to icing writing pens, piping tubes and pouches, all of which are easily obtainable and come in many colours. It's worth spending a few minutes piping the pattern onto the worktop or a sheet of greaseproof paper until you are happy with the result.

For wedding cup cakes: cover the cakes in white icing or tinted to match the colour scheme, then top each with one large white flower, cut from ready-to-roll white icing, rolled thinly. Or pipe intertwined initials in a colour to match the scheme. The simplest and very traditional addition is to top the iced cakes with sugared almonds (a wide range of colours is available as well as gold and silver).

For Christenings or baby showers: cover the cakes in icing tinted lemon, pink or blue and decorate each with a pair of tiny bootees made with white ready-to-roll icing. Take a pea-sized ball of icing, then slightly elongate it; using the fine end of a chopstick, press it into the ball to make the inside of the bootee, making it rounder at the back and shaped slightly higher in front to resemble a slipper-type bootee.

For children's parties: cover the cakes with icing, then top each with a teddy bear made from marzipan (if nuts are allowed) or yellow-coloured ready-to-roll icing thinly rolled and cut with a shaped biscuit cutter (or freehand). Pipe on eyes, ears and mouth and a bow-tie if you have the time.

For Hallowe'en: cover the cakes in orange icing, then pipe a large dark spider on each, using a small cylinder of black liquorice as the body.

For an anniversary party: cover the cakes with icing and then cut out 2 hearts for each cake. Set overlapping on top of each cake.

Making a Party Cake

The dark chocolate sponge cake mixture baked in sandwich tins for Devil's Food Cake (see page 43) can be scaled up or down to make larger or smaller cakes baked in springclip tins, to be filled and covered with a very light maple and marshmallow fluff. For a wedding, three cakes can be assembled to make a three-tier cake to serve 50.

For the sponges	16cm tin	20.5cm tin	24cm tin
cocoa powder	2 tablespoons	4 tablespoons	6 tablespoons
boiling water	85ml	175ml	250ml
bicarbonate of soda	½ teaspoon	1 teaspoon	1½ teaspoons
dark chocolate (70% cocoa solids)	50g	100g	150g
unsalted butter, softened	65g	125g	185g
caster sugar	175g	350g	500g
large free-range eggs, at room temperature	1	2	3
vanilla extract	½ teaspoon	1 teaspoon	1½ teaspoons
plain flour, sifted	150g	300g	450g
soured cream, at room temperature	65ml	125ml	185ml

Preheat the oven to 180°C/350°F/gas 4. Grease the springclip cake tins and line the bases with baking paper.

Make the sponge mixture as instructed on page 43. Bake each cake until a skewer inserted into the centre comes out clean: the 16cm cake will take 55 to 60 minutes, the 20.5cm cake 65 to 75 minutes, and the 24cm cake 75 to 85 minutes.

Remove from the oven, run a round-bladed knife around the inside of the tin to loosen the sponge and leave to cool for 20 minutes. Then unclip the tin and leave the cake to cool completely on a wire rack. When cold, remove the lining paper, wrap the cake in foil and keep until ready to ice.

For the Maple and Marshmallow Fluff
Make up one batch of icing at a time and use immediately.

	16cm cake	20.5cm cake	24cm cake
large free-range egg whites, at room temperature	1	2	3
white caster sugar	175g	350g	500g
maple syrup	2 teaspoons	1½ tablespoons	2 tablespoons
vanilla extract	½ teaspoon	1 teaspoon	1½ teaspoons
cold water	65ml	125ml	175ml

3 round silver or gold
cake cards: 16cm,
20.5cm, 24cm
a large silver or gold
cake board or serving
platter, about 30cm
8 wooden dowels (see
recipe)
dark chocolate
decorations or sugar
flowers (see page 293)

*Tip: Make the
cakes one at a time
and bake separately.
They will taste better
as they mature so
bake a day or two
before assembling.
You will need an
electric mixer (hand-
held or a large, free-
standing mixer).*

To assemble

Put the egg whites and sugar for the icing into a large heatproof bowl and
set over a pan of simmering water. Using an electric mixer, immediately
whisk in the maple syrup, vanilla, water and a pinch of salt. Whisk on full
speed for 7 to 12 minutes or until thick, glossy and meringue-like: the
mixture should hold a soft peak when the whisk is lifted.

Remove the bowl from the pan and keep on whisking for 15 to 20
minutes or until the mixture has cooled, turned white and very thick and
is starting to stiffen up.

Slice each cake horizontally into 2 or 3 layers (depending on how
confident you feel). Put a dab of fluff mixture onto the centre of a cake
card and set one layer of the first cake, cut side up, on it. To make sure
that the dark chocolate cake crumbs don't migrate to the white fluff take
out a third of the mixture and cover the rest. Use the smaller portion
to sandwich the layers. Then using a clean round-bladed knife or icing
palette knife, cover the top and sides of the cake with a very thick layer
of the fluff, swirling it fairly evenly. The fluff will cover up any dips, dents,
cracks or imperfections in the sponge and glue together any loose edges;
you may not need all of the second portion, but keep it well-wrapped for
finishing. Leave the cake to set overnight.

If you are making a 3-tier cake set the largest cake on the large cake
board or platter. Make 4 evenly spaced marks about 6cm in from the
edge of the cake and insert the wooden dowels, pushing them in all the
way through the cake to the card. Then remove the dowels carefully and
cut to size so they are exactly the same height as the cake and icing (you'll
see the point marked by the icing). Replace the dowels into the cake –
they will support the weight of the upper 2 tiers. Do the same with the
middle-sized cake. Layer up the cakes, making sure they are centred. Fill
in any gaps and spaces, marks and dents with the reserved marshmallow
fluff, then decorate. Once assembled use the same day.

If you have a favourite recipe you want to use in the same way you can scale it
up or down by measuring the volume of the cake tin you normally use. If the
cake comes to the top of the tin, then fill it with water to the same level and
measure the volume – say 1 litre. Then measure the volume of a smaller or
larger tin and halve or double, or adapt the recipe as necessary. This is useful
if you're hiring a shaped tin (a numeral, letter or character) from a specialist
shop. The baking times are more tricky to calculate, particularly with odd
shapes, and you need to keep close watch. Be ready to cover the top of the
cake with foil if it is getting too brown. A skewer inserted into the centre of
the cake is the best guide – once it comes out clean then the cake is cooked.

BEST OF THE BAKE-OFF
Chocolate and Raspberry Opera Cake

Cut into at least 20
slices

For the sponge
4 large egg whites plus
    4 whole eggs, at room
    temperature
15g caster sugar
150g ground almonds
150g icing sugar, sifted
25g plain flour
25g cocoa powder
55g unsalted butter,
    melted and cooled

For the raspberry syrup
150g raspberries
75g caster sugar
1 teaspoon lemon juice

**For the French
buttercream**
125g white chocolate,
    broken up
3 large egg yolks, at
    room temperature
55g caster sugar
2 tablespoons water
200g unsalted butter,
    softened, in pieces
vanilla extract, to taste

For the ganache
100g plain chocolate
    (70% cocoa solids),
    broken up
100g unsalted butter,
    softened

Preheat the oven to 200°C/400°F/gas 6. To make the sponge, put the egg whites into the mixer bowl and whisk to soft peaks. Add the caster sugar and continue to whisk until the meringue will hold stiff peaks.

In another large bowl with the mixer on medium speed, whisk together the almonds, icing sugar and whole eggs for about 3 minutes or until light, thick and increased in volume. Sift the flour and cocoa on top and fold in, then fold in the meringue in 3 batches.

Take a cupful of the mixture and fold it thoroughly into the melted butter in a small bowl. Pour this back into the rest of the mixture and fold in until just combined.

Divide the sponge mixture evenly between them, making sure it spreads evenly into the corners where it might get too thin. Bake for 5 to 7 minutes or until the sponge is lightly browned and springs back when gently pressed.

Remove from the oven. Cover 2 wire racks with non-stick baking paper. Flip the pans over onto the racks to turn out the sponge sheets. Carefully peel off the lining paper and leave to cool. Lower the oven to 100°C/200°F/gas ¼.

While the sponge sheets are cooling, make the syrup. Put all the ingredients into an ovenproof dish and warm in the oven for 1 hour, stirring occasionally. Cool, then tip into a food-processor and process until smooth. Sieve to remove the seeds. Set aside.

Next, make the buttercream. Melt the chocolate in a heatproof bowl set over a pan of steaming hot but not boiling water (don't let the base of the bowl touch the water). Remove from the pan and cool. In a large freestanding electric mixer, beat the egg yolks until thick and mousse-like. Meanwhile, put the sugar and water in a small pan and dissolve over low heat, then boil until the syrup reaches 115°C/239°F on a sugar thermometer.

Recipe continues on page 314

100g icing sugar, sifted
2–3 tablespoons
   raspberry liqueur

To assemble
25g dark chocolate
   (70% cocoa solids),
   broken up
300g small fresh
   raspberries

For the glaze
75ml golden syrup
75ml double cream
150g dark chocolate
   (70% cocoa solids),
   broken up

2 baking trays with
   rims, each about 31.5
   x 25.5cm, greased
   and lined with
   baking paper; a sugar
   thermometer

Pour the syrup onto the yolks in a thin, steady stream while beating at top speed. Beat for a further 5 minutes or until the mixture is cool and thick. Gradually beat in the butter followed by the chocolate and vanilla. Chill until firm enough to spread easily.

To make the ganache, melt the chocolate as above, then leave to cool. Meanwhile, beat the butter with the sugar until light and fluffy. Beat in the chocolate and liqueur to taste. If necessary, chill until firm enough to spread.

To assemble, melt the chocolate as above, then leave to cool. Cut each sponge sheet in half and trim off the edges to make 4 rectangles, each 25 x 15cm. Brush one rectangle with the melted chocolate and chill until firm. Then invert it onto a serving board – this is the base layer of the cake. Lightly brush all the sponge layers, including the base, with raspberry syrup and leave to soak for 15 minutes.

Now begin layering up, remembering that each layer must be level. Spread half of the buttercream onto the base layer. Top with half the raspberries, pressing them gently into the buttercream.

Spread the ganache over another sponge layer (on the side brushed with syrup) and place on top of the base layer. Spread the remainder of the buttercream over another layer of sponge (syrup side) and press in the rest of the raspberries, then set this on top of the ganache layer. Top with the remaining sponge layer.

To make the glaze, heat the syrup and cream until almost boiling. Put the chocolate into a heatproof bowl and pour over the hot mixture, stirring constantly until smooth. Leave for 2 minutes, then slowly pour enough over the cake to cover the top, without letting it drip down the sides. Chill until firm, then decorate if wished.

Conversion Tables

For fan assisted ovens, set the oven temperature 20°C lower than stated in the recipes.

Weight

Metric	Imperial	Metric	Imperial	Metric	Imperial	Metric	Imperial
25g	1oz	200g	7oz	425g	15oz	800g	1lb 12oz
50g	2oz	225g	8oz	450g	1lb	850g	1lb 14oz
75g	2 ½oz	250g	9oz	500g	1lb 2oz	900g	2lb
85g	3oz	280g	10oz	550g	1lb 4oz	950g	2lb 2oz
100g	4oz	300g	11oz	600g	1lb 5oz	1kg	2lb 4oz
125g	4 ½oz	350g	12oz	650g	1lb 7oz		
140g	5oz	375g	13oz	700g	1lb 9oz		
175g	6oz	400g	14oz	750g	1lb 10oz		

Volume

Metric	Imperial	Metric	Imperial	Metric	Imperial	Metric	Imperial
30ml	1fl oz	150ml	¼ pint	300ml	½ pint	500ml	18fl oz
50ml	2fl oz	175ml	6fl oz	350ml	12fl oz	600ml	1 pint
75ml	2 ½fl oz	200ml	7fl oz	400ml	14fl oz	700ml	1 ¼ pints
100ml	3 ½fl oz	225ml	8fl oz	425ml	¾ pint	850ml	1 ½ pints
125ml	4fl oz	250ml	9fl oz	450ml	16fl oz	1 litre	1 ¾ pints

Linear

Metric	Imperial	Metric	Imperial	Metric	Imperial	Metric	Imperial
2.5cm	1in	7.5cm	3in	13cm	5in	20cm	8in
3cm	1 ¼in	8cm	3 ¾in	14cm	5 ½in	22cm	8 ½in
4cm	1 ½in	9cm	3 ½in	15cm	6in	23cm	9in
5cm	2in	9.5cm	3 ¾in	16cm	6 ¼in	24cm	9 ½in
5.5cm	2 ¼in	10cm	4in	17cm	6 ½in	25cm	10in
6cm	2 ½in	11cm	4 ¼in	18cm	7in		
7cm	2 ¾in	12cm	4 ½in	19cm	7 ½in		

Spoon Measures

Metric	Imperial
5ml	1tsp
10ml	2tsp
15ml	1tbsp
30ml	2tbsp
45ml	3tbsp
60ml	4tbsp
75ml	5tbsp

Cook's Notes

We use humanely reared meat, free-range chickens and eggs and sustainably-sourced fish and unrefined sugar.

Eggs are large in the UK and Australia and extra large in America unless stated otherwise.

Pregnant women, the elderly, babies and toddlers, and people who are unwell should avoid eating raw and partially cooked eggs.

We use unsalted butter and semi-skimmed milk, unless otherwise stated.

Wash fresh produce before preparation.

almond
    & banana slice 87
    croissants 219
    filling 234
    straws, & palm leaves 216
    tuiles 64–7
apple
    beehives 200
    & pork Somerset pie
        164–5
    quick tarts 188
    simply good pie 201
    sticky maple-, traybake
        92–3
    tarte tatin 204–5
apricot
    Danish pastries 222–5
    honey & hazelnut
        wholemeal loaf 138–9
    & marzipan golden loaf
        cake 36–7
artichoke pizza 132–4

Bakewell cup cakes, cherry
    26–7
Bakewell tarts, mini
    blueberry 186–7
baking tips 14–15, 58–9,
    102–3, 144–5, 178–9,
    208–9, 248–9, 284–5
banana
    & almond slice 87
    fudge layer cake 42
    & raisin pastries 226–7
Battenburg, coffee & walnut
    14, 20–5
beef
    casserole, with dumplings
        172
    & red wine filling 152
biscuits
    almond tuiles 64–7
    baking tips 58–9
    chocolate chunk cookies
        74
    chocolate crackles 80–1
    Christmas 75
    cranberry cooler
        macaroons 86
    florentines 98–9
    iced lemon 69
    macaroon mocktails
        84–6

Mary's brandy snaps
    60–3
melting moments 70–1
mojito macaroons 86
oat & raisin 96
two-chocolate zebras
    82–3
walnut crumbles 68
see also shortbread
black olive & thyme bread
    128–9
blood orange sponge cake 47
blueberry Bakewell tarts,
    mini 186–7
brandy snaps, Mary's 60–3
bread 100–41
    baking tips 102–3
    black olive & thyme
        128–9
    & butter chocolate
        pudding 274
    cheese & onion tear &
        share loaf 110–11
    glazes 114
    a good rustic loaf 112–13
    hazelnut, apricot & honey
        wholemeal loaf 138–9
    lemon babas 137
    monkey 130–1
    old-fashioned London
        loaf 115–17
    Paul's focaccia 118–22
    picnic loaf 124–5
    pizza 132–4
    rum babas 135–7
    sticky buns 140–1
    sweet coconut rolls 126–7
    toppings 114
    white loaf 104–8
buns
    double chocolate 78
    sticky 140–1
butter icing 54
    coffee 21–5
buttercream 28, 39, 55

cakes
    baking tips 14–15, 284–5
    banana fudge layer 42
    blood orange sponge 47
    chocolate & raspberry
        opera 312–14
    chocolate chilli 44–5

chocolate orange mousse
    244–5
Devil's food 43, 310–11
double chocolate marbled
    loaf 52–3
flourless lemon & cream
    roll 33
golden apricot &
    marzipan loaf 36–7
gorgeous lemon cream
    30–2
hazelnut & chocolate
    38–9
large iced fruit 284,
    286–93
lemon poppyseed
    madeira 35
Mary's coffee & walnut
    Battenburg 14, 20–5
panettone 298–9
party 310–11
quick & simple fruit loaf
    29
quick chocolate fudge
    40–1
Simnel 294
speckled mocha 34
sticky orange marmalade
    50–1
strawberry & white
    chocolate cream 48–9
Twelfth Night king 296–7
Victoria sandwich 14,
    16–19
warm chocolate mousse
    255
yule log 295
see also cup cakes
carrot & pistachio traybake
    90
casserole, rich beef, with
    dumplings 172
celebration sherry trifle, a
    302
Chantilly cream 234
cheese
    Gorgonzola & mushroom
        twists 174–5
    & ham croissants 219
    & onion tear & share loaf
        110–11
    three, & spinach pie 173
    see also Stilton

cheesecake
    double chocolate chip
        258–9
    rhubarb & ginger 262–3
    rum & raisin 260–1
cherry
    Bakewell cup cakes 26–7
    warm crumble pie 202–3
chicken spicy pasties 162–3
chilli chocolate cake 44–5
chocolate
    bread & butter pudding
        274
    buns, double 78
    chilli cake 44–5
    chip cheesecake, double
        258–9
    chunk cookies 74
    cooking tips 249
    crackles 80–1
    croissants 219
    Devil's food cake 43,
        310–11
    double marbled loaf cake
        52–3
    fennel & ginger tart 189
    florentines 98–9
    fudge frosting 308
    fudge hot-pot pudding
        276–7
    & hazelnut cake 38–9
    mint macaroons 97
    mocha speckled cake 34
    mousse 270
    mousse cake, warm 255
    mud pie 195
    orange cup cakes 28
    orange mousse cake
        244–5
    Queen of Sheba 278–81
    quick fudge cake 40–1
    & raspberry opera cake
        312–14
    roulade 264–9
    sauce 233
    speckled shortbread 76
    Twelfth Night king cake
        296–7
    twists 226–7
    two-chocolate zebras 82–3
    velvet cup cakes 304–5,
        306–7
    yule log 295

see also white chocolate
choux pastry 208, 229
Christmas
 biscuits 75
 pudding 301
cobbler, peach & ginger 275
coconut
 macaroons 94–5
 sweet rolls 126–7
coffee
 eclairs 232
 mocha speckled cake 34
 Queen of Sheba 278–81
 & walnut Battenburg 14,
  20–5
 & walnut traybake 91
cookies, chocolate chunk 74
crab warm tart 170–1
cranberry cooler macaroons
 86
cream
 Chantilly 234
 lemon cake 30–2
 & lemon flourless roll 33
 mint 86
 mint-chocolate 97
 pastry 235
 strawberry & white
  chocolate cake 48–9
 whipping 249
croissants
 almond 219
 chocolate 219
 ham & cheese 219
 home-made buttery
  217–18
croquembouche, limoncello
 & white chocolate 236–7
crumble pie, warm cherry
 202–3
cup cakes
 celebration 304–9
 cherry Bakewell 26–7
 chocolate orange 28
 chocolate velvet 304–5,
  306–7
 decorations 309
 Earl Grey 46
 icings & toppings 308
 rhubarb & custard 39
 rich vanilla 304
 very lemony 305, 306–7
custard 302
 & rhubarb cup cakes 39

Danish pastries 222–5
Devil's food cake 43, 310–11
double chocolate
 buns 78
 chip cheesecake 258–9
 marbled loaf cake 52–3
drop scones 79
dumplings, with rich beef
 casserole 172

Earl Grey cup cakes 46
easy for kids
 golden apricot &
  marzipan loaf cake
  36–7
 iced lemon biscuits 69
 lemon ice cream
  meringue pie 271
 little stem ginger
  gingerbreads 88–9
 monkey bread 130–1
 oat & raisin biscuits 96
 pizza 132–4
 quick & simple fruit loaf
  29
 quick apple tarts 188
 quick chocolate fudge
  cake 40–1
 yule log 295
easy lemon frosting 308
easy vanilla frosting 308
eclairs 230–2
egg whites, whisking 248–9
elderflower & honeycomb
 tarts 194

fennel, ginger & chocolate
 tart 189
florentines 98–9
flourless lemon & cream
 roll 33
focaccia, Paul's 118–22
folding in 249
frangipane 186–7
fresh raspberry sauce 272
frosting
 chocolate fudge 308
 lemon 308
 vanilla 308
fruit cake
 large iced 284, 286–93
 Simnel cake 294
fruit loaf, quick & simple
 29

ganache 295
ginger
 chocolate & fennel tart
  189
 little stem, gingerbreads
  88–9
 & peach cobbler 275
 & rhubarb cheesecake
  262–3
 stem, shortbread 76–7
glacé icing 69
glazes, for breads 114
gold leaf 285
golden apricot & marzipan
 loaf cake 36–7
good for celebrations
 282–315
 baking tips 284–5
 banana fudge layer cake
  42
 celebration cup cakes
  304–9
 a celebration sherry trifle
  302
 chocolate & raspberry
  opera cake 312–14
 chocolate orange mousse
  cake 244–5
 Christmas pudding 301
 Danish pastries 222–5
 golden apricot &
  marzipan loaf cake
  36–7
 gorgeous lemon cream
  cake 30–2
 hazelnut & chocolate
  cake 38–9
 iced lemon biscuits 69
 large iced fruit cake 284,
  286–93
 limoncello &
  white chocolate
  croquembouche 236–7
 mincemeat lattice tart 300
 panettone 298–9
 party cakes 310–11
 rum babas 135–7
 Simnel cake 294
 speckled mocha cake 34
 strawberry & pistachio
  tart 190–2
 strawberry & white
  chocolate cream cake
  48–9

Twelfth Night king cake
 296–7
yule log 295
good rustic loaf, a 112–13
gorgeous lemon cream cake
 30–2
Gorgonzola & mushroom
 twists 174–5

haddock & watercress quiche
 169
ham & cheese croissants 219
hazelnut
 apricot & honey
  wholemeal loaf 138–9
 & chocolate cake 38–9
home-made buttery
 croissants 217–18
honey, hazelnut & apricot
 wholemeal loaf 138–9
honeycomb & elderflower
 tarts 194
hot lemon curd soufflé
 272–3

ice cream lemon meringue
 pie 271
iced lemon biscuits 69
icing 308
 butter 21–5, 54
 glacé 69
 royal 68

kneading 102, 103

large iced fruit cake 284,
 286–93
lemon
 babas 137
 cream cake 30–2
 & cream flourless roll 33
 curd 32, 33
 curd hot soufflé 272–3
 frosting 308
 ice cream meringue pie
  271
 iced biscuits 69
 lemony cup cakes 305,
  306–7
 Mary's Tarte au Citron
  178, 180–4
 poppyseed madeira cake
  35
 syrup 30

lime, mojito macaroons 86
limoncello & white chocolate
    croquembouche 236–7
little stem ginger
    gingerbreads 88–9

macaroons
    coconut 94–5
    cranberry cooler 86
    mint chocolate 97
    mocktails 84–6
    mojito 86
mango & passionfruit,
    pavlova with 254
maple & marshmallow fluff
    310–11
marmalade orange sticky
    cake 50–1
marshmallow & maple fluff
    310–11
Mary's
    brandy snaps 60–3
    chocolate roulade 264–9
    coffee & walnut
        Battenburg 14, 20–5
    Tarte au Citron 178,
        180–4
marzipan
    & apricot golden loaf cake
        36–7
    Christmas biscuits 75
    coffee & walnut
        Battenburg 14, 20–5
melting moments 70–1
meringue
    baking tips 248
    cooked 248
    Italian 248
    pavlova with mango &
        passionfruit 254
    perfect 250–3
    pie, lemon ice cream 271
    rhubarb pie 196–7
millefeuilles with raspberries
    214–15
mincemeat lattice tart 300
mini blueberry Bakewell tarts
    186–7
mint
    chocolate macaroons 97
    cream 86
mocha speckled cake 34
mojito macaroons 86
monkey bread 130–1

mousse, chocolate 270
mousse cake
    chocolate orange 244–5
    warm chocolate 255
mud pie 195
mushroom & Gorgonzola
    twists 174–5

oat & raisin biscuits 96
old-fashioned London loaf
    115–17
olive, black, & thyme bread
    128–9
onion
    caramelized, Stilton &
        potato pie 153–5
    & cheese tear & share
        loaf 110–11
orange
    blood, sponge cake 47
    chocolate cup cakes 28
    chocolate mousse cake
        244–5
    marmalade sticky cake
        50–1

pains au raisin 226–7
pak choi & salmon quiche
    168
palm leaves & almond straws
    216
panettone 298–9
party cakes 310–11
passionfruit & mango,
    pavlova with 254
pasties, spicy chicken 162–3
pastry
    apple beehives 200
    baking tips 144–5, 178–9
    choux 208, 229
    Gorgonzola & mushroom
        twists 174–5
    hot water crust 144
    puff 208–9, 210–12
    rich shortcrust 178
    shortcrust 146–51
    see also pasties; patisserie;
        pies; quiche; tarts
pastry cream 235
patisserie 206–45
    almond croissants
        219
    baking tips 208–9
    chocolate croissants 219

chocolate orange mousse
    cake 244–5
Danish pastries 222–5
eclairs 230–2
ham & cheese croissants
    219
home-made buttery
    croissants 217–18
limoncello &
    white chocolate
    croquembouche 236–7
millefeuilles with
    raspberries 214–15
palm leaves & almond
    straws 216
Paul's iced fingers 209,
    240–3
profiteroles 230–1, 233
puff pastry 210–12
sweet pastries 226–7
Paul's
    focaccia 118–22
    iced fingers 209, 240–3
    pork pies with quails' eggs
        144, 156–60
pavlova with mango &
    passionfruit 254
peach & ginger cobbler 275
picnic loaf 124–5
pies
    baking tips 144–5, 178–9
    lemon ice cream
        meringue 271
    mud 195
    Paul's pork, with quails'
        eggs 144, 156–60
    rhubarb meringue 196–7
    shortcrust 145, 146–51
    simply good apple 201
    Somerset pork & apple
        164–5
    Stilton, potato &
        caramelized onion
        153–5
    three cheese & spinach
        173
    warm cherry crumble
        202–3
piña colada macaroons 84–5
pistachio
    & carrot traybake 90
    & strawberry tart 190–2
    shortbread 76
pizza 132–4

pork
    & apple Somerset pie
        164–5
    pies, with quails' eggs 144,
        156–60
potato
    caramelized onion &
        Stilton pie 153–5
    new, Stilton, walnut &
        spinach quiche 166–7
profiteroles 230–1, 233
puddings & desserts 246–81
    baking tips 248–9
puff pastry 208–9, 210–12

quails' eggs, with pork pies
    144, 156–60
Queen of Sheba 278–81
quiche
    haddock & watercress
        169
    salmon & pak choi 168
    Stilton, walnut, spinach &
        new potato 166–7
quick & simple fruit loaf 29
quick apple tarts 188
quick chocolate fudge cake
    40–1

raisin
    & banana pastries 226–7
    & oat biscuits 96
    & rum cheesecake 260–1
raspberry
    & chocolate opera cake
        312–14
    fresh sauce 272
    & millefeuilles 214–15
rhubarb
    & custard cup cakes 39
    & ginger cheesecake
        262–3
    meringue pie 196–7
rich beef casserole with
    dumplings 172
rich vanilla cup cakes 304
roulade, chocolate 264–9
royal icing, for piping 68
rum
    babas 135–7
    & raisin cheesecake
        260–1
salmon & pak choi quiche
    168

scones, drop 79
shortbread
    pistachio 76
    speckled chocolate 76
    stem ginger 76–7
    two-chocolate zebras
        82–3
shortcrust pie 145, 146–51
Simnel cake 294
slices, banana & almond 87
Somerset pork & apple pie
    164–5
soufflé, hot lemon curd
    272–3
speckled mocha cake 34
spicy chicken pasties 162–3
spinach
    new potato, Stilton &
        walnut quiche 166–7
    & three cheese pie 173
stem ginger shortbread 76–7
stencils 285
sticky
    buns 140–1
    maple-apple traybake
        92–3
    orange marmalade cake
        50–1
    walnut tart 198–9
Stilton
    potato & caramelized

onion pie 153–5
    walnut, spinach & new
        potato quiche 166–7
strawberry
    & pistachio tart 190–1
    & white chocolate cream
        cake 48–9
sweet coconut rolls 126–7
sweet pastries 226–7
syllabub 302

tarts
    baking tips 144–5, 178–9
    chocolate, fennel &
        ginger 189
    elderflower &
        honeycomb 194
    Mary's Tarte au Citron
        178, 180–4
    mincemeat lattice 300
    mini blueberry Bakewell
        186–7
    sticky walnut 198–9
    strawberry & pistachio
        190–2
    tarte tatin 204–5
    warm crab 170–1
three cheese & spinach pie
    173
thyme & black olive bread
    128–9

tomato topped pizzas 132–4
traybakes
    baking tips 58
    banana & almond slices
        87
    carrot & pistachio 90
    coffee & walnut 91
    quick chocolate fudge
        cake 40–1
    sticky maple-apple
        traybake 92–3
trifle, a celebration sherry
    302
Twelfth Night king cake
    296–7
twists, mushroom &
    Gorgonzola 174–5
two-chocolate zebras 82–3

vanilla
    frosting 308
    rich cup cakes 304,
        306–7
very lemony cup cakes 305,
    306–7
Victoria sandwich 14, 16–19
walnut
    & coffee Battenburg 14,
        20–5
    & coffee traybake 91
    crumbles 68

spinach, new potato &
    Stilton quiche 166–7
sticky tart 198–9
warm cherry crumble pie
    202–3
warm chocolate mousse cake
    255
warm crab tart 170–1
watercress & haddock quiche
    169
whisking 248–9
white chocolate
    & limoncello
        croquembouche 236–7
    & strawberry cream cake
        48–9
white loaf 104–8

yeast 102
yule log 295